No. 2642
$24.95

101 Projects, Plans and Ideas

for the

High-Tech Household

Julie Knott and Dave Prochnow

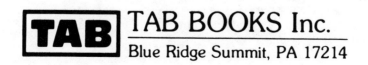

TAB BOOKS Inc.
Blue Ridge Summit, PA 17214

FIRST EDITION

FIRST PRINTING

Copyright © 1986 by TAB BOOKS Inc.

Printed in the United States of America

Reproduction or publication of the content in any manner, without express
permission of the publisher, is prohibited. No liability is assumed with respect to
the use of the information herein.

Library of Congress Cataloging in Publication Data

Knott, Julie.
101 projects, plans, and ideas for the high-tech
household.

Bibliography: p.
Includes index.
1. Household electronics—Amateurs' manuals.
I. Prochnow, Dave. II. Title. III. Title: One
hundred one projects, plans, and ideas for the high-
tech household. IV. Title: One hundred and one
projects, plans, and ideas for the high-tech household.
TK9965.K63 1986   621.381   85-27677
ISBN 0-8306-0342-5
ISBN 0-8306-0442-1 (pbk.)

Contents

Preface

High-tech interior design holds a fascination for everyone. We all have been tempted to purchase a "talking" microwave oven or an unusual lighting system as a source of household stimulation. Granted, these items lend a high-tech atmosphere to any home, but some people desire a more fully implemented high-tech design scheme. This is a plan that is not achieved through the use of only a few individual items. People who are serious about giving their home (whether it is a house, an apartment, or a condominium) a degree of high-tech flare must plan their home's interior design according to this desire.

General questions regarding wall coverings, window treatments, and floor coverings must all be addressed in terms of the high-tech design theme. Even obscure aspects such as the lighting and sound within your home are extremely important and must, therefore, be evaluated and altered to meet the new high-tech criteria you have set. Only after these basic interior design considerations have been planned can you consider other high-tech projects and fixtures that will complete your household.

101 Projects, Plans and Ideas for the High-Tech Household addresses all of these essential aspects of creating a high-tech household—from preparing initial floor plans to employing concepts and projects within individual rooms. As a matter of convention, Chapters 1 through 101 are divided into two distinct parts: Form

(Chapters 1 through 44) and Function (Chapters 45 through 101). Projects within the Form section deal with enhancing the appearance of your home. For example, projects in this section deal with the use of high-tech sculpture and artwork. The Function section contains projects with useful implementations such as an electronic privacy indicator and indicators controlled by sound, temperature, pressure, or a beam of infrared light.

Besides falling into form and function categories, the 101 projects outlined within this book are further divided into electronic and concept oriented projects (these two project types are sprinkled throughout the book). Therefore, in addition to the electronic projects with schematic diagrams and construction notes, projects are included that deal with subjects such as computer-aided floor plan design and high-tech household fire safety.

The greatest benefit of *101 Projects, Plans and Ideas for the High-Tech Household* is that each project is not a concrete template that must be rigidly followed. Instead, each project is a starting point for the creation of highly individualized electronic projects and household concepts. For example, although a schematic diagram is presented for a Door-Open Alarm, the enclosure and installation of this particular project is subject to your own design plan. Because of the individualized implementation for each project, a high-tech interior design theme is also able to reveal a different personality in every household.

However, this book is not written strictly for the electronic project enthusiast. Anyone who is involved with interior design planning, whether professionally or as an individual, will benefit from the concept-oriented project chapters. Likewise, home computer users will find a use for their Apple or IBM computers both in planning their high-tech households and in using their computer as a design sculpture within their homes. Despite the complexity of the electronic projects within this book, most projects remain simple enough for even the electronically inexperienced interior designer or home computer user to build. However, as a point of introduction, Appendix A provides the inexperienced project builder with "Instructions and Tips for Project Preparation."

Finally, in an attempt to help expedite your design planning, Appendix B is devoted to "Computer-aided Interior Design Planning with Apple and IBM Computers." Within this appendix, six of the finest hardware and software products presently available for interior design planning are reviewed. These products are useful to both professional and individual interior design planners. Each product has the ability to both simplify and increase high-tech design productivity.

Acknowledgments

We would like to extend our thanks to the following manufacturers for their loans of both software and hardware. Their support is greatly appreciated.

- —Autodesk, Incorporated for their AutoCAD 2 software.
- —C.Itoh Electronics Corporation for their Model 8510SCP Color Dot Matrix Printer.
- —Data Transforms for their FONTRIX software.
- —Enter Computer, Incorporated for their Sweet-P Model 100 Plotter.
- —International Microcomputer Software, Incorporated (IMSI) for their PC Paintbrush software.

Introduction

A Tour Through
the High-Tech Household

Your home can be either a haven or a hovel; this distinction is made through your approach to interior design. Some people prefer a decoration scheme representing a Dadaistic viewpoint. This crowd buys some of this and some of that without ever really thinking about their home's total appearance. The opposite of this helter-skelter technique is one based on preconception. This group carefully plans each room's final ambience by selectively purchasing the furnishings that will best accomplish the previsualized goal.

Which design system is the best? Without trying to sound judgmental, the orchestrated concept is clearly superior. This definitive statement is based on the degree of harmony generated by each style.

TRADITIONAL VALUES

A properly designed living environment should not tax the owner's senses. Instead, each room must perform its intended function without imposing artificial restraints on its occupant. In other words, a kitchen is used for food preparation (and occasionally dining) and not for guest entertainment. Similarly, every other room has a predetermined task which should dictate its design.

This attitude represents traditional values. Several elements compose the traditional design: careful planning, efficient usage of space, sufficient lighting, and pleasing color patterns. Most of these elements are logical and, as will be discussed later, are present in other interior design schemes as well. Each of the traditional design elements needs very little justification for its employment. Careful planning is the first step for any project, especially one as major as interior design.

Who would dare use space inefficiently? But lighting, color, and patterns are design elements that are frequently overlooked resulting in a poor layout whether it's traditional or high-tech.

HIGH-TECH HISTORY

While these elements are strictly enforced in the traditional interior design concept, today's contemporary design practices occasionally emphasize contradictions. Examples of this philosophy would be Minimalism (sparse, virtually unoccupied interiors) and the "Bauhaus" look (functional, uncluttered, black and white fixtures). The contradictions, however, appear to present an aura of haphazard, makeshift planning reminiscent of the Dadaistic approach. In reality, contemporary design schemes require just as careful planning as traditional ones. The only difference is in the final room appearance.

One example of a contemporary interior design practice centers around the intentional display of a structure's electrical wiring, plumbing, and ventilation duct work. This is an extreme example of high-tech design. Figure I-1 provides an example of this interior design technique. In order to achieve this plan, ceiling tiles are removed, fixtures are placed on the outsides of walls, and clear faceplates are used to cover outlets (this technique is discussed in Chapter 77). Contrary to your initial opinion, this can be a dramatic decoration scheme, but only when expressed under the careful guidance of a previsualized plan. The leading architectural demonstration of high-tech is the Centre Georges Pompidou in Paris, France.

One curious footnote to the history of this movement is its date of origin. Many architects list the Crystal Palace of 1851, London, England, as the first high-tech structure. This date suggests that high-tech is anything but a new concept.

In effect, we have gone full circle back to our original point— good interior design, whether it is traditional or high-tech, requires the development of a solid concept. This concept then forms the template for all future room additions, expansions, and elaborations. Therefore, the major question to be answered is not related to the style issue (traditional versus contemporary), but, more specifically, it is involved with the origination of the concept.

THE IDEA SEED

A concept is an idea, nothing more. This is true in the field of

Fig. I-1. The high-tech display of normally hidden wiring, plumbing, and ventilation duct work.

mathematics, as well as in interior design. The start of this concept (or idea) is fairly subjective and, at present, only theoretical. The human mind contains millions of thoughts, each correlated into a pattern specific for that individual. The creative process, such as the formulation of a concept, begins with a series of chemical and electrical reactions in the brain that in turn examine all of the thoughts which are relevant to the prescribed task. Of course, random "glances" at unrelated thoughts sometimes trigger the so-called creative genius found in certain members of society, but this is a subject for another book. After this reactional examination begins, certain thoughts will combine. Suddenly, an idea occurs and the concept is formed.

Even though this thought process is similar for every person, a group of people confronted with a given task will still come up with several radically different solutions. This is based largely on the individual's thought pattern. Actually, history is replete with simultaneous "invention," but usually each creation presents a different solution.

The development of photography is an ideal illustrative example of this simultaneous solution theory. In 1839 (some historians place 1826 as photography's true origin at the hands of Claude Niepce), an Englishman named William Henry Fox Talbot devised a method for recording "photogenic drawings" on paper. These initial images were reversed with light objects rendered as dark and dark objects represented as light ones (the term "negative" was later coined by Sir John Herschel who developed a process for "fixing" the light sensitive images) from which copy "positive" prints could be made.

Across the English Channel, also in 1839, a Frenchman named Louis Jacques Mande Daguerre devised a method for recording photographic images on metal. These were called daguerrotypes. One key distinction that separated these two discoveries was that Talbot's technique allowed the printing of multiple copies, whereas daguerrotypes were unique and irreproducible. An examination of today's current photographic processes shows that Talbot's method was the champion.

Just as the above photographic conceptual solution varied from person to person, so too everyone's household adopts a different image. Even though all home designs come from the same task—construct a pleasing home atmosphere—the final appearance is derived from each person's unique mental orientation. This type of attitude will allow us to accept both the traditional and the contemporary interior design schemes, as well as the Dadaistic approach, as valid decorative expressions.

FORM AND FUNCTION

With this groundwork established, the high-tech household becomes a credible concept, and form and function are its basal elements. In the high-tech environment, form and function are cornerstones upon which every design plan must be evaluated. This is necessary because of the rampant abuse of the high-tech concept. All too often a product is sold under the guise of a high-tech motif which, upon closer scrutiny, violates one or both of its elemental requirements.

After only a cursory inspection, form and function seem like an odd pair; how can something that is functional also be required to be aesthetically pleasing? In other words, when does a can opener lose its ability to open cans and start looking attractive? Figure I-2 shows the internal structure of a model airplane, which is inherently beautiful while it remains functionally efficient.

To successfully conquer this supposed barrier, many architects have adopted a concept espoused by Louis Sullivan—form follows function. Simply stated, this idea holds the functionalism of an object over its physical beauty. Consequently, before the external appearance of a product is planned, its mechanical, electronic or physical operation must solve its intended problem faultlessly. This is beauty from design.

THE PROJECTS

In this book, both form and function projects are discussed. Over one hundred electronic projects, computer projects, and interior design concepts are grouped into two major book sections: Part I—Form and Part II—Function. More often than not, however, the actual "final" form is left up to the reader. This permits the incorporation of the project into any style of interior design scheme (see Fig. I-3). Therefore, form will truly follow function.

Projects dealing with form and function are a natural for the high-tech household. High-tech interior design, however, will be employed by more users than just the electronic projects enthusiast. For this reason, *101 Projects, Plans and Ideas for the High-Tech Household*, is aimed at three types of readers: the electronic project enthusiast, the computer user, and the interior designer. Each of these special interest categories will find an ample assortment of projects addressing their particular area of expertise and perhaps, for example, a computer user will spot something of interest and construct an electronic project or study an interior design concept.

Finally, it is the household integration of this book's projects, with the appropriate external form, that will make that environ-

Fig. I-2. A well conceived aircraft design demonstrates the principles of beauty from design—form follows function.

Fig. I-3. The completed Musical Mood Maker.

ment high-tech. This is a distinction from other design processes and requires the preparation of a suitable previsualized concept. Stated in a paraphrasing of the bold syntax of the architect Frank Lloyd Wright—a building's furnishings are part of the building and not fixtures dwelling within.

PART 1

FORM

1

Oscillating Sound

A WARBLING OR OSCILLATING SOUND IS CAPABLE OF GENER-
ating many different emotions from the listener. Many people find the gentle oscillations of a "gated" sound to be quite relaxing. One musical instrument that mimics this waveform is the
bagpipe. In the hands of a competent musician, the plaintive wail
of the bagpipe can produce emotions ranging from the eerie to the
remorseful.

Oscillating Sound is able to produce a wide variety of sounds
and sound effects that can imitate instruments like the bagpipe.
This project could be used as a background noise generator or mood
maker.

CONSTRUCTION NOTES

The parts count in Oscillating Sound is extremely low (5), with two
of these parts being integrated circuit (IC) chips (see Table 1-1 for
the parts list). Also needed are a power supply and an 8-ohm
speaker. One IC acts as a gate, the 4011 Quad Two-Input NAND
Gate (Radio Shack #276-2411), while the other is a switch, the 4066
Quad Bilateral Switch (Radio Shack #276-2466). The pin assignment for the 4011 IC is shown in Fig. 1-1, and the 4066 pin assignment is found in Fig. 1-2.

This project (see Fig. 1-3 for the project schematic) will easily

Table 1-1. Parts List for Oscillating Sound.

```
C1- 4.7mf Electrolytic Capacitor
IC1- 4011
IC2- 4066
R1- 100K Potentiometer
R2- 10K Potentiometer
*Use a 4 pin clock crystal oscillator (i.e. S50240)
```

Pin#	Assignment
1	Input
2	Input
3	Output
4	Output
5	Input
6	Input
7	GND
8	Input
9	Input
10	Output
11	Output
12	Input
13	Input
14	V

Fig. 1-1. Pin assignments for the 4011.

Pin#	Assignment
1	In/Out
2	Out/In
3	Out/In
4	In/Out
5	Control B
6	Control C
7	GND
8	In/Out
9	Out/In
10	Out/In
11	In/Out
12	Control D
13	Control A
14	V

Fig. 1-2. Pin assignments for the 4066.

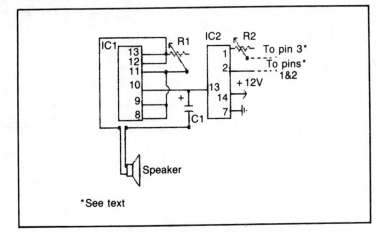

*See text

Fig. 1-3. Schematic diagram for Oscillating Sound.

fit on a large Modular IC Breadboard (Radio Shack #276-174). A greater space savings is afforded by squeezing Oscillating Sound onto a smaller Modular IC Breadboard (Radio Shack #276-175). For a complete tutorial on using these breadboards and transferring a completed project to a soldered printed circuit (PC) board, refer to Appendix A.

OPERATION

There are two adjustment points on Oscillating Sound for altering its output. By turning potentiometers R1 and R2 (together or independently) the final sound can be shaped to the desired "warble." If an amplifier circuit is connected at the speaker point, a more personal operation mode is possible. A pair of headphones connected to this amplifier would then surround the listener with oscillating sound, and isolate him from the noisy outside world.

2

Random Light Generator

P REDICTABILITY CONTRIBUTES TO WHAT SOME SCIENTISTS call the "boredom factor." Basically, the boredom factor develops when an individual can predict the next series of events for a given situation. While this type of prognostication might be useful in certain life threatening environments, predictability literally sucks the life out of a "game of chance."

In order for a game to be enjoyable (and commercially successful), there must be a random element. This random element is usually introduced by the roll of a die, the flip of a spinner, or the drawing of a card. No matter which method is employed, the result is always the same—a random, unpredictable event (unless somebody is cheating). A similar end product is possible with Random Light Generator—without the problem of cheating.

CONSTRUCTION NOTES

The actual random switch activation is performed by a 4017 Decade Counter/Divider IC (Radio Shack #276-2417). A 555 Timer IC (Radio Shack #276-1723) is used for supplying the Random Light Generator's clock frequency. This 555 Timer clock will be connected to pin 13 of the 4017, which is described as the Clock Enable in Fig. 2-1. Pin assignments for the 4017 and the 555 are shown in Fig. 2-1 and Fig. 2-2, respectively.

Fig. 2-1. Pin assignments for the 4017.

Pin#	Assignment
1	Output 5
2	Output 1
3	Output 0
4	Output 2
5	Output 6
6	Output 7
7	Output 3
8	GND
9	Output 8
10	Output 4
11	Output 9
12	Output C
13	Clock Enable
14	Clock
15	Reset
16	V

Random Light Generator's complete schematic is illustrated in Fig. 2-3. Other than the two major ICs, very few additional support components are necessary. Table 2-1 is a complete parts list for Random Light Generator. In a project like Random Light Generator, however, the most prominent component is the display. The 10 LEDs (light-emitting diodes) can be any color (red, yellow, green) and either size (jumbo T-1 3/4 or miniature T-1). One word of caution: when working with LEDs, the proper placement of the anode and cathode must be carefully observed. If the LEDs are not lighting correctly, try reversing the anode and cathode. Finally, the completed project will easily fit on a small Modular IC Breadboard (Radio Shack #276-175).

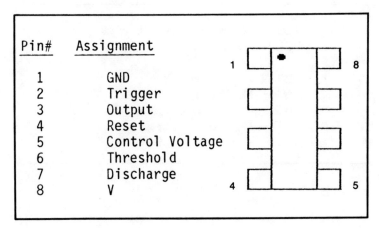

Fig. 2-2. Pin assignments for the 555.

Pin#	Assignment
1	GND
2	Trigger
3	Output
4	Reset
5	Control Voltage
6	Threshold
7	Discharge
8	V

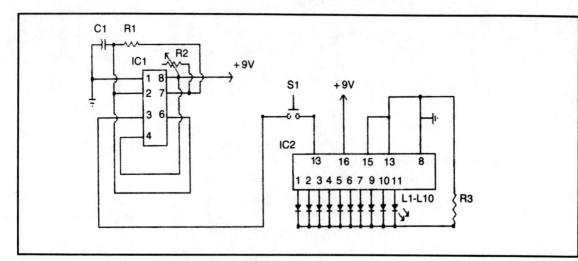

Fig. 2-3. Schematic diagram for Random Light Generator.

OPERATION

One adjustment will be necessary for the successful operation of Random Light Generator. The potentiometer R1 controls the pulse rate of the clock driving the 4017. This pulse rate should be varied until the desired clock cycle is achieved. In order to test the pulse rate, switch S1 is depressed, momentarily held, and then released.

    One possible application for Random Light Generator is an electronic game die. Just assign a number to each of the LEDs. Now whenever a random number is needed, press S1 and then release it. Remember, Random Light Generator is not a true random generator, but a "pseudo-random" generator. This means that the final number or lighted LED is more a product of when your finger releases S1 than random chance. Regardless, Random Light Generator does beat rolling a die.

```
C1- .01mf Capacitor
IC1- 555
IC2- 4017
L1-L10- LEDs
R1- 1K Resistor
R2- 1M Potentiometer
R3- 1K Resistor
S1- Momentary SPST
```

Table 2-1. Parts List for Random Light Generator.

3

Musical Mood Maker

D O YOU LONG FOR A WHIMSICAL DIVERSION FROM A TEDIOUS
day? Many people find a moment of relaxation or pleasure
in sitting down with a cup of hot coffee or a tall glass of iced tea,
in taking a hot shower, or in doing a crossword puzzle. The benefits
derived from each of these activities are a refreshed state of mind
and an elevated mood. But these pastimes also suffer from one common problem: they are surprisingly time-consuming. Obviously, you
normally don't stop in the middle of preparing a meal or balancing
a checkbook to take a shower. There is time, however, to push a
button.

This is where Musical Mood Maker demonstrates its
superiority over a caffeine beverage or a hot shower. Each press
of Musical Mood Maker's button brightens your day with one of
25 different tunes. So when you realize that you're overdrawn at
the bank, just press the button of the Musical Mood Maker. At least
you'll have a smile on your lips as you enter bankruptcy court.

CONSTRUCTION NOTES

Musical Mood Maker is based on the AY-3-1350 Tunes Synthesizer
(Radio Shack #276-1782). Figure 3-1 provides the pin assignments
for the AY-3-1350. This IC contains 25 pre-programmed tunes
which are triggered by a momentary push button SPST (single pole,
single throw) switch (refer to the schematic in Fig. 3-2).

Pin#	Assignment	Pin#	Assignment
1	GND	15	Tune Select Strobe
2	Vcc	16	Switch C Group Select
3	Vxx	17	Restart
4	GND	18	Tune Select 3
5	GND	19	Tune Select 2
6	Door 3	20	Tune Select 1
7	Backdoor	21	Tune Select E
8	Captest	22	Tune Select D
9	Tune Select 4	23	Tune Select C
10	Next Tune	24	Tune Select B
11	Discharge	25	Tune Select A
12	On/Off	26	Clock Out
13	Envelope	27	Oscillator
14	Tune Output	28	Reset

Fig. 3-1. Pin assignments for the AY-3-1350.

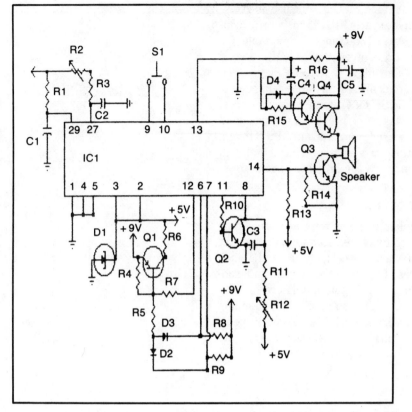

Fig. 3-2. Schematic diagram for Musical Mood Maker.

Table 3-1. Parts List for Musical Mood Maker.

C1— .1mf Capacitor	R3— 3.9K Resistor
C2— 47pf Capacitor	R4— 10K Resistor
C3— .22mf Capacitor	R5— 33K Resistor
C4— 10mf Electrolytic Capacitor	R6— 33 Resistor
C5— 10mf Electrolytic Capacitor	R7— 33K Resistor
D1— 5.1V Zener Diode	R8— 33K Resistor
D2— 1N914 Diode	R9— 33K Resistor
D3— 1N914 Diode	R10— 10K Resistor
D4— 1N914 Diode	R11— 470K Resistor
IC1— AY-3-1350	R12— 1M Potentiometer
Q1— MPS 2907	R13— 2.2K Resistor
Q2— MPS 3904	R14— 33K Resistor
Q3— MPS 3904	R15— 47K Resistor
Q4— MPS A13	R16— 33K Resistor
R1— 100K Resistor	S1— Momentary SPST
R2— 25K Potentiometer	

Of special interest in Musical Mood Maker is the use of 4 transistors (see Table 3-1 for a complete parts list). Transistors are integral to the triggering of each AY-3-1350 tune. For example, Q1 (MPS 2907), a pnp type transistor, controls the flow of +5 volts dc to turn ON the AY-3-1350, allowing a tune to be played.

The Musical Mood Maker circuit also requires one zener diode, the 1-watt, 5.1-volt 1N4733 (Radio Shack #276-565). Furthermore, battery operation of the Mood Maker requires both +5 volts and +9 volts. If battery operation is used, however, an SPST toggle switch needs to be placed on the +5 V source. This switch will prevent excessive battery drain when the project is not in use.

OPERATION

Each press of Musical Mood Maker's tune button triggers one tune from its sequence of 25 tunes, to be played on an 8-ohm speaker mounted within Musical Mood Maker's enclosure. Both the pitch and the speed at which the notes of the tune are played can be adjusted to your taste with the use of two potentiometers.

Varying pitch and speed can create some comical sounding tunes. Whether playing the Deutschland Leid at a breakneck speed, or a stately paced Blue Danube waltz, you will be sure to generate an appropriate mood swing with Musical Mood Maker.

4

Ocean Surf

T HE SEA IS A POWERFUL FORCE IN MANY CREATURES' LIVES. This power can even affect human beings, luring them to seashore vacation spots. What phenomenon explains this strange magnetism? Essentially, it is the ocean's "pulse" that soothes the tired mind. Furthermore, if this pulse is analyzed, the actual surf noise is found to be the prime pacifying element.

This surf noise can be broken down into a small amount of "white noise" and a liberal amount of "pink noise." A common example of a white noise source is the "hiss" produced by a blank television channel. Similarly, running water from a faucet that is equipped with an aerator produces a pink noise sound. These common household examples help explain the surf's large percentage of pink noise.

Ocean Surf is a pink noise generator. This project supplies a constant output of soothing, relaxing pink noise. There are no stray white noise elements, just the gentle sound of breaking waves.

CONSTRUCTION NOTES

Only one IC is necessary for completing Ocean Surf—the S2688 Noise Generator. Additionally, two support components, one resistor and one capacitor, are needed (see the parts list in Table

Table 4-1. Parts List for Ocean Surf.

Table 4-1. Parts List for Ocean Surf.

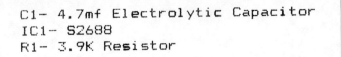

```
C1- 4.7mf Electrolytic Capacitor
IC1- S2688
R1- 3.9K Resistor
```

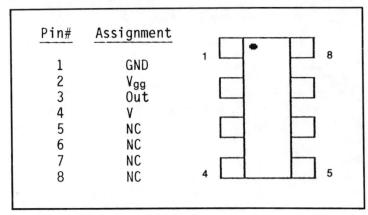

Pin#	Assignment
1	GND
2	V_{gg}
3	Out
4	V
5	NC
6	NC
7	NC
8	NC

Fig. 4-1. Pin assignments for the S2688.

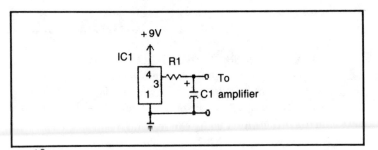

Fig. 4-2. Schematic diagram for Ocean Surf.

4-1). As the pin assignments in Fig. 4-1 show, the S2688 IC is a very simple CMOS (complementary metal-oxide semiconductor) chip. One unfortunate feature of the CMOS IC is the destructive power that static electricity has upon it. Keep this property in mind and handle the S2688 accordingly.

The sound output from the S2688 is extremely weak. Therefore, an external audio amplifier will need to be connected at the points indicated in Fig. 4-2. A home stereo system could be used for maximum Ocean Surf amplification.

OPERATION

Various pink noise qualities are possible with Ocean Surf. The values of the resistor R1 and the capacitor C1 can both be substituted over a wide range for different audio results. Even the supply voltage can be raised and lowered slightly for distinct pink noise changes. Once the final surf sound has been determined, a trip to the seashore will require nothing more than turning on Ocean Surf.

5

Rain

W HICH IS THE BEST SEASON OF THE YEAR FOR SLEEPING?
Spring is the answer, but the reason is quite subtle. One
of the predominant climate conditions present in the spring is rain.
This rain falls in gentle showers throughout the day and into the
night. In effect, a soothing action is produced by the hissing noise
of these April showers. It is this steady pulsing noise that makes
rain and spring the ultimate soporific agents.

The hissing noise that is found in a rain shower is pulsing white
noise. White noise can be produced artificially by tuning a TV or
radio dial to a spot of weak or no reception. Actually, a rain shower
is composed of both white and pink noise. This Rain project, however, will only produce pulsing white noise. For additional noise
projects, Ocean Surf in Chapter 4 is a pink noise project and Wind
in Chapter 6 is a white noise source project.

CONSTRUCTION NOTES

There are many ICs that are capable of producing the pulsing white
noise found in Rain. For this project, a Complex Sound Generator
SN76495 IC (Radio Shack #276-1764) is used. If you use another
sound generation chip, match the pin assignments shown in Fig.
5-1 to the alternate IC. A perfect match is not necessary, but the
pins used for Rain must be similar. One sound generator that is

16

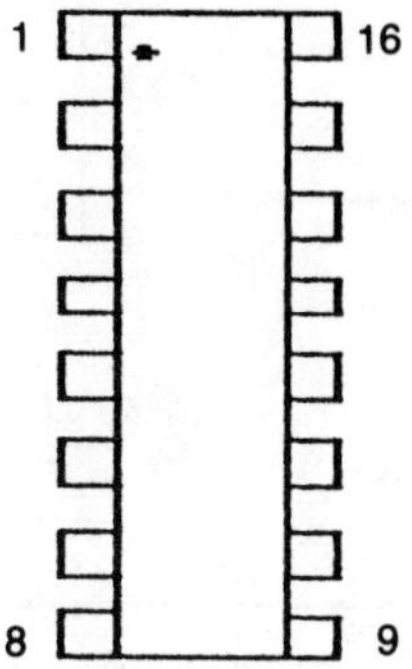

Fig. 5-1. Pin assignments for the
SN76495.

Pin#	Assignment
1	Noise Capacitor
2	Noise Resistor
3	Volume
4	V Reg
5	Audio In
6	Vcc
7	Audio Out
8	GND
9	VCO Capacitor
10	VCO Resistor
11	SLF Resistor
12	SLF Capacitor
13	VCO Select
14	Mixer C
15	Mixer B
16	Mixer A

worth trying is the SN76488N Complex Sound Generator. Most of the pin assignments used for Rain are also present on the SN76488N. Table 5-1 lists the remaining parts required for Rain's construction.

The tonal quality of the white noise can be altered by changing the resistor value connected to pin 5 and the capacitor value attached to pin 6 of the SN76495. For even greater control over the noise output, a potentiometer of a resistance from 100K ohm to 1M ohm, can be substituted for the resistor at pin 5.

An added feature of the SN76495 is its built-in 125-mW audio amplifier that is capable of driving an 8-ohm speaker. This fringe benefit eliminates the need for an external amplifier at pin 13. The presence of this built-in amplifier also presents another point to consider when selecting a substitute sound generation IC.

Table 5-1. Parts List for Rain.

```
C1- .1mf Capacitor
C2- .001mf Capacitor
C3- 10mf Electrolytic Capacitor
C4- 100mf Electrolytic Capacitor
IC1- SN76495
R1- 1M Resistor
R2- 470K Resistor
R3- 1M Resistor
```

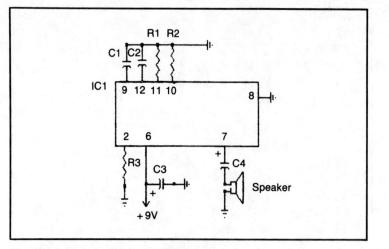

Fig. 5-2. Schematic diagram for Rain.

OPERATION

The pulsing of the white noise in Rain is controlled by the pot on pin 18, R2. Any other resistors or pots attached to pin 5 will only alter the tone of the white noise. Try various combinations of components (resistors, capacitors, and pots) until the desired sound quality is reached.

Rain will "fall" from the moment the battery is connected to pin 12. Therefore, the addition of a switch would be prudent for preventing unwarranted battery drain. After all of the final adjustments have been made and Rain is safely tucked away in a suitable enclosure, throw the switch (or plug in the battery) and step into a somnolent spring shower.

6

Wind

R USTLING LEAVES, MOVING BRANCHES, AND A COLD SHIVER
are all products of the wind. While a warm, lazy breeze during the heat of summer is a welcome relief, the same cannot be
said of a cold, biting wind in winter. Even the sound of the wind
can generate a specific emotion depending on the season of the year.

The sound of the wind is a pure white noise source. One of white
noise's major attributes is the blocking out or the masking of outside sounds. This masking ability is extremely useful when trying
to electronically filter an unwanted frequency. Wind, the white noise
generation project, is the basis for this type of a masking circuit.

CONSTRUCTION NOTES

The white noise produced in Wind is generated by an S2688 Noise
Generator IC. Several other ICs are capable white noise sources
(see Chapter 5).

Any type of audio amplifier can be connected to pins 1 and 3
of the S2688 (refer to the schematic in Fig. 6-1). If an amplifier
is unavailable, the 741C Operational Amplifier IC makes an ideal
low cost alternative. The 741C can be used as the groundwork for
constructing numerous amplifier and frequency filter circuits (see
Fig. 6-2 for the 741C's pin assignments). Table 6-1 lists the parts
necessary for constructing the basic Wind circuit.

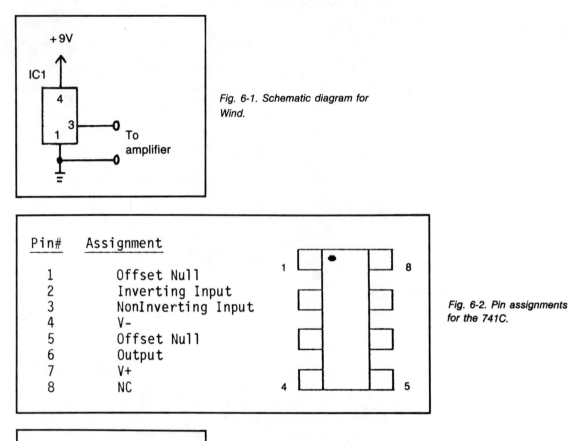

Fig. 6-1. Schematic diagram for Wind.

Pin#	Assignment
1	Offset Null
2	Inverting Input
3	NonInverting Input
4	V-
5	Offset Null
6	Output
7	V+
8	NC

Fig. 6-2. Pin assignments for the 741C.

IC1 — S2688

Table 6-1. Parts List for Wind.

OPERATION

Few, if any, adjustments are necessary for running Wind. The only controls are those inherent to the audio amplification system itself (volume, tone, etc.). Wind (using the S2688) is a consistent, reliable white noise supply. When this performance is coupled with the masking ability of white noise, Wind can easily blow away all annoying sounds.

7

Sound Effects Cube

S YNTHESIZED MUSIC HAS AN INTRIGUING QUALITY THAT HAS maintained its mystery for listeners since Robert Moog popularized his *Moog Synthesizer* in the late 1960s. While modern keyboard synthesizers support IC "brains," touch-button controls, and computer interface options, those early synthesizers depended on their human operators to laboriously patch interface cords to create each new sound.

Regardless of the method used to create the electronic melody, an electronically generated signal (usually white noise) is the basis for all sounds. It is how the signal is modified or processed that makes the final sound emulate a saxophone's wail or an alien creature's howl. A synthesizer's method of processing signals is through an oscillator, such as one or both of the following types: voltage-controlled oscillator (VCO) or super-low-frequency (SLF). The eerie strains of self-composed synthesized music can drift through your high-tech household with the use of Sound Effects Cube—and you don't even need archaic patch cords.

CONSTRUCTION NOTES

The "brain" of Sound Effects Cube is the SN76495 Complex Sound Generator (Radio Shack #276-1764). This IC not only generates the tones to be processed, but it also provides two types of

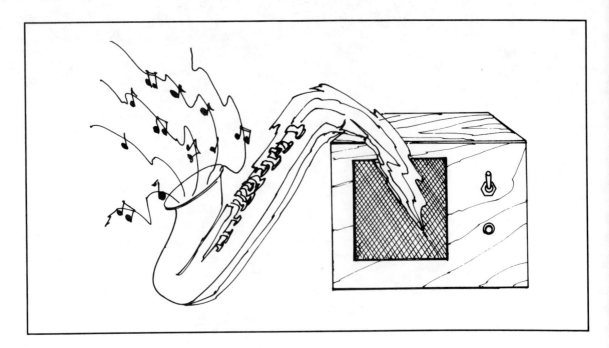

Table 7-1. Parts List for Sound Effects Cube.

```
C1-  .001mf Capacitor
C2-  .1mf Capacitor
C3-  10mf Capacitor
C4-  100mf Electrolytic Capacitor
C5-  .001mf Capacitor
C6-  .1mf Capacitor
C7-  10mf Capacitor
C8-  .001mf Capacitor
C9-  .1mf Capacitor
C10- 10mf Capacitor
IC1- SN76495
R1-  56K Resistor
R2-  50K Potentiometer
R3-  1M Resistor
R4-  33K Potentiometer
R5-  5K Potentiometer
S1-  3-position Rotary
S2-  SPST Toggle
S3-  SPST Toggle
S4-  SPST Toggle
S5-  SPST Toggle
S6-  3-position Rotary
S7-  3-position Rotary
```

oscillators to modify a generated sound signal: a VCO and a SLF. One useful parameter that can be explored with Sound Effects Cube is varying the voltage sent to the VCO to alter the frequency of the tone. The additional parts required to complete Sound Effects Cube are listed in Table 7-1.

For connecting the VCO capacitors with pin 9 of the SN76495 or the SLF capacitors with pin 12 (see the schematic in Fig. 7-1), DIP (dual in-line package) switches, rotary switches, or direct breadboard connections can be used. The two switch types (DIP and rotary) can be mounted on the project's cube enclosure for easy access.

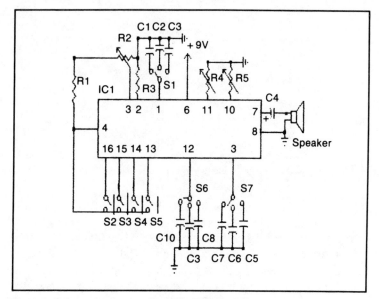

Fig. 7-1. Schematic diagram for Sound Effects Cube.

OPERATION

Volume for Sound Effects Cube is controlled with a potentiometer varying the voltage on pin 3 between .4 and 3.5 volts. Tonal quality of the notes are shaped by using a combination of settings on the SLF capacitor, VCO capacitor, SLF resistor, VCO resistor, VCO select, noise capacitor, and the three mixers (A on pin 16, B on pin 15, and C on pin 14).

8

Wall Sound Panel

WITHIN THE DESIGN STRUCTURE OF THE HIGH-TECH HOUSE-hold, artistic projects stimulate the sense of hearing as well as the sense of sight. If a third sense, that of touch, is also involved, the viewer becomes an active element in the project. Wall Sound Panel is sensitive to the touch of a human hand. Musical tones are the direct result of an interaction between the participant and Wall Sound Panel.

The greatest fascination generated by Wall Sound Panel is that a participant activates the project's circuit. A sandwich of vertically and horizontally placed wires, covered by plastic sheeting, creates a pressure sensing area for the project. When the surface is touched, a circuit is completed. Applying pressure to different areas on the face of Wall Sound Panel generates a variety of musical tones.

CONSTRUCTION NOTES

The single IC used in the Wall Sound Panel is the 555 Timer (Radio Shack #276-1723). By substituting capacitors with different values from the ones presented in Parts List (Table 8-1), it is possible to achieve alternative tones from Wall Sound Panel. The circuitry used to drive Wall Sound Panel's tones (see Fig. 8-1) is only one portion of the completed project. A pressure sensing surface (as illustrated in the schematic) must also be constructed.

Table 8-1. Parts List for Wall Sound Panel.

```
C1- 4.7mf Electrolytic Capacitor
C2- .001mf Capacitor
C3- .005mf Capacitor
C4- .01mf Capacitor
C5- .1mf Capacitor
C6- 10mf Capacitor
IC1- 555
R1- 100K Potentiometer
R2- 1K Resistor
```

Wiring Wall Sound Panel's pressure sensing area is time consuming, but quite simple. Three sheets of semi-rigid plastic material are cut to identical dimensions (e.g. three 10 inch by 10 inch pieces). Lightweight *ABS plastic sheeting,* which is ideal for this application, is available from local hobby stores (see Appendix A for further information on ABS plastic). One sheet supports horizontal contact wires, another supports vertical contact wires, and the third provides a nearly complete barrier between the horizontal and vertical sheets. This barrier permits contact between the two wired sheets when pressure is applied directly to open areas selectively placed in the barrier.

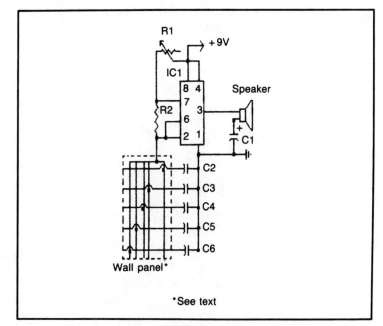

Fig. 8-1. Schematic diagram for Wall Sound Panel.

Glue four pieces of wire wrap wire, which have had 10 inches of their insulative material removed from the center section of each wire, vertically on one sheet of plastic and four, similarly prepared, horizontally positioned wires on another sheet of plastic. Be sure to leave enough insulated wire extending from the plastic sheeting to connect the pressure sensing area with the rest of Wall Sound Panel's circuitry. Cyanoacrylate glue is the best adhesive for gluing the wire to the plastic sheeting (see Appendix A for the use of cyanoacrylate glue).

The barrier sheet is created by placing the remaining plastic sheet over the two plastic grid sheets and marking the intersection points of their wires. Cut a 1/8 to 1/4 inch hole in the barrier sheet at each point of intersection. Sandwich the three sheets so that each wired grid sheet faces the middle barrier sheet. To finish the project, place the supporting circuitry in a separate enclosure next to the pressure sensing area.

OPERATION

Wall Sound Panel is activated by a light touch on the pressure sensing area's surface. When the exposed wires of the top grid sheet are pressed against the exposed wires of the bottom sheet, a circuit is completed and the appropriate tone sounds. The locations of the contacts are easily seen if clear plastic sheeting is used for the pressure sensing area. An opaque plastic, however, requires the participating viewer of Wall Sound Panel to randomly touch their way through sound creation unless the appropriate spots are marked on the plastic sheeting.

9

Drum Cube

A SIDE FROM HUMMING ALONG, WHAT DO MOST PEOPLE DO when they hear a song? They tap their feet and/or tap their fingers, provided, that is, that they like the music. A further analysis of this "extremity percussion" shows that the greatest degree of activity is generated in emulation of the drums and bass (the back beat).

Drums and drumbeats have a deep-rooted fascination for human beings. This adulation is partly responsible for the widespread misconception that anyone can play the drums. While most of us long for the status of a Ringo Starr, very few of us will ever attain such a regal position. For millions of frustrated Lenny Whites, there is Drum Cube.

Essentially, Drum Cube is a simple drum sound synthesizer that can be built in several different configurations. Only the basic drum sound producing circuitry is shown in this project. First evaluate your syncopation needs and then add the required drum sounds for a custom Drum Cube "kit."

CONSTRUCTION NOTES

There are no ICs in Drum Cube. One npn transistor, MPS A06, produces the synthesized drum sound and another MPS A06 amplifies the final drum sound output. Table 9-1 is a parts list for Drum Cube.

Table 9-1. Parts List for Drum Cube.

```
C1-  .01mf Capacitor
C2-  .01mf Capacitor
C3-  .01mf Capacitor
C4-  1mf Capacitor
C5-  4.7mf Electrolytic Capacitor
Q1-  MPS A06
Q2-  MPS A06
R1-  100K Resistor
R2-  22K Resistor
R3-  4.7K Resistor
R4-  470K Resistor
R5-  47K Resistor
R6-  47K Resistor
R7-  25K Potentiometer
```

A metal plate described in Fig. 9-1 as *Input* should be formed as one of the faces in the final Drum Cube construction. This will give ample room for pounding out your special beat.

An even better Drum Cube is possible by combining three of these circuits into the same container, yielding three cube faces for drumming.

These Drum Cube circuits are combined, with slight C2 and C3 capacitor value changes, and fed together to the amplifier input. No more than three Drum Cubes should be joined in this fashion, however.

A Deluxe Drum Cube version is possible with the MM5871

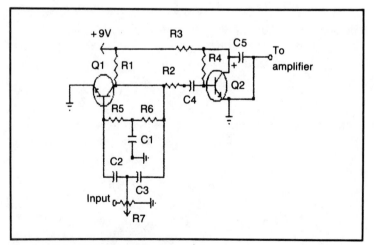

Fig. 9-1. Schematic diagram for Drum Cube.

Rhythm Pattern Generator IC. This drum chip has five drum sounds (snare, bongo, bass, wood block, and brush noise) and six tempo patterns (rock, slow rock, bossa, swing, samba, and waltz). The only problem is the scarcity of this IC.

OPERATION

If the Drum Cube has been properly assembled, tapping on the cube face (or faces, if more than one Drum Cube circuit has been used) will bring forth a beat. Adjust the potentiometer R7 to vary the "touch" of the Drum Cube's face switch (Input). Now, you can belt out that Motown, low down, get down kind of sound, just by bopping your beat, on the Drum Cube.

10

Voice Sculpture

ART HAS A TRADITION THAT PRODUCES STRICT RULES. EVEN the so-called impromptu or spontaneous art forms adhere to a set of guidelines. Consequently, when a new art form begins, its proponent's first expression is often a desire to eliminate all rules. This course will not be followed, however, during the introduction of the revolutionary now art form, Voice Sculpture.

In its inactive state, Voice Sculpture bears an uncanny resemblance to a dead rectangular box (of your own design). But, a touch to its action switch causes Voice Sculpture to come to life and utter one of 33 different, preprogrammed words. These inactive/active qualities make this an art form unlike any other. Therefore, when Voice Sculpture is placed in the high-tech household, traditional art barriers are not removed, instead new audio vistas are created.

CONSTRUCTION NOTES

Voice Sculpture makes use of a unique IC pair: the SP0256 Speech Processor and the SPR016 External Speech ROM (Read Only Memory) (Radio Shack #276-1783). The 16-pin SPR016 (see Fig. 10-1 for pin assignments) stores 36 key words for direct voice processing in the bigger 28-pin SP0256 (see Fig. 10-2). Table 10-1 lists the remaining parts required for Voice Sculpture.

Pin#	Assignment
1	GND
2	C3
3	NC
4	ROM Clock
5	NC
6	NC
7	CS1
8	CS2
9	ROM Enable
10	Serial Out
11	V
12	NC
13	NC
14	Serial In
15	C1
16	C2

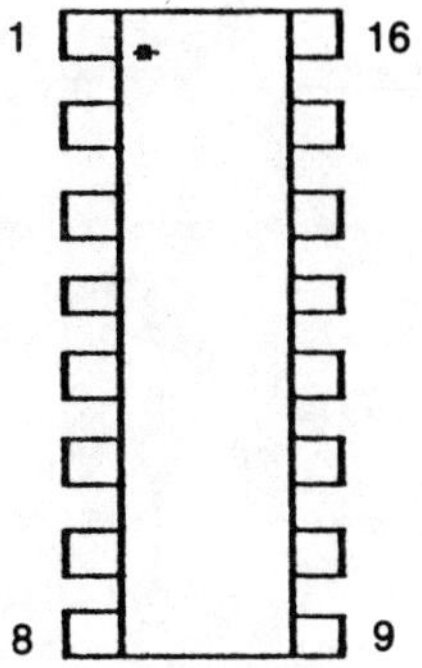

Fig. 10-1. Pin assignments for the SPR016.

The External Speech ROM IC in Voice Sculpture is the key to the production of fully formed words and phrases. This chip receives the address signal coded by the DIP switch S1 (see Fig. 10-3), and sends a serial 8-bit output to the Speech Processor. The SP0256 then forms and connects the allophones that are represented by the serial data into the required word.

Pin#	Assignment	Pin#	Assignment
1	GND	15	A4
2	Reset	16	A3
3	ROM Disable	17	A2
4	C1	18	A1
5	C2	19	Strobe Enable
6	C3	20	Address Load
7	V	21	Serial In
8	Standby	22	Test
9	Load Request	23	V
10	A8	24	Digital Out
11	A7	25	Standby Reset
12	Serial Out	26	ROM Clock
13	A6	27	Oscillator 1
14	A5	28	Oscillator 2

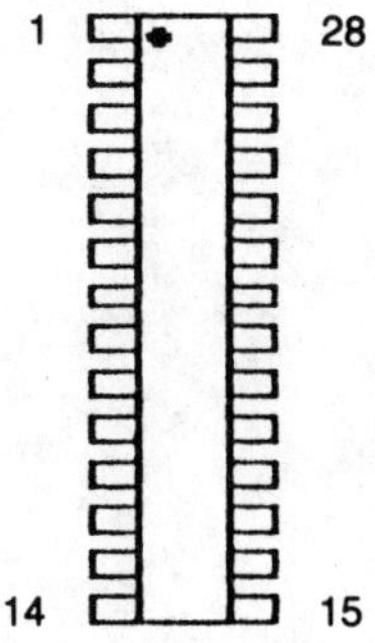

Fig. 10-2. Pin assignments for the SP0256.

Table 10-1. Parts List for Voice Sculpture.

```
C1-  .1mf Capacitor
C2-  47pf Capacitor
C3-  47pf Capacitor
C4-  .022mf Capacitor
C5-  .022mf Capacitor
C6-  10mf Electrolytic Capacitor
CL1- 3.12 MHz Crystal
IC1- SP0256
IC2- SPR016
R1-R8- 100K Resistor
R9- 100K Resistor
R10- 33K Resistor
R11- 33K Resistor
S1- 8-position DIP
```

The crystal CL1, connected between pins 27 and 28 of the SP0256, controls the tone of Voice Sculpture. Different frequency values of crystals can be substituted at CL1's location for various vocal results.

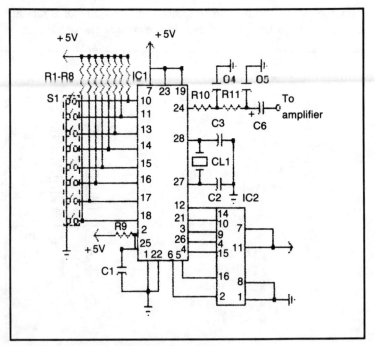

Fig. 10-3. Schematic diagram for Voice Sculpture.

OPERATION

Only positions 3-8 are used in the 8-position DIP switch, S1. These six switches control the selection of words spoken by Voice Sculpture in its active state. For circuit testing purposes, set all six switch positions "OFF." Now, when Voice Sculpture is activated with a momentary switch, across SP0256's pins 8 and 20 (see Fig. 11-1 for the proper connection application), the word "Oh" will be heard through the amplifier.

Experiment with all 36 entries in Voice Sculpture's vocabulary. These entries are all 8-bit decimal coded addresses, with position 8 of S1 representing the low bit and position 3 being the high bit. Using this representation, the 36th entry has a decimal code of 35 with an S1 positioning of 8, 7, and 3 "ON" and 6, 5, and 4 "OFF."

11

Jabbering Robot

R OBOTS, BY THEIR VERY NATURE, ARE SUITABLE OCCUPANTS
for the high-tech household. Unfortunately, when robots are
assigned to their appointed duties they inevitably fall into a slave
category. This robotic servitude usually mandates a practical application and deprives the home environment of a potential mobile
entertainer. Robot butlers and maids, beware and make way for
the Jabbering Robot.

Utilizing any form of a motorized platform, the Jabbering Robot
carts around the room and stammers out a perfectly nonsensical
utterance. All of these shenanigans are under a human being's
thoughtful control, but please temper your expectations of Jabbering Robot's household role. It may not serve any functional purpose, but then neither do most dogs and cats.

CONSTRUCTION

Only the voice part of Jabbering Robot is presented in this project.
Virtually any chassis and motor combination will propel your vocal
friend. Therefore, be creative. The main IC that wags Jabbering
Robot's tongue is the SP0256 Speech Processor (Radio Shack
#276-1784). Figure 11-1 and Table 11-1 provide the schematic and
parts necessary for making its vocal tract.

The support components connected to pin 24 of the SP0256

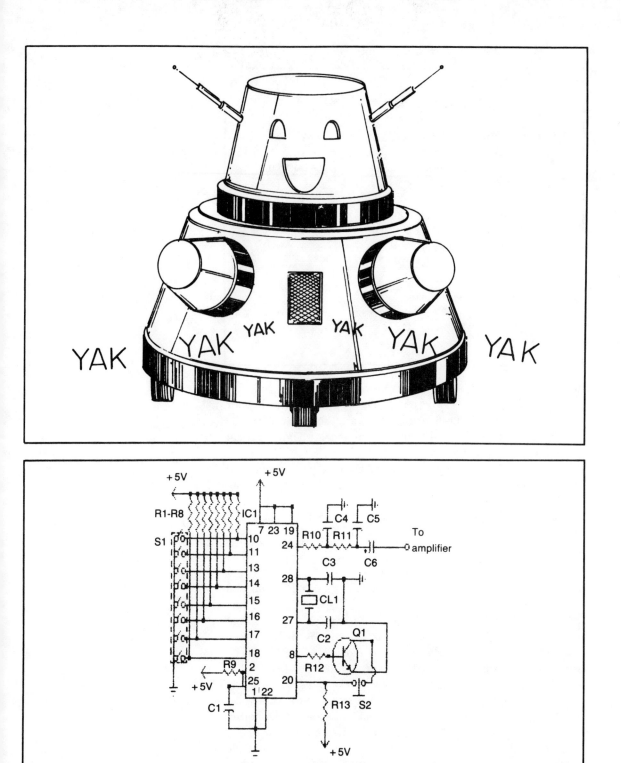

Fig. 11-1. Schematic diagram for Jabbering Robot.

Table 11-1. Parts List for Jabbering Robot.

```
C1-  .1mf Capacitor
C2-  47pf Capacitor
C3-  47pf Capacitor
C4-  .022mf Capacitor
C5-  .022mf Capacitor
C6-  10mf Electrolytic Capacitor
CL1- 3.12 MHz Crystal
IC1- SP0256
Q1-  MPS 3904
R1-R8- 100K Resistor
R9-  100K Resistor
R10- 33K Resistor
R11- 33K Resistor
R12- 10K Resistor
R13- 10K Resistor
S1-  8-position DIP
S2-  Momentary SPST
```

form a low pass filter. This filter turns the IC's digital signal into an analog one before the output reaches the amplifier. If your amplifier sports a built-in low pass filter, these parts can be eliminated. Experiment with this arrangement before a final soldered circuit is constructed.

There are 64 possible allophones and assorted pauses contained within the SP0256. Each of these speech parts is controlled via an 8-bit address input through S1. Only positions 3-8 are required for activating all 64 speech parts. Position 8 (a decimal 1) is the low bit and position 3 is the high bit (a decimal 32).

OPERATION

Use S1 for selecting Jabbering Robot's daily speech. Positions 3-8 of the 8-position DIP are set either "ON" or "OFF." This arrangement determines the binary address sent to the SP0256 which, in turn, outputs the selected allophone or pause. Obviously, spoken pauses are silent and should probably be avoided. All of the Speech Processor's pauses are located in decimal addresses 0-4.

When the desired speech part has been selected and properly programmed with S1, Jabbering Robot is ready to roam. Just activate your mobile chassis and gibberish will soon fill the house. After your guest has become established, a name will be in order. Dogs and cats have names, so why can't this little unintelligible fellow have one? *Lewis* somehow sounds most appropriate for a Jabbering Robot.

12

Pulsing Tones

S OUND PRODUCED WITH A THROBBING TONE WILL STIMU-
late even the most staid listener. This pulsing beat emulates
the chronometer of the human body—the heart. In fact, the human
body can be subtly affected by slight variations in this musical pulse.
These effects usually manifest themselves in altered pulse rates,
heightened breathing activities, and enhanced sensations.

With so much power contained inside the strains of pulsating
sound, no high-tech household would be complete without a suitable
throbbing tone generator. The possible applications are endless.
Think of a soft, gentle pulse helping to erase the tensions developed from a strenuous day. Just such a mental massage is obtainable
through Pulsing Tones.

CONSTRUCTION NOTES

Pulsing Tones needs only 8 parts for completion (see Table 12-1),
two of which are ICs. Also required is a speaker and a power supply. One of these ICs produces the circuit's timing and the other
generates the tonal sound. The 555 Timer chip is the pulse or timing IC, while the 74LS123 Dual One-Shot IC is the tonal output
processor. The pin assignments for the 74LS123 are given in Fig.
12-1.

A wide range of sounds are producible with Pulsing Tones as

Table 12-1. Parts List for Pulsing Tones.

```
C1- 4.7mf Electrolytic Capacitor
C2- 1mf Electrolytic Capacitor
IC1- 555
IC2- 74LS123
R1- 100K Potentiometer
R2- 1K Resistor
R3- 100K Potentiometer
R4- 220 Resistor
```

soon as power is applied to the circuit. A switch will provide selective power application. Most of these sounds can be created with little or no modification to the original circuit described in Fig. 12-2. Furthermore, there are four circuit areas that are ripe for alteration: potentiometer R1, capacitor C1, potentiometer R3, and capacitor C2.

Different values for each of these components will produce different sounds. At this point, value selection and combination are wide open for experimentation. One other possibility worthy of exploration, however, is the substitution of resistors for pots R1 and R3. An endless tonal range is possible. This, in fact, would be an ideal Pulsing Tones enhancement.

Pin#	Assignment
1	Input A
2	Input B
3	Clear
4	Output
5	Output
6	Capacitor
7	Resistor/Capacitor
8	GND
9	Input B
10	Input A
11	Clear
12	Output
13	Output
14	Capacitor
15	Resistor/Capacitor
16	V

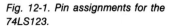

Fig. 12-1. Pin assignments for the 74LS123.

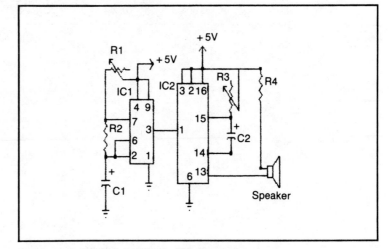

Fig. 12-2. Schematic diagram for Pulsing Tones.

OPERATION

The proper operation of Pulsing Tones will be dependent on the final desired sound. As discussed in the above CONSTRUCTION NOTES, R1 and R3 are variables and C1 and C2 values can be determined by the user.

No matter what the finished circuit arrangement is, Pulsing Tones will always be adjustable and unique. This "open" type of circuitry is ideal for custom tone generation or for designing that special sound to pulse away today's troubles.

13

Pulsing Light

L IGHT SERVES TWO PURPOSES IN THE HIGH-TECH HOUSE-
hold: functional illumination and mood creation. Various light
forms cause different effects on people. Soft room lighting sets a
calm room atmosphere. Spot illumination aids in preparing a useful
working environment. Artistic lighting, however, offers the greatest
influence over a viewer's attitude.

The rhythmic strobing of Pulsing Light is almost hypnotic as
its calming action affects the viewer. The LEDs of this project flash,
one after another, in a bar that can be either wall mounted or independently enclosed for table top display.

CONSTRUCTION NOTES

IC4, a 74154 4-Line to 16-Line Decoder (see Fig. 13-1), IC3, a
74LS193 4-Bit Up-Down Counter (see Fig. 13-2), and IC1, a 555
Timer (Radio Shack #276-1723) are the three main ICs used in Pulsing Light. It is the 74LS193 that triggers the pulsing LEDs in sequence. The 74154 performs the actual lighting of the LEDs. All
switching in Pulsing Light is conducted by IC2, a 7400 Quad Two-
Input NAND Gate (Radio Shack #276-1801) (see Fig. 13-3).

The rate at which Pulsing Lights pulsates is controlled by the
555 Timer. By choosing a resistor of a different value than that
given in the Parts List Table (Table 13-1) or by substituting a poten-

Pin#	Assignment		
1	Output 0	13	Output 11
2	Output 1	14	Output 12
3	Output 2	15	Output 13
4	Output 3	16	Output 14
5	Output 4	17	Output 15
6	Output 5	18	Input E1
7	Output 6	19	Input E2
8	Output 7	20	Input D
9	Output 8	21	Input C
10	Output 9	22	Input B
11	Output 10	23	Input A
12	GND	24	V

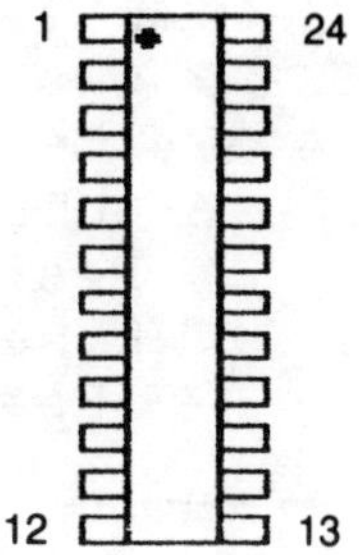

Fig. 13-1. Pin assignments for the 74154.

Pin#	Assignment		
1	Input B	9	Input D
2	Output B	10	Input C
3	Output A	11	Load
4	Count Down	12	Carry
5	Count Up	13	Borrow
6	Output C	14	Clear
7	Output D	15	Input A
8	GND	16	V

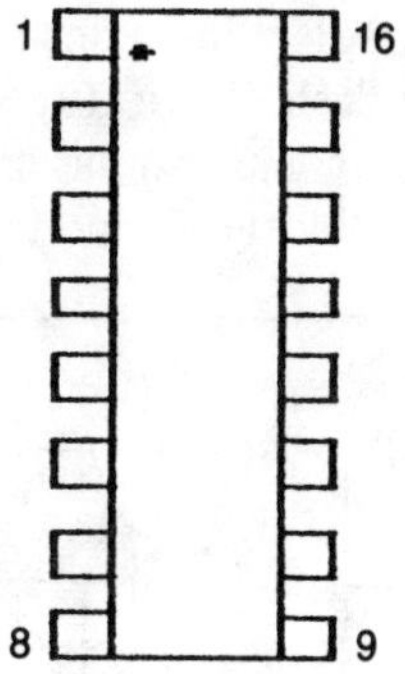

Fig. 13-2. Pin assignments for the 74LS193.

Pin#	Assignment		
1	Input	8	Output
2	Input	9	Input
3	Output	10	Input
4	Input	11	Output
5	Input	12	Input
6	Output	13	Input
7	GND	14	V

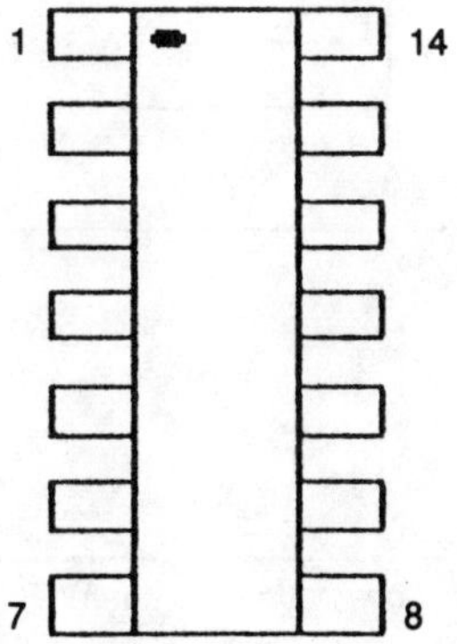

Fig. 13-3. Pin assignments for the 7400.

Table 13-1. Parts List for Pulsing Light.

```
C1- 1mf Electrolytic Capacitor
IC1- 555
IC2- 74LS193
IC3- 7400
IC4- 74154
L1-L16- LEDs
R1- 1K Resistor
R2- 100K Resistor
R3- 470 Resistor
```

tiometer for the resistor R1 (see Fig. 13-4), connected to the 555 Timer, a new pulsation rate can be set.

OPERATION

Operation of Pulsing Light is refreshingly simple—just place the finished project in its desired location and sit back to watch Pulsing Light flash. Wave after wave of continuous visual delight awaits you with Pulsing Light. But be careful, you may find yourself transfixed by the hypnotic rhythm of the LEDs.

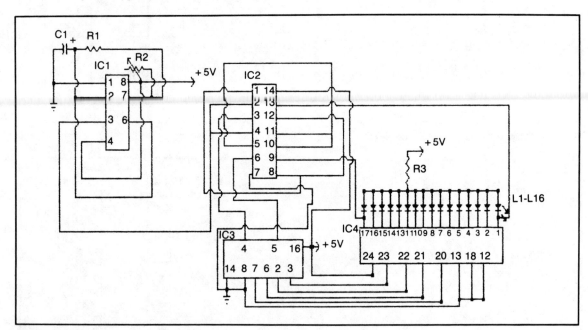

Fig. 13-4. Schematic diagram for Pulsing Light.

14

LED Number Blocks

BLOCKS ARE A PART OF EVERYONE'S CHILDPLAY. GRANTED, some of today's neo-synthetic blocks have replaced the more traditional wooden variety, but the educational value is still present. Blocks teach the growing mind some of the elementary principles in mathematics, language, architecture, and science. As the mind grows, the block takes on more of an aesthetic form and less of an educational role.

In the high-tech household, use of the block shape can capitalize on this new aesthetic value. LED Number Blocks serve as a contemporary statement of a traditional form. They should be thought of as a high-tech substitute capable of providing the educational, as well as the aesthetic, roles afforded by their wooden kin.

CONSTRUCTION NOTES

LED Number Blocks consists of five separate circuits—one for each face of the block (the empty face serves as a display base). A single face is represented by the schematic diagram in Fig. 14-1. The display in this circuit is driven by a 7447 BCD To Seven-Segment Decoder/Driver (Radio Shack #276-1805). Figure 14-2 gives the pin assignments for the 7447. Table 14-1 lists the parts for LED Number Blocks.

Two types of digital displays will work with the 7447 IC: com-

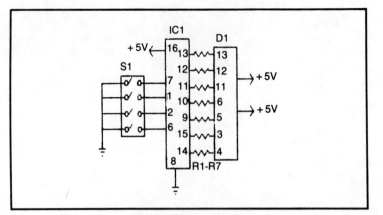

Fig. 14-1. Schematic diagram for LED Number Blocks.

Pin#	Assignment
1	Input B
2	Input C
3	Lamp Test
4	BI/RBO
5	RBI
6	Input D
7	Input A
8	GND
9	Output e
10	Output d
11	Output c
12	Output b
13	Output a
14	Output g
15	Output f
16	V

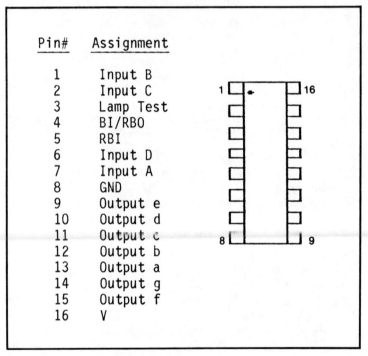

Fig. 14-2. Pin assignments for the 7447.

Table 14-1. Parts List for LED Number Blocks.

```
D1- Common Anode 7-segment Display
IC1- 7447
R1-R7- 330 Resistor
S1- 4-position DIP
```

Table 14-2. DIP Switch Settings
for All Possible Seven-Segment Display Digits.

DIGIT	DIP Switch Settings—"ON"
1	1
2	2
3	1&2
4	3
5	1&3
6	2&3
7	1,2&3
8	4
9	1&4

mon anode and common cathode. Use the common anode (active low) digital display for working with LED Number Blocks. Each display fits a 14-pin IC socket. These sockets should be attached directly to the LED Number Blocks' five "active" faces.

The circuit for one face should be placed on a small piece of an *Experimenter's PC Board* (Radio Shack #276-170). Refer to Appendix A for help in cutting this board and selecting the cube construction material. Arrange the power supply and the five 7447 driver boards inside the cube structure. Prepare every cube face with a 14-pin socket that has the required seven wires running from the socket to the appropriate 7447 driver board connections.

As an option, a mercury switch can be placed inside LED Number Blocks. This switch will prevent both battery drain and excessive wear on the displays. Orient the mercury switch parallel to one of the cube display faces with its switch active base fixed against the blank base face. Then, for activation of the mercury controlled LED Number Blocks, just turn the block onto its blank base side. Conversely, place LED Number Blocks on one of its display faces to deactivate.

OPERATION

The DIP switches on each of the 7447 driver boards must be manually set for a specific number. Table 14-2 lists all of the possible digits and their corresponding DIP switch settings. There are six additional unlisted settings that will provide some interesting non-digit displays for experimentation purposes.

After the DIPs have all been set and the faces attached to the cube structure, LED Number Blocks is ready for operation. The flexibility of interchangeable face values (through DIPs) lends this high-tech wooden block substitute considerable credence. Who knows what incredible educational achievements will be stimulated in a growing mind with LED Number Blocks?

15

LED Light Cube

I N THE AGE OF ELECTRONIC COMMUNICATION, ONE MIGHT think that there is little room for such an old fashioned object as a paperweight. Computer generated bits and bytes travel along telephone wires sending messages in a new paperless form. Actually, one offshoot of the computer community is an overabundance of computer printed documents, requiring even more paperwork than before the age of electronic communication. But a valid reason for paperweights remains, whether the user owns a computer or not.

LED Light Cube provides a paperweight that reflects the electronic technology behind the paper's output. Alternatively, this cube makes a suitable piece of artwork for desktop or table top display. Contained within a clear or opaque enclosure are a number of LEDs and support circuitry to drive the flashing LEDs.

CONSTRUCTION NOTES

Operation of LED Light Cube is directly controlled by the 3909 LED Flasher/Oscillator (see Fig. 15-1). The only other support materials required for the project are a few resistors, a capacitor, a battery, and of course, the LEDs themselves (see Parts List Table 15-1).

Figure 15-2 is a schematic diagram of LED Light Cube's driving circuitry. LEDs for filling LED Light Cube can be selected from any of the three common LED colors—red, green, or yellow. The

Pin#	Assignment
1	Fast RC
2	Out
3	NC
4	GND
5	V
6	R
7	NC
8	Slow RC

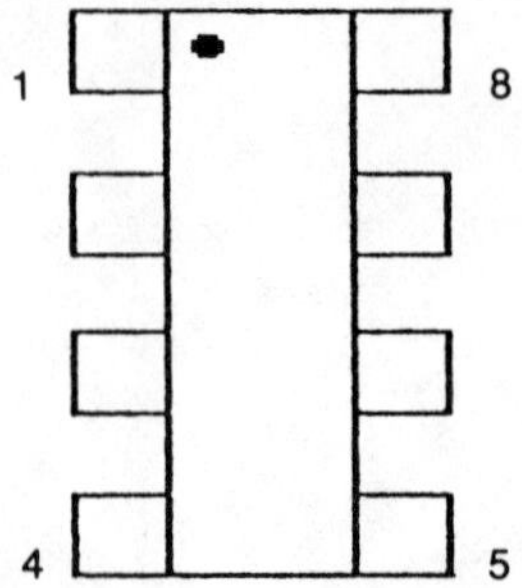

Fig. 15-1. Pin assignments for the 3909.

sizes of the LEDs will also affect the project's final appearance. Mixing jumbo LEDs with the miniature and regular sized LEDs creates a mottled light look for the final displayed project. The cube enclosure for LED Light Cube is constructed of heavyweight, clear or opaque plastic sheeting as described in Appendix A. Ideal positioning of the LEDs within the cube enclosure is a random spacing of the LEDs throughout the cube's interior.

Although all of the LEDs in LED Light Cube circuit pulse at the same rate, it is possible to create a cube with LEDs flashing at staggered rates. With the addition of a nearly identical second circuit based on its own 3909 IC, a second set of flashing LEDs are added to the cube. A new flash rate for this second circuit is selected by using a capacitor, C1, of a different value than that used in the first circuit.

OPERATION

Once a battery is in place within the LED Light Cube, your high-tech paperweight is fully functional. The simple and silent operation of LED Light Cube permits it to blink ceaselessly on the top of your desk or table adding a bright extra dimension to your environment.

Table 15-1. Parts List for LED Light Cube.

```
B1- 1.5-3V Battery
C1- 1000mf Electrolytic Capacitor
IC1- 3909
L1- LED
R1- 680 Resistor
R2- 220 Resistor
R3- 33 Resistor
```

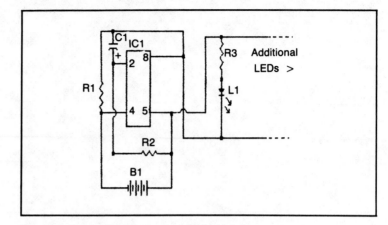

Fig. 15-2. Schematic diagram for LED Light Cube.

16

Flashing Fiber Optic Lamp

J UST AS ELECTRONIC SIGNALS CAN TRAVEL ALONG A COPPER
wire, light can travel through a thin filament of plastic or glass
fiber optic material. While this plastic or glass media is commonly
used to transmit data such as telephone signals, fiber optic filaments
can also be used effectively to create a decorative lighting fixture.
Although fiber optic filaments are only a few millimeters in
diameter, light passing through a filament is visible as a point of
light at the end of the fiber optic strand. It is this quality of fiber
optic filaments that make them ideal for artistic electronic application. A number of fibers gathered together and illuminated at a base
can be used to create a starburst display with a tiny pinpoint of
light at each filament's end. Flashing Fiber Optic Lamp is a spectacular demonstration of what happens when the illuminated starburst is made to blink.

CONSTRUCTION NOTES

A single IC, the 3909, causes the LED of Flashing Fiber Optic Lamp
to blink. To achieve the maximum amount of light at the end of
each fiber optic filament, a high intensity LED should be used. One
LED particularly suited to this purpose is the TLR-107 High-
Brightness Red LED with Fresnel Lens (Radio Shack #276-033)
(see Fig. 16-1). A complete list of parts for Flashing Fiber Optic

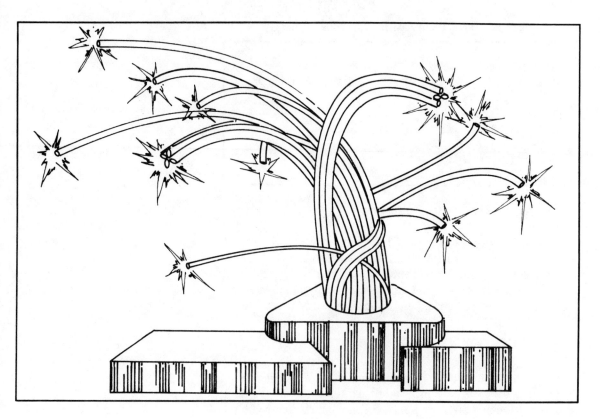

Lamp is contained in Table 16-1.

Fiber optic material is available from many electronics stores in single filament strands. The fiber optic material should be cut into many strands of a suitable length so that the strands bend down and flare out into an attractive display when they are held together at their base. A group of 200 to 400 filaments makes a suitable spread of light. Choose any size grouping of fibers you desire, how-

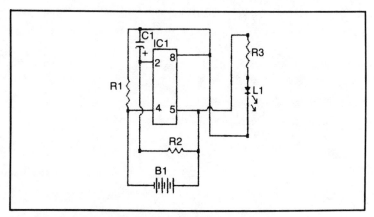

Fig. 16-1. Schematic diagram for Flashing Fiber Optic Lamp.

Table 16-1. Parts List for Flashing Fiber Optic Lamp.

```
B1- 1.5-3V Battery
C1- 1000mf Electrolytic Capacitor
IC1- 3909
L1- LED
R1- 680 Resistor
R2- 220 Resistor
R3- 33 Resistor
```

ever, as long as they can be adequately illuminated by the LED light source.

The filament ends can be bound together and the entire bound unit can be placed in a base containing the 3909 and LED circuitry. When bundling the fiber optic strands together, be sure to leave the filament ends exposed so that they are easily illuminated by the light source. The bundled end should be placed directly over the flashing LED.

OPERATION

To heighten the sense of enjoyment stimulated by Flashing Fiber Optic Lamp, view the lamp in a slightly darkened room. As a faint breeze stirs the delicate glass fibers, the moving pinpoints of light truly become a three dimensional starburst of beauty.

17

Fiber Optic Lamp

O CCASIONALLY, AN ITEM OF FUNCTIONALITY IS ALSO CON-
sidered an item of beauty. Fiber optic material can be considered one of these rare occurrences. Although a fiber optic filament is a simple, hair-thin strand of glass or plastic, it can be
combined with other filaments and a light source to become a
gorgeous light sculpture. This is the intended design goal for Fiber
Optic Lamp.

A flared bundle of fiber optic filaments is the main element of
Fiber Optic Lamp. The bundle of fiber optic filaments extends from
a base containing a light source. If a colored light source is selected,
light appearing at the end of each filament emits this color.

CONSTRUCTION NOTES

No ICs are necessary for the Fiber Optic Lamp. A light source,
some fiber optic material, and a suitable power supply (matching
the requirements of the chosen light source) are the basic requirements for this project.

Preparing the fiber optic filaments for mounting within an
enclosure requires the fiber optic material to be cut into several
hundred strands. If all of the fibers are cut in equal lengths, their
pattern, when flared out after installation, will be roughly
hemispherical. If the filaments are cut in a variety of different sizes,

however, the flared pattern will be more random.

Heat shrinkable tubing makes a wonderful binding agent for a bundle of fiber filaments. Just cut a 1 inch piece of tubing and pack the fibers inside quite closely. Adjust the fiber ends until they are flush with the bottom end of the heat shrinkable tubing and apply the heat of a hair-dryer to the tubing. The resulting bound packet of filaments is ready for mounting within an enclosure of your choice. A hole cut in the top of your enclosure should have a diameter sufficient to hold the fiber bundle, which should be placed directly above the internal light source.

OPERATION

Place the completed Fiber Optic Lamp in your selected room environment and activate its light source. Fiber Optic Lamp is attractive as a sculpture when it is displayed in a lighted room, but the elegance of the lighted fiber optic filaments is accentuated when the lamp is displayed under dimmed lighting conditions. The whole mood of a room can be altered by the addition of this soothing light sculpture.

18

3-D Wall Mural

A RT CAN BE LUMPED INTO TWO BROAD CATEGORIES: TWO-dimensional (2-D) and three-dimensional (3-D). A painting, a photograph, and a drawing are all 2-D works of art. Sculptures, quilts, and buildings represent the 3-D category. This definition remains useful until an object is discovered that violates both boundaries.

3-D Wall Mural is just such an outcast. The traditional mural is a painting (also photographs and drawings) which is, using the previously established classification system, 2-D art. When a mural has another dimension added to its features, however, this new level of art is now neither 2-D nor 3-D, but rather it is 3-D Wall Mural.

CONSTRUCTION NOTES

The actual construction consists of the selective arrangement of fiber optic bundles (see Chapters 16 and 17 for fiber optic bundle construction) on a base. An independent lamp is then fixed to the bottom of each fiber optic bundle. Finally, a suitable power supply is connected to all of the lamps and the mural is activated.

Even though the construction of 3-D Wall Mural sounds relatively mundane, there are hundreds of creative design applications that can make the finished mural an exciting work of art. Three important areas where the greatest amount of inspiration

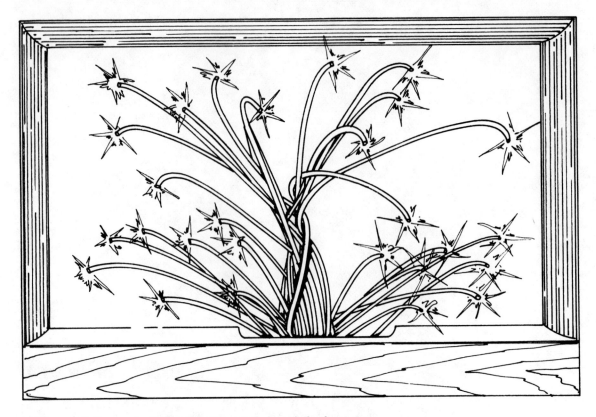

can be applied are: the base, the fiber optics, and the lamps.

First, choose a base that will complement the final mural. Heavy gauge plastic sheeting, such as Plexiglas, has a lot of merit, but wood should not be automatically excluded. Secondly, the fiber optic bundles do not all have to be the same length. Various height bundles will give the mural a texture. Lastly, lamps with various colored lenses or gel filters will make each fiber optic bundle a unique entity. The final product will provide an amazing visual treat when a flow of air mixes several colors of fiber optic strands.

OPERATION

Like any piece of art, 3-D Wall Mural's operation is in its enjoyment. Ideally, placement should be in a room location with heavy traffic. This will set up the necessary air currents for mixing the filaments from the fiber optic bundles. With 3-D Wall Mural in full operation, one other problem still remains—is it 2-D or 3-D?

19

Weather Balloon Sculpture

S OFT SCULPTURES ARE AN ATTRACTIVE DECORATION IN A high traffic environment. Aside from their resistance to accidental damage, soft sculptures also interact well with people. For example, a large, soft sculpture presents a less imposing figure than a comparably sized "hard" sculpture. As mentioned earlier (see Introduction), this is an important consideration when designing a high-tech interior.

A soft sculpture that is a derivative from an unlikely source is Weather Balloon Sculpture. The final art object is a combination of light, size, and movement. The light comes from an internal source that will be described shortly and the size comes from the balloon itself. The movement is a curious by-product of all soft sculptures—people enjoy touching them. Possessing an almost lifelike quiver, even the gentlest touch sends Weather Balloon Sculpture into animated movement.

CONSTRUCTION NOTES

A circuit similar to that used in Flashing Fiber Optic Lamp (see Chapter 16) generates the light in Weather Balloon Sculpture (see Fig. 19-1). The 3909 LED Flasher/Oscillator (Radio Shack #276-1705) is the IC that flashes the LEDs placed inside the sculpture. A complete parts list is provided in Table 19-1.

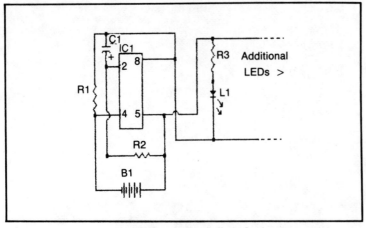

Fig. 19-1. Schematic diagram for Weather Balloon Sculpture.

There are three popular sizes of weather balloons readily available: 3, 8, and 16 feet in diameter. While any size is usable, the 3 foot diameter version is the most practical for this sculpture. A lot of air is required to fill a weather balloon. The best method is to reverse the air flow of a vacuum cleaner and fit the balloon's air-fill hole over this outlet. Beware of overinflation. A stretched balloon skin is extremely delicate and with very little provocation it will explode.

In order for the flasher lights to be visible on the exterior of the weather balloon, high-intensity LEDs must be used. TLR-107 type LEDs (Radio Shack #276-033 and #276-070) are ideal for this purpose.

One final construction area for consideration is the container holding the 3909 and its LEDs. An extremely small box is necessary for slipping through the air-fill hole and neck of the weather balloon. Dimensions should be approximately 3 inches by 2 1/2 inches by 2 inches. Since the weather balloon is susceptible to punctures, thoroughly eliminate all sharp ends from the LED box.

Table 19-1. Parts List for Weather Balloon Sculpture.

```
B1- 1.5-3V Battery
C1- 1000mf Electrolytic Capacitor
IC1- 3909
L1- LED
R1- 680 Resistor
R2- 220 Resistor
R3- 33 Resistor
```

OPERATION

After the balloon is inflated, insert the working (no need for an on/off switch) 3909 flasher box through the air-fill hole and neck and into the central sphere. Make sure the flasher is working properly prior to insertion. Seal the balloon's air-fill opening against air leakage and orient the flasher box in an upright position. Weather Balloon Sculpture is now ready for high-tech display. In order to enhance this soft sculpture's longevity, adopt the following house rule: no guest shall carry anything sharper than their wit in the vicinity of Weather Balloon Sculpture.

20

Tube Lights

L IGHT IS USUALLY EMPLOYED WITHIN A HOUSEHOLD IN ITS
most functional capacity: illumination for work and recrea-
tion. But decorative lighting serves an important purpose by adding beauty to an environment. Tube Lights is an example of a
handsome use of decorative lighting techniques.

With Tube Lights, a river of light can be poured across a floor
or draped over a piece of furniture, or a stick of light can be placed
in a corner. This impossible-sounding feat is accomplished with a
few feet of plastic tubing and a number of LEDs. The product of
this combination is a tube of light that can be positioned in any
suitable manner within any room of your house.

CONSTRUCTION NOTES

No ICs are required for the construction of Tube Lights. However,
if a special LED is chosen, an IC is included within this project to
perform an LED blinking function. This IC is contained within the
tiny enclosure of the Blinking LED (Radio Shack #276-036). Selection of this special LED greatly simplifies construction of Tube
Lights as well as making the tube's contents less bulky—the need
for additional support components, such as resistors, within the tube
is eliminated.

Construction of Tube Lights is extremely simple. Select a piece of transparent tubing having an open center diameter of at least 1 inch. Either flexible plastic tubing or a rigid plastic tube makes an excellent enclosure for the blinking LEDs. Cut this tubing to your desired length.

Both a power wire and a grounding wire must run the length of the tube to allow the placement of LEDs throughout the tube. One simple method is to create a ladder structure consisting of the two wires with the LEDs soldered into place between them for installation within the tubing. The two wire lengths must each be cut approximately 5 inches longer than the piece of plastic tubing, so they can reach their associated power and grounding sources. Be sure to keep the number of LEDs used in Tube Lights within the power output capabilities of your selected power source.

Care must be taken so that the width of the constructed LED ladder remains within the diameter restrictions of the plastic tubing. A long wire fed through the tubing and hooked over the first "rung" of the LED ladder assists greatly in pulling the connected LEDs through the plastic tubing. The LED ladder should be held in place by fastening it to the two ends of the plastic tube. One tube end can then be capped with a suitable piece of plastic sheeting. All that remains is to connect Tube Lights to its power source at the other end.

OPERATION

Operation of Tube Lights is mostly a matter of interior design. Tube Lights is a self-contained light sculpture. Its placement within a house may be as casual as "tossing" the project on the floor and displaying it in the configuration in which it lands. Highly structuralized interior design settings might require a more preconceived tubing placement, however. Remember, anyplace in the high-tech household requiring a bit of creative, artistic floor lighting is a perfect home for Tube Lights.

21

LED Alphabet Blocks

W HETHER THEY ARE MADE FROM WOOD OR PLASTIC, AL-
phabet blocks appear in some incarnation in almost every
household. The need to endlessly pick up these educational
playthings is the bane of every parent's life. Alphabet blocks can
create an unsightly, cluttered mess in a living room. Salvation can
be found in objects that meet with parental approval for living room
play, as well as educational value. These are LED Alphabet Blocks.
Furthermore, these blocks are attractive even to adults without
children.

A transparent cube backlit by LEDs forming alphabetic
characters is infinitely more enjoyable than the customary faded
wooden blocks familiar to most families. An entire set of LED
Alphabet Blocks can be made to replace the wooden letters. The
blinking LEDs of the cube are automatically turned off by an internal power switch, whenever the cube is inverted, to conserve
battery power.

CONSTRUCTION NOTES

The LEDs of each LED Alphabet Block face provide their own internal ICs to control their ability to blink. A mercury switch, such
as the one sold by Radio Shack (Radio Shack #275-027) breaks off
power to the circuit when the project is inverted (see Fig. 21-1 for

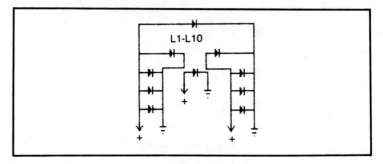

Fig. 21-1. Schematic diagram for LED Alphabet Blocks.

the schematic requirements of one block face), and consequently provides a concealed power ON/OFF switch.

Approximately 10 LEDs can be used to form each letter. Six faces must be prepared for each block by cutting out squares of your chosen dimensions from heavy gauge clear plastic sheeting. LEDs are mounted on each face of the block by drilling holes in the plastic at the appropriate locations for LED placement. LED PANEL LAMP HOLDERS (Radio Shack #276-080) are used to secure the LEDs to each plastic panel. The LEDs of each block face are connected in parallel to the power supply so that each face blinks separately from the others.

The cube's faces are constructed around the internally mounted mercury switch and battery power source (see Chapter 14 for tips on mercury switch installation). A second set of slightly larger plastic block faces can be placed around LED Alphabet Block to protect the LEDs.

OPERATION

Using LED Alphabet Blocks is child's play, literally as well as figuratively. Just turn the cube until the internal mercury switch engages and permits all of LED Alphabet Block's faces to blink. When you are ready to put the block away, simply turn the cube until the mercury switch is inverted and the blinking stops. You may find that LED Alphabet Blocks stimulate a child's imagination more than the original wooden blocks ever did. If you're not careful, you might even be tempted to play with the blocks yourself.

22

Solar Music

T HE SUN IS A SOURCE OF MANY DIFFERENT PHYSICAL PHE-
nomena. Light, heat, and radiation are the most common products from this star. It is possible, however, to create other, more
bizarre events using the sun as a catalyst. The only problem is that
an external device is required to experience these other properties.

One of the more common external devices capable of inter-
preting this new celestial data is the silicon solar cell. This
remarkable wafer translates the sun's rays into usable electricity
that can be applied to a number of different high-tech projects (see
Chapter 23). Another project that utilizes the solar cell's power is
Solar Music. This sun powered oscillator is inexpensive to build
and free to operate.

CONSTRUCTION NOTES

The audio oscillation in Solar Music is produced by the 3909 LED
Flasher/Oscillator IC (Radio Shack #276-1705). Four Silicon Solar
Cells (Radio Shack #276-124) connected in series supply the free
power to make solar music. The Solar Music components are given
in Parts List Table 22-1.

There are numerous design elements that can be experimented
with for making the desired Solar Music. The values of resistor
R1 and capacitor C1 are both open to such alteration (see Fig. 22-1).

Table 22-1. Parts List for Solar Music.

```
C1- 1mf Electrolytic Capacitor
IC1-3909
SC1- Silicon Solar Cell(s)
R1- 100K Potentiometer
R2- 100 Resistor
```

Similarly, the number of solar cells can be increased, up to a maximum of 12 serially arranged cells.

It is even possible, with a little experimentation, to turn Solar Music into a musical keyboard. Each "key" in this solar synthesizer is made from a momentary (normally open) SPST switch and a different valued potentiometer. The switch is placed between the variable leg of the pot and the connection of C1 and pin 8 of the 3909. One of the other legs of the pot is connected to ground. All of the remaining "keys" are attached in parallel to the first. Each pot can then be adjusted to create a different tone when its key is pressed.

OPERATION

When the wiring is completed, place Solar Music (or, at least, its solar cells) in direct sunlight. An audible noise should be heard immediately. If not, adjust the pot R1. You keyboard fans will have to depress one of the SPST buttons to generate your solar music.

Various intensities of sunlight will alter the musical tone. Additional tone changes can also be made by tuning R1. There are many potential uses for Solar Music other than those that are purely recreational. One such use would be a weather indicator. The tone

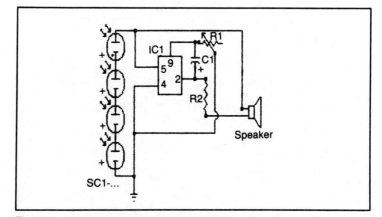

Fig. 22-1. Schematic diagram for Solar Music.

will change in relation to the intensity of the sun's light, indicating the presence of cloudy versus sunny weather. But no matter which task is assigned to Solar Music, its greatest quality is that it will never waste one cent of irreplaceable energy.

Mysterious Mover

H AS ANYONE EVER VISITED YOUR HOUSE AND ADMIRED AN object on a coffee table? It was probably the appearance or subject matter of the object that captured their attention. One sure way to catch someone's eye with a conversation piece is to have the object move without any prompting from you. Mysterious Mover provides countless moments of fun, as this unusual object begins roving about on top of a table on its own accord.

Mysterious Mover is dependent on light as the impetus to do its roving. Solar cells mounted on the top of the project's enclosure drive internally mounted motors that move the Mysterious Mover. When sufficient light is present, Mysterious Mover starts traveling and entertains your guests.

CONSTRUCTION NOTES

A series of small Silicon Solar Cells (Radio Shack #276-124) performs the tasks of both triggering and powering Mysterious Mover. As light hits the solar cells, power is generated to an internal drive system. A compact enclosure easily accepts both the internal drive system and the external mounting of the solar panels powering Mysterious Mover.

Mysterious Mover's method of travel depends on the type of drive system you want to install. Miniature electronic motors and gears, available from local hobby stores are well suited for this purpose. Refer to Appendix C for a source guide to this type of equipment. Depending on your ingenuity, Mysterious Mover can be designed to roll or crawl, or maybe even hop. Just be sure to use enough solar cells to support the selected form of locomotion.

OPERATION

Mysterious Mover is not a nocturnal creature. When its environment is dark, Mysterious Mover is neither mysterious nor moving. At the first evidence of strong sunshine or full room light, Mysterious Mover is on the prowl. You can control Mysterious Mover during the daylight, however, by caging it in a dark place.

Electronic House Pet

C OMPANIONSHIP IS AN EXPENSIVE "HOBBY." THERE ARE TEL-
ephone calls to be made, lunches to attend, promises to be
kept; the list goes on and the expenses keep climbing. These are
just a few of the reasons why many people purchase pets. Granted,
there is an initial outlay of money for the creature itself, but many
folks overlook this momentary inconvenience for the reward of a
friendly wet-nosed kiss.

Even in this idyllic relationship, there comes a times when the
owner has second thoughts. The economics of daily meals, the
cleanup after daily meals, and the impromptu baby-sitting are all
factors that contribute to the disfavor of the average pet. What's
needed is a pet that requires nothing, but snaps to life at the whim
of the owner—enter Electronic House Pet.

CONSTRUCTION NOTES

A speech synthesizer, the SP0256 Speech Processor (Radio Shack
#276-1783), gives the Electronic House Pet a tongue for greeting.
The vocabulary for the speech synthesizer is contained on an aux-
iliary support ROM (read only memory) chip (SPR016). Additionally, a 386 Low Voltage Audio Power Amplifier (Radio Shack
#276-1731) amplifies the digital output of the Speech Processor (see
Fig. 24-1). Activation of the pet's vocal cords is accomplished by

an optional mercury switch (refer to Fig. 24-2). Parts List Table 24-1 lists the components required for your pet's construction.

Even though the actual Electronic House Pet enclosure is open to your design, consideration must be given to the placement of the mercury switch. This attention needs to be specifically directed to the method used for bringing the pet to life. In other words, the mercury switch will cause Electronic House Pet to utter a phrase, but only after the switch has been tilted. Therefore, design both

Pin#	Assignment
1	Gain
2	-Input
3	+Input
4	GND
5	Out
6	V
7	Bypass
8	Gain

Fig. 24-1. Pin assignments for the 386.

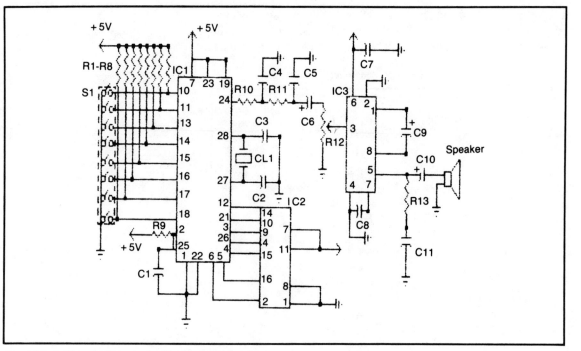

Fig. 24-2. Schematic diagram for Electronic House Pet.

```
C1-  .1mf Capacitor
C2-  47pf Capacitor
C3-  47pf Capacitor
C4-  .022mf Capacitor
C5-  .022mf Capacitor
C6-  10mf Electrolytic Capacitor
C7-  .1mf Capacitor
C8-  .1mf Capacitor
C9-  10mf Electrolytic Capacitor
C10- 100mf Electrolytic Capacitor
C11- .1mf Capacitor
CL1- 3.12 MHz Crystal
IC1- SP0256
IC2- SPR016
IC3- 386
R1-R8- 100K Resistor
R9-  100K Resistor
R10- 33K Resistor
R11- 33K Resistor
R12- 10K Potentiometer
R13- 10 Resistor
S1-  8-position DIP
```

Table 24-1. Parts List for Electronic House Pet.

a "working pet" side and a "dead pet" side. Then place the mercury switch parallel to the dead side for activation only when the pet is placed on its working side. This is far simpler than it sounds.

Table 24-2. SPR016's ROM Vocabulary Listing.

DIP Switch Settings—"ON"	ROM Phrase
NONE	Oh
8	One
7	Two
7&8	Three
6	Four
6&8	Five
6&7	Six
6,7&8	Seven
5	Eight
5&8	Nine
5&7	Ten
5,7&8	Eleven
5&6	Twelve
5,6&8	Thirteen
5,6&7	Fourteen
5,6,7&8	Fifteen
4	Sixteen
4&8	Seventeen
4&7	Eighteen
4,7&8	Nineteen
4&6	Twenty
4,6&8	Thirty
4,6&7	Forty
4,6,7&8	Fifty
4&5	It is
4,5&8	A.M.
4,5&7	P.M.
4,5,7&8	Hour
4,5&6	Minute
4,5,6&8	Hundred hour
4,5,6&7	Good morning
4,5,6,7&8	Attention please
3	Please hurry
3&8	Melody 1
3&7	Melody 2
3,7&8	Melody 3

OPERATION

There are 36 different words in Electronic House Pet's ROM vocabulary. The possibilities range from the intelligent "Oh" to the definitive "It is." Table 24-2 lists each of these phrases along with their accompanying switch settings.

Select the phrase that suits both your pet and yourself, adjust the volume with R12, and test your pet's sensitivity (physical, not emotional). The ultimate companion is now ready for service. Throw away the doggie bones, forget about having to clean the upholstery, have no concerns about walking blindly into a dark room, for the only thing this pet will ever consume is batteries.

25

Crawling Robot

Y OU ENTER THE LIVING ROOM OF YOUR HOME AND WALK
past an end table. Suddenly, a small metal box comes to life.
Scurrying about the floor in a prescribed pattern, this box's
animated appearance simulates the activity of a living being. The
only difference is that this "being" is a robot.

A robot that can respond to a given stimulus sound like a
creature that can only inhabit a science fiction story line. Robots,
however, are now in the domain of reality. In fact, many of the
"real" robots currently being manufactured have features that are
most sophisticated than those ever dreamed of for their fictional
brethren. A small sample of a robot's true ability is demonstrated
in the "brain" of Crawling Robot.

CONSTRUCTION NOTES

Crawling Robot is divided into two separate parts: the "brain" and
the main body. To function, the brain senses motion or vibration
and activates the main body which drives the robot. Several types
of motion detectors are commercially available for giving Crawling Robot its brains. On the low-cost scale are the Auto Motion-
Detector (Radio Shack #49-520) and Vibration Detector (Radio
Shack #49-521) while at the higher cost end are the Ultrasonic
Motion-Sensor (Radio Shack #49-303) and the Passive Infrared Sensor (Radio Shack #49-530).

Each of these detection sensors offers a degree of sensitivity adjustment that will have to be set for proper robot operation. Basically, the function of the motion detector is to act as a switch between the power supply and the main body.

The main body, on the other hand, provides the "muscle" for moving Crawling Robot. This robot body region consists of two small electric motors (one for driving the left side and another for driving the right side) connected to the movable appendages (wheel or legs) via a series of gears.

Finally, these two robot body parts, the brain and the main body, are assembled inside a suitable enclosure. As has been frequently stated in this book, heavy gauge plastic sheeting, such as Plexiglas, is a marvelous construction material for this type of work. Other alternatives for this structural composition are wood and moldable, stretched formed styrene plastic. Appendix A details the methods used for working with these materials.

OPERATION

In order to ensure proper operation of the Crawling Robot, the sensitivity of the motion sensor must be adjusted for the room's environment. Additionally, the intended crawling path must be carefully charted. Object avoidance is one area where this robot's brain is deficient. When the "education" of Crawling Robot is complete, anyone moving past its lair will stir it into a spectacular display of real robotics.

26

Computer Environment

L ARGE NUMBERS OF MICROCOMPUTERS ARE FINDING THEIR
way into domestic households. Unfortunately, most of this
hardware quickly falls into disuse. The leading reason for this in-
activity most often surrounds the erroneous thought that there are
few "real" applications for a computer. The truth is that microcomputers *are* powerful and this power manifests itself in data processing.

No matter what type of data are being processed, from numbers
and words to ideas and pictures, the computer is the supreme machine. Contrary to many people's thoughts, however, the computer
does need to improve its performance in the area of "passive entertainment" before it will ever be widely accepted. An examination
of television and stereo equipment sales demonstrates the benefit
of a successful passive entertainment campaign (the non-
entertainment value of TVs and stereos is negligible). Luckily, this
improvement is not hardware oriented, but, rather, it is software
oriented.

Currently, there is a need for software that lends an aura of
passive entertainment to the computer (refer to Chapter 27 for this
type of program written for the Apple *II*e computer). Computer
Environment is a short program that accomplishes this goal. Basically, the IBM PCjr computer is transformed into a surf-sound
generating machine, without user input.

```
10 SCREEN 0:RANDOMIZE:CLS:KEY OFF:SOUND ON
20 Z=INT(RND*(4))
30 FOR G=1 TO Z
40 H=INT(RND*(5))
50 FOR I=3 TO 15
60 FOR J=1 TO H
70 NOISE 5,I,J
80 NEXT J
90 NEXT I
100 FOR I=15 TO 3 STEP -1
110 FOR J=1 TO H
120 NOISE 4,I,J
130 NEXT J
140 NEXT I
150 NEXT G
160 GOTO 20
```

Fig. 26-1. Program listing for Computer Environment.

PROGRAM NOTES

Computer Environment uses the elaborate sound synthesizer IC of the IBM PCjr to pulse white noise into a "surf-like" sound (see the program listing in Fig. 26-1).

The RANDOMIZE statement in line 10 begins each Computer Environment startup on a different numerical value. This random number seed is then used for determining the values of variables Z and H. Z is used in G which sets the number of wave swells, while H is used in J for establishing the duration of each swell. The variable I runs the volume of each swell from low (3) to high (15). This same process is performed again, but in reverse order, in line 100.

The actual wave sound is produced in lines 70 (rising) and 120 (falling). NOISE is a statement for generating various degrees of white noise. This statement's values may range from 0 to 7. Any of these values may be substituted for the 5 in line 70 and the 4 in line 120. Another statement that may also be added experimentally to these same two lines is SOUND (e.g. SOUND 110,J,I,0). All of these changes will result in dramatic sound alterations.

OPERATION

After Computer Environment has been typed into the IBM PCjr using IBM Cartridge BASIC (Beginner's All-purpose Symbolic Instruction Code), and saved onto a floppy disk, the program may be run (type RUN and press ENTER). Before the PCjr clears the screen and activates the sound, you will be prompted for a random number seed from −32768 to 32767 (type in a value and press ENTER). The screen will now go blank and the sound of crashing waves will fill the air. Computer Environment will run until the program is manually stopped (press Fn followed by the B key).

27

Computer Images

T HE LACK OF PASSIVE ENTERTAINMENT CAPABILITY IS A microcomputer's single biggest failing. Actually, this problem rests squarely on the shoulders of software manufacturers. They have been made painfully aware of the public's lack of interest in standard microcomputer related activities (only 10% of the United States' households have a microcomputer and even less buy software regularly). Therefore, software manufacturers keep falling faster than the Chapter 11 Bankruptcy courts can catch them, but they still don't make the people's product—passive entertainment software.

In order to express the value of passive entertainment in more concrete terms, study the function of stereo equipment at a party. How many people would use a sound system that required a crank for operation? It's bad enough that LP platters have to be periodically flipped (which is why people buy cassette drives with auto-rewind), but imagine a social gathering where everyone took turns cranking the stereo. Sure, it's ludicrous, but virtually all computer software on the market requires user input or cranking. How boring!

Computer Images is an Apple IIe computer program that runs completely without user input. Once started, this program creates fantastic high-tech images until stopped. Best of all, the whole program is only 16 lines long.

```
1    REM   APPLE IIe SHAPE TABLE
10   FOR X = 7676 TO 7689
20   READ Y
30   POKE X,Y
40   NEXT X
50   POKE 232,252: POKE 233,29: HGR2
60   HCOLOR= 3
70   FOR R = 0 TO 32
80   FOR S = 1 TO 255
90   ROT= R
100   SCALE= S
110   DRAW 1 AT 140,96
120   FOR Z = 1 TO 10: NEXT Z
130   XDRAW 1 AT 140,96
140   NEXT S: NEXT R
150   GOTO 50
160   DATA   1,0,4,0,54,63,36,37,8,46,40,54,63,0
```

Fig. 27-1. Program listing for Computer Images.

PROGRAM NOTES

Even though Computer Images *might* work on other Apple computers (II + and *IIc* owners, use this program at your own risk), the extensive use of the POKE statement and assorted memory assignments could lead to a program "crash." Therefore, for consistent results run Computer Images on an Apple *IIe* computer (see the program listing in Fig. 27-1).

Computer Images achieves its unique visual quality from the Applesoft BASIC's shape table graphics feature (Fig. 27-2 and Tables 27-2 and 27-3). Table 27-1 lists all of the steps used in the creation of this program's shape table. By following this procedure other user created shape definitions can be substituted.

Program lines 10 through 40 load the shape definition and index into the Apple's memory. The data for this definition are stored in the DATA statement of line 160. After the shape is loaded, line 50 tells the program where to find the shape table by using two POKE statements. The HGR2 statement at the end of line 50 ac-

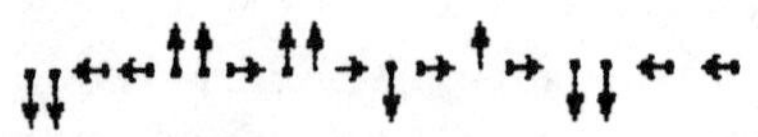

Fig. 27-2. Stretched vectors used in shape table construction example.

Table 27-1. Step-by-Step Shape Table Construction Procedure.

1. Draw a stretched vector map similar to Fig. 27-2.
2. Convert the vectors into a binary representation.
3. Translate the binary representation into a hexadecimal format.
4. Change the hexadecimal values into their decimal counterparts.
5. Determine the shape table index.
6. Choose a suitable memory location for storing the shape table and use READ, POKE, and DATA statements to place this data into the memory location.
7. The proper programming syntax is the shape table index followed by the shape table data.
8. Program the shape table's starting address.

tivates the second high-resolution graphics screen (known as "page 2").

Everything printed on the screen is colored white-1 (for maximum visibility on any type of monitor) with the HCOLOR = statement of line 60. Then, two FOR-NEXT loops generate different values of the rotation statement, ROT = , and the scale statement, SCALE = . Finally, the shape definition is drawn (line 110) and then erased (line 130), repeatedly all over the screen.

Table 27-2. Shape Table Value Conversion.

BINARY VECTOR SECTIONS			HEXADECIMAL	DECIMAL
C	B	A	Values	Values
00	110	110	36	54
00	111	111	3F	63
00	100	100	24	36
00	100	101	25	37
00	001	000	08	8
00	101	110	2E	46
00	101	000	28	40
00	110	110	36	54
00	111	111	3F	63
00	000	000	00	0

Table 27-3. Shape Table Index Values.

```
TOTAL NUMBER OF SHAPES---> = 1 (BYTE 0)
UNUSED---> = 0 (BYTE 1)
SHAPE TABLE BEGINNING LOWER BYTE---> = 4 (BYTE 2)
SHAPE TABLE BEGINNING UPPER BYTE----> = 0 (BYTE 3)
SHAPE TABLE VALUES... (BYTE 4...)

FINAL SHAPE TALBE INDEX VALUE = 1,0,4,0
```

OPERATION

As with any good form of passive entertainment, starting Computer Images is a snap—just type RUN and press RETURN. This program will now run until it is manually stopped (press and hold CONTROL, then press RESET).

Computer Images continually generates high-tech designs. The visual magnitude of this short program is so great that every computer owner should see a demonstration. Computer Images makes the computer more than just a piece of high-tech decoration. If for nothing else, this program could be used at a party as a background visual treat. The sole drawback to this practice, however, is that like moths to a flame, Computer Images will draw the entire crowd into an arc in front of the Apple's screen. Goodbye—party, hello—computer passive entertainment.

28

Computer Room Painting

AN EXTREMELY INFLUENTIAL INGREDIENT THAT SHAPES A room's atmosphere is the color of its walls. Although one's reaction to a room's color is often subconscious, color definitely affects one's perception of a room's design. For example, a pale wall color gives a room a light, open appearance. On the other hand, a particularly dark or strong color brings a small, closed feeling to a room.

While the importance of wall coloring in a room's overall design is undeniable, it is often difficult to arrive at the appropriate paint shade to match the room's decor. A solution to this problem is found in Computer Room Painting.

Computer Room Painting is a BASIC program that makes use of your Apple or IBM computer's color monitor screen to display a set of random "room" color panels. This large color palette allows you to previsualize a room's total color by using the screen colors as reference values. After all, it's much simpler to manipulate colors on a computer's screen than on a room's wall.

PROGRAM NOTES

The Computer Room Painting program is provided in two versions. One program version runs on the Apple *II*e, and the other runs on either the IBM PC or the IBM PCjr computers. Regardless of the

```
1    REM   APPLE IIe VERSION
10    HOME : GR
20    FOR X = 0 TO 15
30    COLOR= X
32    FOR A = 0 TO 39
34    FOR B = 0 TO 39
36    PLOT B,A: NEXT B: NEXT A
40    GET A$
50    NEXT X
60    GOTO 10
```

Fig. 28-1. Apple program listing for Computer Room Painting.

computer system on which Computer Room Painting is run, the desired color selection results are achieved only with a color monitor. Computer owners possessing monochrome monitors are not completely ignored by Computer Room Painting, however. The green or amber textured patterns achieved with a monochrome monitor are also attractive in themselves.

The Apple *II*e version of Computer Room Painting (see Fig. 28-1) begins by preparing the screen. Line 10 homes the screen's cursor and sets the graphics mode. Sixteen colors are then displayed on the Apple's graphics screen. These colors are selected in line 20 and represented by the variable X. A loop is formed (ending with line 50) with this variable to cycle through the computer's 16 colors. Finally, the current color is altered in line 30.

Plotting of the screen color occurs in lines 32, 34, and 36. Variable A in line 32 controls the vertical plotting value and variable B in line 34 selects the horizontal plotting value. Line 36 then performs the actual plotting. The GET statement in line 40 waits for you to press any key before plotting the next screen's color. Because of the GOTO statement in line 60, this program will restart and continue to cycle through its color palette, as long as you keep pressing keys.

Careful design considerations allow the IBM version of Computer Room Painting to be used on either the IBM PC or the IBM PCjr (see the program listing in Fig. 28-2). Screen preparation is performed by line 10. In this line, the graphics screen is set to 0, the screen is cleared, function key labels are turned off, and the width of the screen is set to 40 characters.

A loop is established in line 20 (through line 50) to run through IBM's palette of colors. Line 30 sets the color for each loop and positions the cursor at the upper left corner of the screen. Color is printed across the screen with lines 32, 34, and 36. Lines 32 and 34 of the IBM version perform the same functions as the similar

```
10 SCREEN 0:CLS:KEY OFF:WIDTH 40
20 FOR X=0 TO 15
30 COLOR X,X,0:LOCATE 1,1
32 FOR A=1 TO 27
34 FOR B=1 TO 40
36 PRINT CHR$(32);:NEXT B:NEXT A
40 A$=INKEY$:IF A$="" THEN 40
50 NEXT X
60 GOTO 10
```

Fig. 28-2. IBM program listing for Computer Room Painting.

lines in the Apple program version. Color is created in this line by printing a series of blank space characters with CHR$(32). Line 40 awaits a key press to trigger printing of the next screenful of color. After the entire color palette has been observed, the program and therefore the color sequence is repeated due to the GOTO statement in line 60.

OPERATION

The only requirements for running the Apple version of Computer Room Painting are an Apple *II*e, a color composite monitor, and the Applesoft BASIC programming language. For the IBM program version, the requirements are an IBM PC or an IBM PCjr, a color monitor, and the IBM BASIC programming language.

With one of the complete computer systems listed above, just type in your computer's version of Computer Room Painting and then enter the RUN command. At each completion of an Apple color screen, a flashing box prompts you for a key press to continue with the next screen color. The IBM program version does not provide such a prompt. After the IBM screen is filled, any key press brings on the screen's next color. Either version of the program can be stopped by performing a system reset.

29

Dot Matrix Printer Creations

F REEHAND SKETCHES ALLOW THE DESIGNER A CHANCE TO
plan a room's appearance on paper long before any interior
remodeling or furniture arranging actually occurs. Not all people
are equally adept at drawing a floor plan, however. Many people
have superb design ideas, but their manual dexterity prevents them
from drawing these designs on paper. Thanks to its extensive block
graphics character set, the C.Itoh Electronics Model 8510SCP Color
Dot Matrix Serial Impact Printer is ideal for making design sketches, with no human sketching prowess required (see Appendix
B for a full evaluation of this printer). The block graphics characters
of the 8510SCP can be joined together to form neatly prepared room
layouts or designs.

Dot Matrix Printer Creations is a BASIC program that runs
on your IBM computer and demonstrates the layout and design
capabilities of the C.Itoh 8510SCP color printer. By applying the
techniques used within this program, you can custom design your
own sketches using the block graphics characters of this printer.

PROGRAM NOTES

Dot Matrix Printer Creations performs 8 program loops that illustrate the 8510SCP's graphics characters in the 8 colors the
printer is capable of producing (see Fig. 29-1). Appropriate line

```
10 SCREEN 0:CLS:WIDTH 80
20 PRINT "DOT MATRIX PRINTER CREATIONS"
30 LPRINT CHR$(27)CHR$(99)CHR$(49);
40 LPRINT CHR$(27)CHR$(62);
50 LPRINT CHR$(27)CHR$(84)CHR$(49)CHR$(52);
60 FOR X=48 TO 55
70 LPRINT CHR$(27)CHR$(67)CHR$(X)
80 FOR Y=1 TO 40
90 LPRINT CHR$(236)CHR$(237);:NEXT Y
100 LPRINT:LPRINT TAB(15);CHR$(224)CHR$(32)CHR$(224)CHR$(32)CHR$(225)CHR$(32)CHR
$(227)CHR$(32)CHR$(224)CHR$(32)CHR$(224);
110 LPRINT TAB(58);CHR$(224)CHR$(224)CHR$(225)CHR$(227)CHR$(224)CHR$(224)
120 LPRINT TAB(37);CHR$(228)CHR$(229)CHR$(230)
130 NEXT X
```

Fig. 29-1. Program listing for Dot Matrix Printer Creations.

spacing and printing direction are also maintained within this program.

A software reset of the printer is performed in line 30 to ensure the accurate acceptance of the print controlling instructions in the following lines. Line 40 tells the printer to print unidirectionally. This unidirectional printing is important when multiple line graphics characters are used to form a single design template. Because the block graphics characters are designed to intersect when placed adjacently, printing these characters on multiple lines forms a congruous character (provided the appropriate line spacing has been selected). Unidirectional printing ensures a continuous, non-ragged intersecting line.

Also related to the printout's final appearance is the use of customized line feed spacing. Line 50 selects 14/144 inch line spacing. With this line spacing selected, characters from two adjacent lines meet with no gap between them. It is possible to experiment with the line feed spacing by substituting different values into the last two character codes of line 50.

The FOR-NEXT loop beginning in line 60 and ending in line 130 causes 8 repetitive printings of the graphics characters in lines 90-120. The values chosen for the variable X within this loop serve to both increment the X loop and to select the printing color in line 70. The LPRINT statement is used for direct printing of characters by their CHR$ code values in lines 90-120.

Remember that Dot Matrix Printer Creations serves only as a demonstration and guide for the use of graphics characters on the C.Itoh Electronics 8510SCP color printer. By using this program as a reference template, you can create your own design sketches on this printer, in any color(s) you choose.

OPERATION

Whether you own an IBM PC or an IBM PCjr, Dot Matrix Printer

Creations will run on your computer. The only other requirement is a C.Itoh Electronics 8510SCP color printer. In order to access the graphics character set, DIP switch number 2, position 6 must be set to the *open* position. Be sure that your 8510SCP printer is connected to your IBM computer and that the printer is on-line (Selected) before running this program by simply typing the RUN command and pressing the ENTER key. A bit of constructive alteration to this demonstration program is all that is necessary to make the C.Itoh's 8510SCP color printer your colorful design sketch pad.

30

Framable Plotter Works

P ERIPHERALS ARE THE HARDWARE LINK BETWEEN A COM-
puter system and the final product. Granted, software provides the computer with its "brains," but it still requires the "muscle" of a peripheral to see a project through to its completion. In
the arcane lingo of the computer world, the term peripheral encom-
passes a vast assortment of hardware "goodies." Modems, dot matrix printers, disk drives, plotters, joysticks, graphic tablets and
mouses are all peripherals (some people even include humans in
this list). Judging from this partial hardware listing and all of the
associated functions that these devices perform, a computer without peripherals would be nothing more than an isolated toy.

One of the peripherals from this list that receives the least attention is the plotter. Scarcity and high price are the two most commonly cited reasons for this neglect. This unfortunate misconception prevents many microcomputer owners from producing high
quality, precision graphics from even the simplest of computer
systems. Debunking myths is a difficult task, but Enter Computer,
Inc. manufactures an inexpensive plotter that produces expensive
results—the Sweet-P Model 100 Personal Plotter (a complete review of this plotter is in given Appendix B).

Precise line drawing, 4 interchangeable pen colors, and the
ability to use standard typing paper are all valuable features that
enable the Sweet-P to make high-tech art. This new wave in art

starts with an IBM PCjr or PC computer, a Sweet-P plotter, and Framable Plotter Works.

PROGRAM NOTES

Framable Plotter Works (see Fig. 30-1) takes a random number seed from the user and turns the Sweet-P into a Sweet-Picasso. This random number seed is requested by the RANDOMIZE statement in line 10. The variables X, Y, and S then use this seed to determine the plotter coordinate values (X and Y) and the STEP statement (S). This STEP statement is used in conjunction with variables A and B and their associated FOR-NEXT loops to increment the plotting of each line.

All commands sent to the Sweet-P with the IBM PC must be embedded in LPRINT statements. This programming practice activates the Sweet-P's built-in command language. These two letter instructions represent a valuable savings to any programmer wishing to exploit the features of this plotter. Line 30 is the first use of this plotter code. In this case, the RE; command resets the plotter to its initialized state.

Lines 70-160 of Framable Plotter Works deal with the actual

```
10 SCREEN 0:CLS:WIDTH 80:RANDOMIZE
20 PRINT "FRAMABLE PLOTTER WORKS"
30 LPRINT "RE;"
40 X=(INT(RND*(1250))+400)
50 Y=INT(RND*(919))
60 S=(INT(RND*(10))+5)
70 FOR A=200 TO 400 STEP S
80 LPRINT "LN";A+A;",900,";X;",";Y;";"""
90 LPRINT "DR";A;",";X;";"""
100 LPRINT "DA";X-A;",919;"""
110 NEXT A
120 FOR B=100 TO 200 STEP S
130 LPRINT "LN 1250,";B+B;",";X;",";Y;";"""
140 LPRINT "DR";B;",";Y;";"""
150 LPRINT "DA 0,";B;";"""
160 NEXT B
170 INPUT "ANOTHER PICTURE (Y/N)";A$
180 IF A$="N" THEN END
190 PRINT "LOAD A NEW SHEET OF PAPER"
200 PRINT "PRESS ENTER"
210 INPUT "";A$
220 GOTO 10
```

Fig. 30-1. Program listing for Framable Plotter Works.

Fig. 30-2. A sample printout from the program listing in Fig. 30-1.

plotting. Only three additional plotter commands are used: LN;, DR;, and DA;. These commands draw a line, draw a relative line, and draw an absolute line, respectively. One unfortunate omission from the otherwise fine Sweet-P manual is the use of variables in programming with the plotter command language. Lines 80, 90, 100, 130, 140, and 150 demonstrate how to incorporate variables into this language through LPRINT.

Finally, lines 170 through 220 prompt the user for another picture. If no further plotting is needed, the program ends. If another image is desired, however, Framable Plotter Works starts over again through the GOTO statement in line 220.

OPERATION

After Framable Plotter Works is typed into the memory of your IBM PC or PCjr, save a copy onto a floppy disk. Now load the Sweet-P with paper, a pen in a color of your choice, and turn on the power. Framable Plotter Works is started by typing RUN and pressing ENTER (or use F2). The program will now prompt you for a random number seed. Any number may be entered; try 209 and then press ENTER.

The Sweet-P will now go busily about its task of making you a High-Tech image. Figure 30-2 is an example of this program's output. When all of the excitement is over, you will be prompted for another picture. First remove your piece of synthetic art and press the upper right Sweet-P keyboard control. Now determine your needs for additional art and answer the prompt accordingly, Y(es) or N(o). If your choice is "N," the program is over and you can begin contacting the local art galleries to negotiate the sale of your plotter artwork. If your need for art is unsatisfied, choose "Y" and follow the program's instructions.

Don't delay, however. Soon the art market will be glutted with Sweet-P's work and the price of plotter art will plummet. Therefore, be a leader—instigate the Framable Plotter Works' revolution . . . before it's too late.

31

Light As Art

EVERYONE RECALLS THOSE BRIGHT, PRIMARY COLORED TEM-
pera paints which were set out carefully at the front of an
elementary school classroom for art period. Primary colors were
soon transformed into secondary colors, however, when a careless
classroom artist dipped a blue, paint-laden brush into the jar of
yellow paint. The other classmates fumed, either silently or
vociferously, as they reluctantly painted their pictures' suns the
resultant pea-soup green color.

Color is important to adults in a different way than it is to
children. Household color design depends equally on both color
pigments (as in wall paint or fabric coloring) and colored light (as
in colored mood lighting). The key ingredients which separate pig-
ment generated color from light generated color are the methods
in which the types of colors are combined and the resulting secondary colors formed. The familiar red, yellow, and blue primary pig-
ment colors give way to the red, green, and blue primaries of colored
light addition. Computer owners will recognize these primary colors
of light addition if they are familiar with RGB (red, green, blue)
monitors. It is the carefully controlled addition of these three colors
that yield the large variety of colors on your monitor screen.

By projecting two primary light sources together onto a common surface, the complementary color of the third primary color

Table 31-1. Light Addition Combinations and Their Results.

ADDED PRIMARY COLORS	RESULTANT COLOR
Blue+Green	Cyan
Blue+Red	Magenta
Green+Red	Yellow
Blue+Green+Red	White

is produced. this definition may sound stuffy, but in practice it can be quite beautiful. Light As Art provides a means for capturing this beauty within a household environment.

CONSTRUCTION NOTES

Track lighting spotlights provide a suitable illumination source for Light As Art while also being mobile units for its display (refer to Chapter 91 for tips on track lighting installation). Three primary colored photo gels (red, green, and blue) are mounted over the face of three track lighting spotlights—one gel per light. Each gel covered spotlight is turned on and focused on a wall surface. A white or pale colored wall works best for displaying Light As Art.

OPERATION

Creative display of Light As Art is dependent only on your own imagination. Two methods, one bold and one subtle, have proved to be particularly popular, however. The projected light from the gel covered spotlights can be pointed at different spots across a wall. Each color will slightly overlap and be made to mingle with the other primary colors creating the bold approach. The final wall image is a flattering combination of primary and secondary colors.

A more subtle approach is to focus all of the gel covered spotlights so that they overlap on the same portion of wall space. A single white spot of illumination is all that can be seen initially, because white light is composed of all three primary colors. As soon as someone walks in front of one of the lights, however, some mysterious shadows begin to emerge. The person's figure masks the light from one of the gel colored spotlights and permits the other two colors to combine. The person's "shadow" is produced in the form of the complementary color of the obscured light source. Multicolored shadows can be intentionally created by selectively placing objects in the light's path from a chosen color gel. Table 31-1 illustrates the outcome of primary color addition.

94

32

Chemical Light

A DARKENED ROOM IS TREACHEROUS TO NAVIGATE, ESPEcially in your bare feet. You know that the light switch is around here someplace, but OUCH; you forgot that it was above the end table. Identification of large and painful landmarks (or is that housemarks?) is difficult to implement without upsetting a room's delicate high-tech design. Large warning signs are impractical and an elaborate lighting system is costly. A viable alternative is Chemical Light.

The properties of phosphorescent paint make it ideal for the selective "labeling" of troublesome and dangerous objects. This paint phosphoresces (generates light) after exposure to "regular" light. However, there is no need for any external power sources and there's no problem with heat dissipation. Chemical Light, therefore, enhances room safety exclusive of the overhead associated with the other systems.

CONSTRUCTION NOTES

Very little needs to be said about the application of Chemical Light. This fluid behaves similarly to any housepaint in application. Before any phosphorescent paint is applied to the selected surface, however, a compatibility test should be performed.

Spread a small amount of Chemical Light on a superfluous piece of similar material. After the paint has dried, visually examine the material for any abnormal reaction. This would also be the correct time to test the phosphorescence of the paint. Don't be satisfied with mediocre results. Experiment with different brands of phosphorescent paint until you find one meets with your approval.

OPERATION

While the room's lights are on, either electrical or sunlight, Chemical Light is "charging." As the amount of ambient light lessens, the intensity of Chemical Light appears to increase. Finally, when you enter the darkened room, Chemical Light identifies the location of objects with its soft green glow. Thank you, Chemical Light.

33

Interior Night Sky

DESPITE THEIR AGE, STARS HOLD A CERTAIN HIGH-TECH appeal. This celestial fascination is more than a recent fad spurred on by popular science fiction movies—it is the age-old human inquisitiveness about the unknown universe.

For those who just can't get enough of the awe inspiring stars (due to cloudy skies or bright city lights), planetariums exist for both educational and entertainment value. But, quite often, planetariums are even less accessible than the stars themselves. Whether one's curiosity is mild or insatiable, bringing a simulation of the night sky into a household environment is an intriguing concept. Planning an Interior Night Sky is one way of overcoming the problems of a cloudy night sky or a distant planetarium.

CONSTRUCTION NOTES

The easiest, most convenient, and most effective method to simulate the night sky is to buy a constellation projecting device. Several manufacturers sell these units. For example, Radio Shack sells a Constellation Finder (Radio Shack #60-2325) that projects an assortment of seasonal constellation configurations.

If you find the enclosure, display, or cost of a purchased constellation projector unsatisfactory for your particular household environment, it is possible to construct your own Interior Night Sky.

The only materials required are an opaque, hollow hemisphere punctured with the constellation shapes, an interior light source, and a base for the finished unit. An item such as the hollow hemisphere is easily created by stretch forming a sheet of opaque, moldable styrene plastic (refer to Appendix A for stretch forming techniques).

A final finishing touch that adds realism to the Interior Night Sky is a photocell control for the device. With a photocell monitoring the room's light level, Interior Night Sky's constellations will appear only when the room is dark enough for them to be properly viewed. The unit will likewise turn itself off when there is too much light in the room.

OPERATION

A room with a white or light colored ceiling provides the best surface for viewing Interior Night Sky. The height of your constellation projecting unit can be altered to achieve the most realistic appearance of constellations on the ceiling. Optimal viewing results can be produced by dimming the room lights. Now, you can sit back and enjoy Interior Night Sky within the comfort of your home.

34

Wall Kaleidoscope

MOVEMENT ADDS LIFE TO ANY ROOM. WHETHER IT'S A breeze coming through an open window which blows a curtain or a large balloon gracefully migrating across the room (see Chapter 19), this animated action makes the room come alive.

This lifelike quality can produce a variety of different emotions completely independent of the movement itself. In other words, a moving curtain in a bedroom could induce drowsiness, whereas the same action in the kitchen could enhance work output. Granted, these effects are subjective, but the stimulus is readily identifiable. Bowing to the possible pressures of different interpretations, let's just say that movement has a definite effect on a room's occupants.

Based on these arguments, movement inside a room would be a welcome high-tech design addition. Wall Kaleidoscope artificially provides this ingredient in the form of an inexpensive mural.

CONSTRUCTION NOTES

The parts list in Table 34-1 is deceptive. Even though only a modest number of inexpensive parts are necessary to construct Wall Kaleidoscope, their assembly must be precise for flawless operation.

Two elements of Wall Kaleidoscope's construction deserve close attention: the electric motors and the gears. Mabuchi electric motors (see Fig. 34-1) are recommended for driving the movable

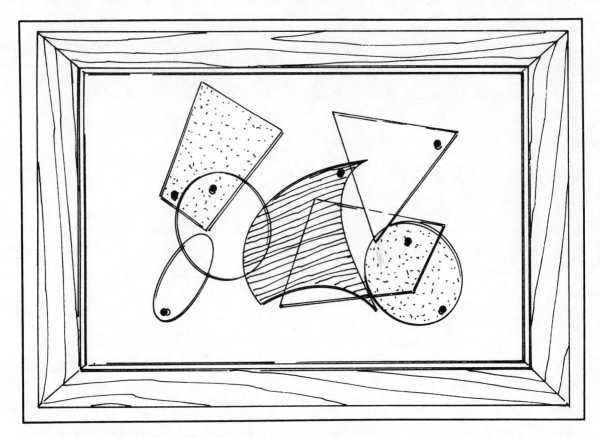

panels. They are reliable, readily available, and cheap. Substitute another brand if Mabuchi motors are impossible to locate. This product substitution should not alter the performance of Wall Kaleidoscope.

The gear selection process for Wall Kaleidoscope is an exercise in mental planning. This planning relates to how the motors are supposed to move the panels. There are hundreds of gear types and thousands of gear arrangements. The "correct" combination for your Wall Kaleidoscope will probably only come from experimentation. Figure 34-2 provides some examples of gears and gear arrangements. Additionally, Appendix C lists various sources of gears and electric motors. The best construction technique is

Table 34-1. Parts List for Wall Kaleidoscope.

```
-Balsa Wood
-Heavy gauge plastic sheeting
-Electric motors
-Assorted gears
```

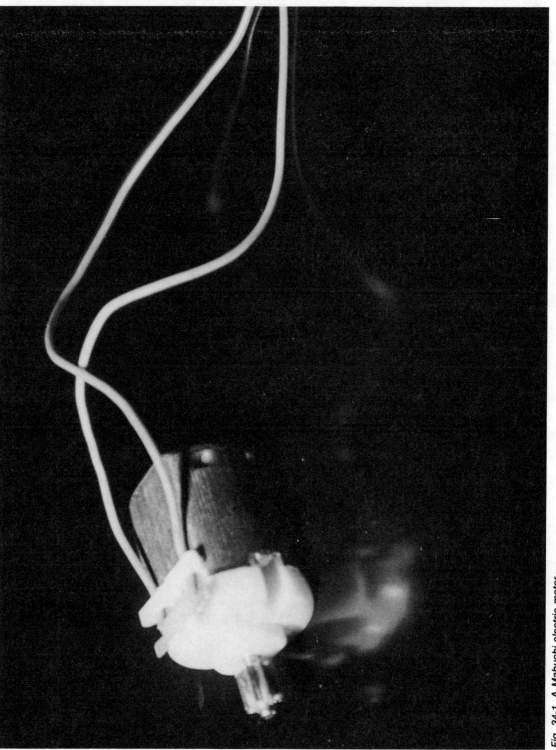

Fig. 34-1. A Mabuchi electric motor.

Fig. 34-2. Proper gear alignment is vital for successful electric motor operation.

to purchase several motors and a gear assortment. After completing the desired configuration, see if it works to your satisfaction.

OPERATION

Make sure that Wall Kaleidoscope is enclosed inside a sound proof base, unless the sound of little electric motors grinding away hour after hour is music to your ears. This base will also need appropriate ventilation for the motors. When the final location for Wall Kaleidoscope has been determined (near an electrical outlet) and it has been mounted on the wall, throw the switch.

Slowly, the muffled sound of the electric motors, the mural's base, and the moving panels will all dissolve into the room leaving behind only their presence in movement. From this moment on, the emotions of the room's occupants will be shaped by Wall Kaleidoscope.

35

Rotating Light Cube

THROUGHOUT RECENT YEARS, MOTION AND LIGHT HAVE been combined in many forms, from light-catching mobiles to the agelessly popular LAVA LITE for household adornment. Oddly enough, it is not the light intensity of these motion oriented devices that gives products like the Lava Lite their fame; one certainly cannot read a book by the illumination of a Lava Lite. Rather, it is the warm glow and the steady, rhythmic movement that draws one's attention to a motion oriented light. The observer of a moving light sculpture is concerned equally with the light's structure as well as the mood that the light generates.

One need not rely on a purchased light sculpture to create a soothing atmosphere for their household. An artistic light source can be self-created with very few materials. Rotating Light cube is an easily built self-created light sculpture. A motor slowly rotates a cube containing a steadily glowing light source, creating Rotating Light Cube.

CONSTRUCTION NOTES

The cube housing the light source of Rotating Light Cube can be constructed from any suitable material. Heavy gauge plastic sheeting is especially well suited for Rotating Light Cube because it is available in a variety of different colors in either a translucent or transparent style. You may even choose a different color or style of plastic for each face of Rotating Light Cube. One design feature that should be incorporated into the construction of the cube is a system of ventilation holes that adequately dissipate the heat created by your chosen light source.

A base for Rotating Light Cube can be formed from the same material used to create the cube itself. Within Rotating Light Cube's base should be a motor suitable for driving the illuminated cube in a circular motion. A small electric hobby motor, such as the Mabuchi variety, will rotate the cube. Through the addition of appropriate gears, the electric motor's speed can be slowed and the cube's rotation speed can be designed to suit the mood of the room.

A selected light source for Rotating Light Cube should be large enough to illuminate the enclosure but small enough to stay within the heat restrictions of the enclosure's materials. Grain of wheat bulbs, such as Radio Shack's Colored Mini Lamps (Radio Shack #272-1098), are one type of lighting that produce a moderate degree of light without producing too excessive heat.

OPERATION

Enjoyment is the only instruction for operating Rotating Light Cube. The gentle rotation of an illuminated geometric shape will make Rotating Light Cube the soothing center of attention for any room.

36

Mirror/Light Sculpture

S CULPTURE IS ART WITH DIMENSION. THIS DIMENSION IS achieved through the selective manipulation of three-dimensional objects. Whether made of clay, wood, or metal, the final sculpture exhibits length, width, and height (or depth). Regardless of the medium, a sculpture's dimension can be expressed by a variety of different means.

An artist working with clay opts for a bust. Dimension, in this case, would be demonstrated in the final work's lifelike quality. Another artist feels that a static arrangement of steel sheet and wire produces a desired theme. Here, the interwoven steel panels and wire lines generate the required dimension. Truly exciting sculpture, however, strays away from these classical interpretations of dimension. This neo-sculpture utilizes unlikely construction elements for obtaining dimension.

Of the many possible construction elements, light is by far the most unlikely. Granted, light by itself would be difficult to employ as the sole media, but when light is tempered with other construction elements, a high-tech sculpture is the result. Mirror/Light Sculpture takes the element of light and combines it with mirrors to form a three-dimensional piece of art.

CONSTRUCTION NOTES

Only three materials are necessary for Mirror/Light Sculpture (and

Fig. 36-1. A Mirror/Light Sculpture made from a front surfaced, silvered mirror.

two of these you have probably already guessed): a light source, a mirror assortment, and a base for holding the sculpture. The first of these materials, the light source, is an open category. In other words, virtually any light source may be used. One light source that is especially worthy of consideration is that produced by a laser (light amplification by stimulated emission of radiation). If proper safety precautions are observed (laser light is dangerous to vision), lasers can produce a light sculpture without needing any ancillary materials.

The choice of mirrors is almost as broad as that for the light source. There are front surfaced and rear surfaced mirrors, silvered and colored mirrors (see Fig. 36-1 for a rear silvered mirror example). By combining several of these mirror types into the final Mirror/Light Sculpture the proper dimension is obtained.

Finally, the base structure that will house the light source and support the mirrors must be strong enough to withstand the rigors of display. Most of the materials mentioned in Appendix A are suitable for constructing this base. Just be sure to include a ventilation supply in the final design. Otherwise, Mirror/Light Sculpture will become Melted/Blob Sculpture.

OPERATION

Placement and subsequent operation of Mirror/Light Sculpture is dependent on the type of light source. Once the arrangement has been made and Mirror/Light Sculpture is fixed in its regal position, let the power flow. Immediately, a new dimension will fill the room—the dimension of mirrored light.

37

Bathroom Lenses

A SAD STORY IS PLAYED OUT IN BATHROOMS EVERYWHERE. Mom struggles to apply makeup evenly, dad nicks his chin shaving, sister drops and looses her contact lenses, and brother gets away with drying his poorly washed hands on the new white towels. These common bathroom calamities occur due to the lack of one essential resource—adequate lighting.

A bathroom is the room of the house where family members prepare themselves to meet the rest of the world. Under the poor lighting conditions of most bathrooms, it is virtually impossible to critically appraise one's appearance as much as a business or school day requires. Short of installing outdoor floodlights over the bathroom mirror, what can one do to alleviate this problem of poor lighting?

Fortunately, steps can be taken to enhance your present bathroom lighting facilities. That's right, no expensive and time consuming room renovation is required. Bathroom Lenses employs Fresnel lenses to amplify the light produced by your bathroom lighting fixtures.

CONSTRUCTION NOTES

The Fresnel lens is unique among lenses in its ability to focus light by using a very thin focal length over a large area. A typical Fresnel lens consists of a thin plastic sheet etched with concentric focusing circles.

By covering your current bathroom fixtures with a custom fitted Fresnel lens sheet, the amount of light in your bathroom is dramatically increased. Fresnel lenses can be purchased in dimensions large enough to fit the ceiling lighting panels of bathrooms with dropped ceilings. Stability is added to the Fresnel lens if the edges of the lens are glued to the original ceiling lighting panel.

Bathrooms with wall mounted lighting fixtures can also benefit from Bathroom Lenses. All you need to do is prepare a suitable mounting structure for the Fresnel lens. Your particular mounting structure is completely dependent on the type of lighting fixtures that your bathroom contains. A basic wooden or Plexiglas internal framework, however, would provide an adequate starting point. The lens can then be mounted on this framework. A similar mounting structure can also be used to enclose an appropriate light source.

OPERATION

As soon as you turn on your bathroom light switch (or separate Bathroom Lenses power supply switch), Bathroom Lenses goes into operation. Grooming is carefree with the new-found confidence you gain with Bathroom Lenses. There is no longer any worry about makeup application, shaving, or contact lens insertion. But, most importantly, little brother will get his just reward when mom and dad "see the light" about those soiled white towels.

38

Photographic Murals

SILVER NITRATE SALTS CAN FREEZE AN UNSEEN INSTANCE or monitor a dangerous event. These are the same salts that record birthday parties and line the pages of wedding albums. The process for making these lasting memories is the chemistry of photography. Additionally, silver nitrate is the light sensitive compound found in photographic emulsions. All of this scientific formulation goes together and contributes to the sensitive eye of the camera.

Hardware is the ugly side of photography. Even with the best chemistry and the finest films certain subject matter will still elude the poorly equipped photographer. For example, stopping the flight of a bullet would be an impossible feat without using an electronic strobe light. Likewise, high quality photographic work demands a healthy supply of both superb chemistry and the appropriate support hardware.

After all of the preparation is complete and the image has been captured on film, the next step is the presentation. There is one type of presentation that is highly suitable for the high-tech household—Photographic Murals. These photographs should not be confused with the average wallet-sized pic. Photographic Murals are a minimum of 16 inches by 20 inches, with a size of at least 20 by 24 inches being ideal.

TECHNIQUE NOTES

There are two distinct steps in the production of Photographic Murals. First is the snapping of the photographic image. Numerous decisions go into the execution of this process. The camera, lighting, and film are all variables that must meet the requirements for the particular subject matter.

The second step is strictly chemistry related. The film is developed and the proper negative for making the mural is selected. The mural is nothing more than a special enlargement. Printing photographic enlargements is a fine art, however, that is mastered by very few individuals. Therefore, it is strongly recommended that a professional lab be used to print the mural.

High-tech subject matter for Photographic Murals should be carefully chosen. While Junior petting a bunny might represent a fine photograph, it is not suitable for high-tech display. A better source is in the field of electronics. Any of a number of calculator displays, ICs, and circuit board tracings make ideal Photographic Murals subject matter. Table 38-1 lists the equipment necessary to make a photo from an electronic source.

After the film has been exposed, it is processed and an enlargement is made. Choosing the correct negative for enlargement is not a casual affair. If a flawed negative is used, the final blurry mural will be detrimental to the entire interior design scheme. Use a contact or proof sheet coupled with a strong hand magnifier lens to pick the highest quality negative for enlargement.

PRESENTATION

Displaying a mural 20 by 24 inches or larger is not an easy proposition. Before framing, the enlargement is dry mounted onto a

Table 38-1. Equipment List for Photographic Murals.

```
--SLR (Single Lens Reflex) Camera; preferably 35mm
--2 Electronic Strobe Lights
--1 Strobe Slave
--Bellows
--Macro Lens
--Sturdy Tripod
--Bellows Focusing Rail
--Cable Release
--Lens Shade
--Light Meter
```

piece of foam core board. This backing will lend some rigidity to the final picture. Most competent processing labs offer a dry mounting service. As an alternative, and with proper protection for the photograph, a regular household iron can be used to apply dry mount tissue to the mural.

Finally, the mural is displayed on your wall. Either a "frameless" frame or an aluminum frame are perfect for this purpose. The frameless frame consists of two pieces of glass or UF-3 Plexiglas (which filters out harmful ultraviolet rays) held together by small metal clips (e.g. GALLERY CLIPS). Alternatively, the aluminum frames (e.g. NIELSON ALUMINUM FRAMES) can hold the mural in a more conventional manner (around the picture's perimeter). Now hang the mural in a position of pride. Who knows, maybe Photographic Murals will help you develop into a high-tech art connoisseur.

39

Visible Human Sculptures

W HAT COULD BE MORE HIGH-TECH THAN THE HUMAN BODY? The human form has been slowly modified and perfected over a period of more than 4 million years. With such an extensive design history, it is obvious that the current human form is perfectly specialized for its environment. You might even say that the human body is the ultimate achievement in both form and function.

Throughout the history of civilization, the human body has been a favorite subject of sculptors. From the works of Michelangelo to those of Brancusi, the human form has been exalted in carefully chiseled stone. When sculpted from a modern material in a modern style, the human form is especially suited for addition to a high-tech environment.

With Visible Human Sculptures, the modern material is plastic and the modern style is the product of a scientific approach. Unlike the ancient sculptures which celebrated external human characteristics, Visible Human Sculptures give credit to the body's internal anatomy. Solid marble is forsaken for a clear plastic skin so that internal organs can be visibly displayed.

CONSTRUCTION NOTES

Visible Human Sculptures are available in kit form from a variety of manufacturers. Commonly known as the VISIBLE MAN and

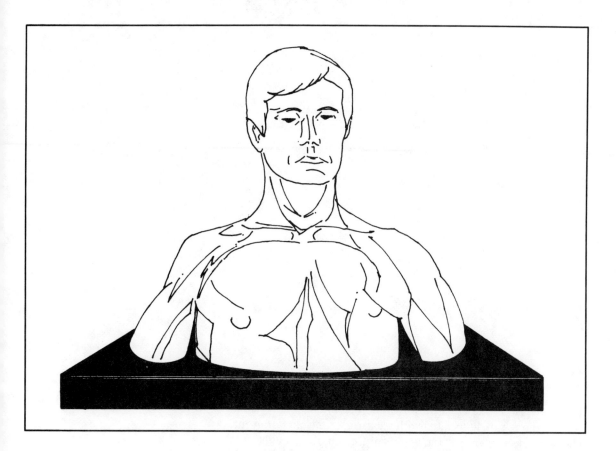

the VISIBLE WOMAN, these kits provide a clear plastic body for each sculpture into which accurate internal organs are placed. Preparing Visible Human Sculptures for display is a matter of assembling the kits and choosing a suitable display method.

Possible display options include an opaque or a translucent display base. A simple opaque display base forms a stand for holding the sculptures. If, however, a translucent material is used for the base you might consider providing a light source to illuminate the sculptures. Alternatively, place a mirror underneath the Visible Human Sculptures so that all portions of the figures can be seen.

OPERATION

Visible Human Sculptures need not be completely assembled when they are placed on their display base. Part of the fun of displaying Visible Human Sculptures is allowing viewers to interact with the sculptures by adding some of the parts. The strongest point that can be made in favor Visible Human Sculptures is that, unlike the human form, Visible Human Sculptures can be created in considerably less time than 4 million years.

40

Odor Maker

C ERTAIN ODORS STIMULATE SPECIFIC MEMORIES. THESE memories are associated with a location, time, and/or event. The odor doesn't serve as the dominant force in the thought, it is only a trigger for the recollection. Coupled with this memory stimulation, odors can also create an air of pleasantness. The scents of pine, wood smoke, and cooking cinnamon all contribute to a warm feeling of Christmas. Likewise, the smell of wet grass soaked by a summer rain fills the air with a fresh cleansed odor reminiscent of youth. These are the memories of odor.

Based on their memory stimulation ability, odors play an important role in the high-tech household. By using the proper scents, the "feeling" or mood of a room can be shaped. Odor Maker provides the selective placement of specific scents in a room to create a desired effect. Also, you can chase away unwanted smells with Odor Maker.

CONSTRUCTION NOTES

There are three techniques for producing odors: natural, chemical, and mechanical. The natural technique was mentioned above. Heating herbs, boiling fluids, and burning woods are all natural odor producers. Unfortunately, most natural odors require the expenditure of some form of energy for the release of their scents.

In contrast, the chemical generation of odor is performed with sprays, sticks, and ointments. These contain high concentrations of oils which emit the natural odors they represent. The major drawback to this technique is its limited lifespan.

The final odor making technique, mechanical, is the best for prolonged household usage. This method uses odor "record players" to fill a room with the desired scent. Portability, prolonged use, and selectable odors are all valuable features that make odor record players ideal Odor Makers.

A large scent record library is available for odor record players. Therefore, when a pine odor is needed for a given room, just "play" the pine forest record. Similarly, several other scents can be produced with an odor record player. Once the odor record is loaded into the player, 15 minutes of highly concentrated scent are emitted. This is ample time to either clear a room of an undesirable scent or prepare a room to receive guests.

OPERATION

Natural and chemical odor production is messy and impractical but mechanical scent production offers the versatility and convenience necessary when using scents as an integral part of room design. Odor record players quickly scent a room immediately following the insertion of the odor record of choice. That's all there is to it. Now you can sit back and let your nostrils take over—as Odor Maker helps you remember a seashore visit.

41

Thermal Mural

WHAT WOULD YOU CALL ART THAT CAN CHANGE ITS AP-
pearance? One correct answer is Thermal Mural. This art
work can actually change its colors over a period of time. No magic
or repainting is necessary to perform this transformation. Just flick
a switch and watch Thermal Mural turn into a freaked-out cha-
meleon.

Thermal Mural's physical elasticity comes from the unique
temperature property of liquid crystal. This sensitive chemical
changes its color in response to a change in temperature. Two factors make liquid crystals valuable for High-Tech design applications like Thermal Mural: they can be purchased in flexible sheets
and they can be manufactured with specific temperature tolerances.

CONSTRUCTION NOTES

Only liquid crystal sheets with specifically defined temperature
scales should be used for Thermal Mural. Any resultant color
change will be dependent on these temperature scales.

There are two methods of triggering Thermal Mural's color
change: natural and electrical. The method of choice will be determined by the display location of Thermal Mural. A mural will require dramatic changes in the environmental temperature for a
proper liquid crystal reaction. A cool wall that receives its share

of direct (warm) sunshine would be such a location (see Chapter 42 for further examples of natural liquid crystal color triggering).

If Thermal Mural is to be displayed in a climate controlled environment, however, the electrical method will be necessary. Using this method, the liquid crystal color can be altered by activating randomly placed light bulbs located behind the mounting base that holds Thermal Mural. As each of these light bulbs warms, a grouping of crystals in close proximity to it will change colors. Delicate color shadings are possible through the electrical method.

OPERATION

The optimal operation of Thermal Mural produces gradual color changes. Small, irregularly cut pieces of liquid crystals in the mural are the ingredients most often overlooked. The beautiful mosaic created by these liquid crystal pieces makes Thermal Mural worthy of placement in the high-tech household, and the color changing ability is an unexpected plus. If liquid crystals give you a fever for experimentation, Chapter 50 has a more functional application for these thermal tinters.

42

Liquid Crystal Wall Hanging

T EMPERATURE PLAYS A SUBSTANTIAL ROLE IN ANY HOUSE-
hold. Wintertime, in most parts of the country, brings on an
icy chill which invades even the most lavishly insulated households
to some degree. This chill affects a home's occupants by sending
them running for sweaters and electric blankets. Summertime elicits
another, equally intense temperature change on a household.
Granted, air-conditioning has become a standard luxury for most
homes, but people are still sensitive to this drastic climatic
temperature change.

To most people, temperature concerns are essential considerations during the structural planning or remodeling of a household,
but they do not play much part in the interior design of the home.
These people do not realize that their home's temperature can be
made to influence an individual's room's beauty. Liquid Crystal Wall
Hanging is a heat sensitive panel that indicates a room's "mood"
as well as reflecting the moods of the room's occupants.

CONSTRUCTION NOTES

The functioning element of Liquid Crystal Wall Hanging is a sheet
of heat sensitive liquid crystal. Liquid crystal sheets are available
in several different sensitivity ranges. Within the sensitivity range
of each liquid crystal sheet, the liquid crystal changes its color ac-

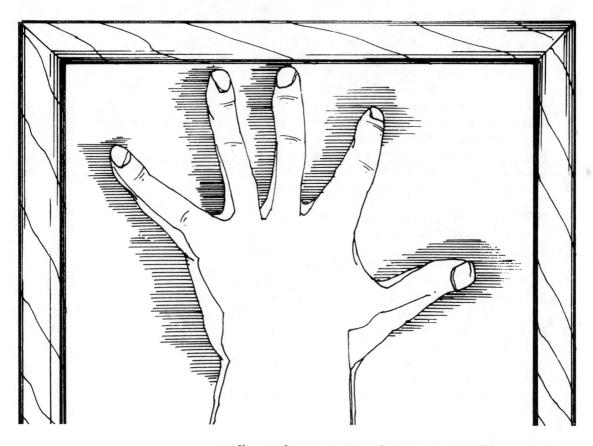

cording to the temperature that surrounds it. When each sheet registers the coldest temperature that it can sense, a color is displayed. For example, this color might be black for a particular liquid crystal sheet. When a sheet detects the warmest temperature in its range, another color is displayed, for example—blue. A variety of other colors exist between these two extremes.

The liquid crystal sheet chosen for Liquid Crystal Wall Hanging should reflect a temperature range that is common within your household. This selection will ensure that your Liquid Crystal Wall Hanging transmutes through the wide range of its potential colors when placed in its viewing area within a room.

Liquid Crystal Wall Hanging is prepared by placing the selected liquid crystal sheet within an appropriate frame. Be sure that the liquid crystal is not completely insulated within the chosen frame. The color changes of a liquid crystal sheet are dependent on receiving temperature signals directly from the environment or by human touch.

OPERATION

Liquid Crystal Wall Hanging is not merely a passive indicator of a room's temperature. Although Liquid Crystal Wall Hanging is an attractive display piece in itself as its color shifts with a room's temperature, this is only one possible display technique. The very placement of Liquid Crystal Wall Hanging will influence its display color. For example, placement of Liquid Crystal Wall Hanging in direct line with a window's incoming sunlight will cause the area in contact with the sunlight to change color (provided the temperature change is dramatic enough to affect the sensitivity of your chosen crystal). If Liquid Crystal Wall Hanging is placed on a wall near a heating duct or a hot water pipe, the wall's altered temperature will be reflected by the color changes of the liquid crystal sheet.

The most pleasing and entertaining display method for Liquid Crystal Wall Hanging, however, is created by viewer participation. Liquid Crystal Wall Hanging is particularly influenced by the touch of a human hand. Place a warm hand against the surface of Liquid Crystal Wall Hanging and watch the affected area of the liquid crystal sheet dramatically change color. When you remove your hand, observe the slow change in color as your finger's impressions dissolve into one color after another.

With Liquid Crystal Wall Hanging, you can be completely in tune with your living environment. You'll have a new sign of spring to observe as your Liquid Crystal Wall Hanging mutates from it's usual somber wintertime tones, into the bright hues indicating springtime warmth.

43

Tesla Coil

A COMMON MISCONCEPTION ABOUT ART IS THAT VERY FEW works of art also demonstrate a practical side equal to their beauty. Real beauty can come from technical subject matter just on the merit of its successful solution to a design problem. This *beauty from design* or *form follows function* philosophy is readily apparent in the Tesla Coil.

How much more practical can you get than lighting a fluorescent tube by just touching one end of it to a Tesla Coil? This is not the only dimension of the Tesla Coil, however. The gleaming copper wiring wrapped around the central core makes the Tesla Coil a standout high-tech sculpture. However, there is more than meets the eye with this art form. A flick of a switch transforms this sedate statue into a 100,000 volt screaming voltaic pile. Think of the "shock" guests will receive when the dual personality of the Tesla Coil is exposed.

OPERATION

Construction of a Tesla Coil is unnecessary with the large number of readily available, inexpensive models currently being manufactured. All Tesla Coils exhibit the same features and abilities found in the original version designed by Nikola Tesla. One quick point needs to be made about the voltages produced by the Tesla Coil.

Granted, "kilo-voltages" (thousands of volts) are produced. If carefully handled, however, this voltage will not be harmful to either you or anyone else occupying the room. Just be smart and don't try and take a shower with the Tesla Coil.

A reassessment of art might be in order with the introduction of the Tesla Coil. This reevaluation is needed due to the dual life of part-time sculpture and part-time scientific tool becoming more acceptable in interior design (see Chapter 44). In fact, this type of art is now more of a standard than a rarity in high-tech. This lofty status deserves a new name to enhance its recognition. In the case of the Tesla Coil, high-voltage art is more applicable than high-tech.

44

Van de Graaff Generator

DEVICES FOR SCIENTIFIC EXPERIMENTATION ARE AN EXCEL-
lent source for interior design materials. This is not a sug-
gestion to place beakers filled with colored water in your window
sills or to use a Bunsen burner as a birthday candle. There is one
particularly attractive device that would serve to add some hair-
raising activity to your household. The sensuous design features
of this device are not intentional—rather, they are a result of form
following a preconceived scientific function. What scientific object
could deserve a place of display in a carefully planned household
decor? The answer lies in the Van de Graaff Generator.

The Van de Graaff Generator is a shapely beauty. It's most
attractive features are a long, narrow waistline capped off with an
attractive domed forehead. When coupled with its polished,
metallic, blemish-free exterior skin, the final result is stunning
beauty.

The adjective "stunning" is also appropriate to describe the
function of the Van de Graaff Generator. The product of the Van
de Graaff Generator is static electricity caused by the positively
charged particles emitted from the unit's domed top. While a Van
de Graaff Generator will not actually "stun" a person standing near
a running unit, the static electricity created by the device will
literally raise the person's hair.

Physicist R.J. Van de Graaff's first Van de Graaff generator was considerably larger than the experimental units available today. It stood at a height approximately three times that of an average adult. Modern units can be purchased which are only two or three feet tall—a perfect size for table top display.

Preparing the Van de Graaff Generator for display is a matter of finding a suitable location for the unit. Because of its relatively low height, the Van de Graaff Generator is too small to be placed directly on a floor. Placement on a table top or on a specially constructed display pedestal greatly enhances the appearance of the Van de Graaff Generator within a household setting.

You may decide to use the Van de Graaff Generator only as a form to be displayed. If you intend to operate the device as well as display it, be sure that the Van de Graaff Generator is not operated near electrostatically sensitive equipment such as a computer or a television set.

The Van de Graaff can add a "spark" to any gathering. Just turn on the Van de Graaff Generator, place your hands near its globe, and show off your high-tech bouffant hairdo.

PART 2

FUNCTION

45

Cyclic Doorbell

D INGDONG. THIS IS THE STANDARD AMERICAN DOORBELL greeting. As unimaginative as this sound is, few people know of the possible alternatives. One alternative commercially available is the song or tune doorbell. This doorbell has several full length tunes stored in its computer memory for "programmable" selection by the user. The only catch is that the *same* tune is heard every time the doorbell button is pressed (that is, until a new tune is selected). Eventually, even this doorbell becomes boring.

Actually, the best alternative is Cyclic Doorbell. This, too, is a tune version, but with an exciting improvement—a *different* tune is played each time the button is pressed. There is a total of 25 tunes, played in a cyclic order, with one tune sounding for each press of the doorbell button. Two additional features that make this project particularly attractive are ease of construction and low cost. In fact, Cyclic Doorbell costs under $25 in parts (see Table 45-1) and takes only one night to build.

CONSTRUCTION NOTES

Cyclic Doorbell is centered around the AY-3-1350 Tunes Synthesizer IC (Radio Shack #276-1782). The low voltage requirement for the AY-3-1350 makes it ideal for either battery or line voltage supply. In order for Cyclic Doorbell to be practical, however, line

Table 45-1. Parts List for Cyclic Doorbell.

```
C1-  .1mf Capacitor
C2-  47pf Capacitor
C3-  .22mf Capacitor
C4-  10mf Electrolytic Capacitor
C5-  10mf Electrolytic Capacitor
D1-  5.1V Zener Diode
D2-  1N914 Diode
D3-  1N914 Diode
D4-  1N914 Diode
IC1- AY-3-1350
Q1-  MPS 2907
Q2-  MPS 3904
Q3-  MPS 3904
Q4-  MPS A13
R1-  100K Resistor
R2-  25K Potentiometer
R3-  3.9K Resistor
R4-  10K Resistor
R5-  33K Resistor
R6-  33 Resistor
R7-  33K Resistor
R8-  33K Resistor
R9-  33K Resistor
R10- 10K Resistor
R11- 470K Resistor
R12- 1M Potentiometer
R13- 2.2K Resistor
R14- 33K Resistor
R15- 47K Resistor
R16- 33K Resistor
S1-  Momentary SPST
```

voltage is used in this explanation.

Part layout (see Fig. 45-1) can become cramped if Cyclic Doorbell is shoehorned into a single breadboard or Experimenter's PC Board. Two boards mounted side by side will provide more than enough space for housing the AY-3-1350 and its support parts. If space is at a premium, however, a single board approach might be your only choice. Using a tight part layout and careful soldering technique there is ample room for single board assembly. Refer to Appendix A for suggestions and tips on accomplishing this board consolidation.

When installing the completed Cyclic Doorbell in your home,

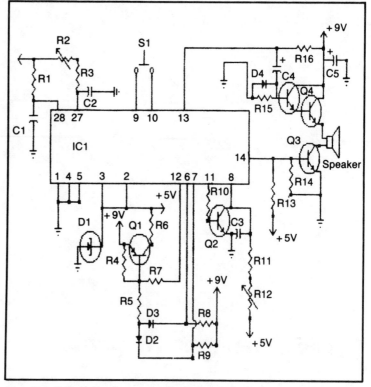

Fig. 45-1. Schematic diagram for Cyclic Doorbell.

use the existing doorbell wiring. In other words, connect one wire from the current doorbell's button to pin 10 of the AY-3-1350 and the other wire to the circuit's ground. Additionally, connect the former doorbell's power supply lines to the mains of transformer T1 (BEWARE of lethal line voltage). Be sure to observe the correct voltage polarity and only reconnect the doorbell's main power *after* the installation is complete.

One optional supplement for this circuit is an amplifier for the 8 ohm speaker. If deemed necessary, this unit should be connected between the emitter of transistor Q1 and the collector of transistor Q2.

OPERATION

Two potentiometers control the pitch and speed of the tunes. These two controls should be independently adjusted for whatever tonal qualities are important in your doorbell sound. Cyclic Doorbell is now ready to operate with a unique tune greeting each visitor at your door, that is, until the 26th person appears.

46

Cyclic Telephone Ringer

A TELEPHONE CALL IS THE MOST FREQUENT INTRUSION INTO the home. Unfortunately, this is not always a pleasant experience. Aside from the nature of the call itself, the electromechanical telephone ring is a loud, brash assault on a human's ears. While this might be an "occupational hazard" common to all homes, the high-tech household offers a melodic alternative.

Every time the telephone "rings" in the high-tech house a short musical score is heard. A simple circuit called Cyclic Telephone Ringer makes this possible. In operation, Cyclic Telephone Ringer plays a different tune each time the telephone rings. This minor modification of the telephone's ringer circuitry makes receiving a telephone call much more enjoyable.

CONSTRUCTION NOTES

The Tunes Synthesizer IC AY-3-1350 (Radio Shack #276-1782) is the heart of Cyclic Telephone Ringer. An additional support IC, the Ring Detector/Driver TCM1512A (Radio Shack #276-1302), intercepts the telephone's voltage changes that represent a "ring" and switches "on" the Tunes Synthesizer for a tune instead of a ring (see Fig. 46-1). A schematic diagram, Fig. 46-2, for Cyclic Telephone Ringer shows the parts' placement.

Two 6-inch breadboards will have to be used to construct Cyclic

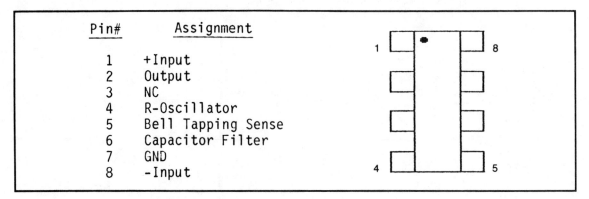

Pin#	Assignment
1	+Input
2	Output
3	NC
4	R-Oscillator
5	Bell Tapping Sense
6	Capacitor Filter
7	GND
8	-Input

Fig. 46-1. Pin assignments for the TCM1512A.

Telephone Ringer. This will provide a large work area to house the ICs, their support components (see Table 46-1), and the power supply. In fact, a separate breadboard housing the 8V transformer used for supplying this project's power would be a wise design plan. Remember, extreme caution should be exercised when working with the line voltage connected to Cyclic Telephone Ringer.

A significant improvement in the final construction of Cyclic Telephone Ringer would be the installation of two sets of telephone

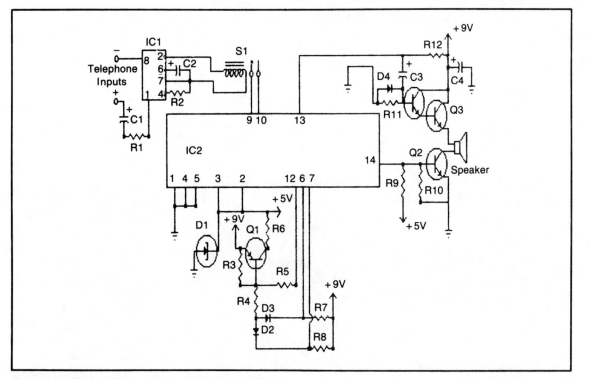

Fig. 46-2. Schematic diagram for Cyclic Telephone Ringer.

133

```
C1-  1mf Electrolytic Capacitor
C2-  10mf Electrolytic Capacitor
C3-  10mf Electrolytic Capacitor
C4-  10mf Electrolytic Capacitor
D1-  5.1V Zener Diode
D2-  1N914 Diode
D3-  1N914 Diode
D4-  1N914 Diode
IC1- TCM1512A
IC2- AY-3-1350
Q1-  MPS 2907
Q2-  MPS 3904
Q3-  MPS A13
R1-  2.2K Resistor
R2-  100K Resistor
R3-  10K Resistor
R4-  33K Resistor
R5-  33K Resistor
R6-  33 Resistor
R7-  33K Resistor
R8-  33K Resistor
R9-  2.2K Resistor
R10- 33K Resistor
R11- 47K Resistor
R12- 33K Resistor
S1-  SPST Relay
```

jacks in the project's chassis. Use the same type of jacks that serve as the connections for the wall plate and your telephone. Both of the jacks should have all of their wires serially connected together except for the positive and negative lines on the input jack. This jack will need to have its positive and negative lines attached to their respective connection points on the TCM1512A (it is unnecessary to connect the positive and negative lines of the output jack). A major selling point of this dual jack installation is that no modification of either the wall mount or the telephone will be needed for the connection and subsequent operation of Cyclic Telephone Ringer.

OPERATION

If the idea of a chorus of telephones all playing the same tune sounds like cacophony to your ears, Cyclic Telephone Ringer can also function in a more discreet manner. For example, some homes have several telephone lines, each with its own number. In this case, how can you identify which line is ringing and which isn't? By using Cyclic Telephone Ringer selectively on one specific incoming line, identification will be a snap. No matter what the reason is for using Cyclic Telephone Ringer, you are bound to enjoy answering a telephone that is belting out Beethoven's 9th Symphony instead of the archaic "brr-ring."

47

Musical Message Pager

I N ANY HOUSEHOLD THAT IS OCCUPIED BY MORE THAN ONE
resident, discreet paging can become a problem. How do you
locate someone that is wanted on the telephone? Do you feel comfortable yelling a person's name when his or her guest arrives at
the door? This method will undoubtedly place the paged person in
an embarrassing and uncomfortable situation. Have you ever tried
to explain a loud scream to a deafened business client? A second,
far less obnoxious solution is to press the button of Musical Message
Pager.

In operation, Musical Message Pager can use up to three buttons to play three different tunes. Up to three people within a
household are each assigned one of the specific musical scores for
paging purposes. Now, instead of yelling "Hey, you," when a high-
tech occupant is summoned, a single keypress of Musical Message
Pager will convey the same message with the William Tell Over-
ture (or another tune of your choice). This feature makes Musical
Message Pager the ideal summoning device. After all, discretion
is the better part of paging.

CONSTRUCTION NOTES

All of the musical scores produced by Musical Message Pager are
stored in an AY-3-1350 Tunes Synthesizer (Radio Shack

Table 47-1. Tune and Chime List for the AY-3-1350.

Toreador	William Tell
Hallelujah Chorus	Star Spangled Banner
Yankee Doodle	John Brown's Body
Clementine	God Save the Queen
Colonel Bogey	Marseillaise
America, America	Deutschland Leid
Wedding March	Beethoven's 5th
Augustine	O Sole Mio
Santa Lucia	The End
Blue Danube	Brahms' Lullaby
Hell's Bells	Jingle Bells
La Vie en Rose	Star Wars
Beethoven's 9th	Westminister Chime
Simple Chime	Descending Octave Chime

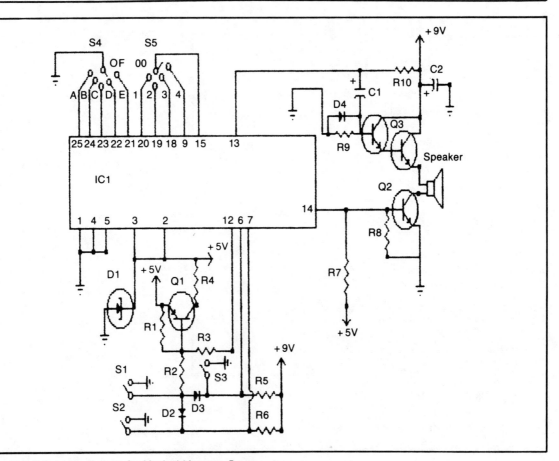

Fig. 47-1. Schematic diagram for Musical Message Pager.

#276-1782). There are a total of 25 tunes and 3 chimes that can be played with this IC. Table 47-1 contains a list of these possible melodies.

Musical Message Pager can be either battery operated or powered by household current. If batteries are used, both a 9V battery and a 5V battery pack are required. The proper connection points are marked on the schematic diagram (see Fig. 47-1). Using household current, however, requires an 8V transformer to be connected to all of the same points outlined for battery usage. No matter which power method is used, a simple SPST power switch is placed on the main positive power lead going to the circuit. A complete list of Musical Message Pager's parts is found in Table 47-2.

If you find that the volume of Musical Message Pager's sound output is insufficient, an amplifier can be added. Amplifying circuitry can be installed directly inside Musical Message Pager's chassis or a remote amplifying unit (connected via an appropriate cable) can be used.

Table 47-2. Parts List for Musical Message Pager.

```
C1-  10mf Electrolytic Capacitor
C2-  10mf Electrolytic Capacitor
D1-  5.1V Zener Diode
D2-  1N914 Diode
D3-  1N914 Diode
D4-  1N914 Diode
IC1- AY-3-1350
Q1-  MPS 2907
Q2-  MPS 3904
Q3-  MPS A13
R1-  10K Resistor
R2-  33K Resistor
R3-  33K Resistor
R4-  33 Resistor
R5-  33K Resistor
R6-  33K Resistor
R7-  2.2K Resistor
R8-  33K Resistor
R9-  47K Resistor
R10- 33K Resistor
S1-  Momentary SPST
S2-  Momentary SPST
S3-  Momentary SPST
S4-  6-position Rotary
S5-  5-position Rotary
```

OPERATION

With Musical Message Pager suitably installed at a convenient location, all that remains is to assign each person a tune. After everyone has finally agreed on their "theme song" and the proper switch (S4 and S5) positions have been selected, just press the button (S1, S2, or S3) that corresponds to the person being paged. The high-tech household will be filled with the echoing notes of that person's tune. This could create a new problem, however. The paged person's guest is bound to inquire, "What's the name of that song?"

48

Musical Light Switch

D O YOU FEEL FAMOUS? IF YOU THINK SO, THEN A FLOURISH of music should mark your entrance into a room. Unfortunately, this type of audio announcement is difficult to achieve without hiring a musical conductor or a live-in band. This problem is corrected through one virtue of the high-tech household—flexibility. By using some circuit wizardry, the room itself will signal your entrance with a prerecorded musical score.

For the sake of convenience, this musical message can be triggered by a common action, such as turning on a light switch. The result is a Musical Light Switch. In operation, Musical Light Switch plays a repetitive musical chime with each switching on of the room lights. This makes Musical Light Switch the perfect mating of fanfare and function.

CONSTRUCTION NOTES

The chime portion of Musical Light Switch is generated by the AY-3-1350 Tunes Synthesizer IC (Radio Shack #276-1782). This chip is interfaced to any electrical switch with a minimum of support parts (see Table 48-1).

Power for the Tunes Synthesizer is pulled from the line voltage driving the light bulb. Transformer T1 (refer to Fig. 48-1) reduces the normal house current to an acceptable 8 volts. Great

Table 48-1. Parts List for Musical Light Switch.

```
C1-  10mf Electrolytic Capacitor
C2-  10mf Electrolytic Capacitor
D1-  5.1V Zener Diode
D2-  1N4001 Diode
D3-  1N914 Diode
D4-  1N914 Diode
D5-  1N914 Diode
IC1- AY-3-1350
Q1-  MPS 2907
Q2-  MPS 3904
Q3-  MPS A13
R1-  10K Resistor
R2-  33 Resistor
R3-  33K Resistor
R4-  33K Resistor
R5-  33K Resistor
R6-  33K Resistor
R7-  2.2K Resistor
R8-  33K Resistor
R9-  47K Resistor
R10- 33K Resistor
S1-  Momentary SPST
T1-  8V Transformer
```

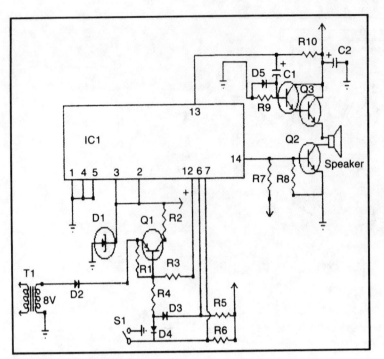

Fig. 48-1. Schematic diagram for Musical Light Switch.

care should be taken during the circuit's testing phase because of this voltage level.

There is no need for a power switch in Musical Light Switch. The flow of current into the circuit from the activation of the light switch causes the chime to sound. This feature reduces the dimensions of the final project to a size suitable for a light switch box.

Finally, if the sound output from the AY-3-1350 is inadequate for a room's environment (i.e., a noisy room), an audio amplifier should be attached to pin 14 (Tune Output). This action should be carefully planned because it will increase the final size of Musical Light Switch. One last consideration about an amplifier centers on its power requirements. A battery powered amplifier will need periodic access for battery replacement.

OPERATION

Musical Light Switch can be either a part of the actual light or placed as a separate accessory unit. Once in place, a delicate chime will permeate the air every time the light bulb is turned on. This melodic message only sounds for every "on" but not for the "offs." Therefore, the status of a light switch is indicated visually, as well as aurally. Musical Light Switch is a practical aid to an individual with limited sight and a delightful addition to any high-tech household.

49

Musical Alarm

O BNOXIOUS SOUNDS ARE THE BANE OF EVERY LIVING DAY. Quite often, sound is used as a method of communication. For example, a sound can signal the beginning or ending of an event. It is the manner in which a tone communicates a message that influences a person's daily attitude swings from minor irritation to extreme tension. Sirens announce the arrival of police cars, ambulances, and fire trucks. Bells alert listeners to bank robberies and the end of class periods. Ringing tones signify telephone calls and oven timers. Sound is an extremely effective device for relating these types of messages, but the unrelenting assault of noises on the human eardrums can become intolerable.

Partial relief from abrasive noise can be found in the form of a pleasant sounding alarm device. Instead of reacting to an incessantly ringing bell, you could be answering a gently playing musical tune. As long as both methods achieve the same result, most people would gladly choose the musical tune over the nerve-racking sound of a bell. Musical Alarm provides the tuneful solution.

Every household has the need for alarms. A practical alarm application might be as simple as a notification that someone is snooping in the kitchen cabinet containing the cookie jar. For this example, Musical Alarm is the perfect indicator to pleasantly remind a dieter or child that the cookie jar is off limits. Musical Alarm, triggered by the opening of a cabinet door, starts the gentle alarm tune.

CONSTRUCTION NOTES

Musical Alarm plays a chime tune from the AY-3-1350 Tunes Synthesizer whenever a switch (see Fig. 49-1) is activated. The Tunes Synthesizer is the only IC used in the Musical Alarm circuit. Table 49-1 provides a list of components that are required to complete this project.

A line voltage power supply is recommended for this circuit. A constant power source ensures that your circuit will always actively await a triggering signal.

A triggering switch can be selected which most suits the application to which Musical Alarm will be applied. A wide assortment of switches, including those that break a magnetic contact (Radio Shack #49-497 and #49-496), those that react to glass breakage (Radio Shack #49-516), those that react to a momentary contact (Radio Shack #49-517, #49-513 and #49-528), and those that react to vibration (Radio Shack #49-521), are adaptable for use with Musical Alarm.

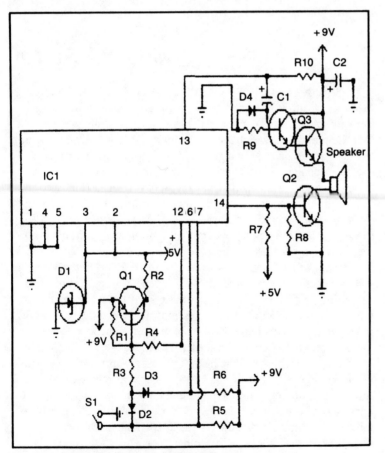

Fig. 49-1. Schematic diagram for Musical Alarm.

Table 49-1. Parts List for Musical Alarm.

```
C1-  10mf Electrolytic Capacitor
C2-  10mf Electrolytic Capacitor
D1-  5.1V Zener Diode
D2-  1N914 Diode
D3-  1N914 Diode
D4-  1N914 Diode
IC1- AY-3-1350
Q1-  MPS 2907
Q2-  MPS 3904
Q3-  MPS A13
R1-  10K Resistor
R2-  33 Resistor
R3-  33K Resistor
R4-  33K Resistor
R5-  33K Resistor
R6-  33K Resistor
R7-  2.2K Resistor
R8-  33K Resistor
R9-  47K Resistor
R10- 33K Resistor
S1-  Momentary SPST
```

OPERATION

Once Musical Alarm has been installed in its selected position, a disturbance of the accompanying triggering switch causes Musical Alarm to sound its chime warning.

50

Wall-Mounted
Room Thermometer

T HE MERCURY THERMOMETER IS A FUNCTIONAL DEVICE
found in most homes for monitoring environmental
temperature changes. The ability to monitor temperature is important, not only to the comfort of a home's residents, but also to the
well-being of household furnishings. Extremely hot or cold
temperatures have a deleterious effect on fabrics, wood, and electronic equipment over time.

Although it is undeniably useful, the mercury thermometer is
not very attractive, especially if it is displayed within a room sporting a high-tech decor. If you wish to monitor your home's
temperature, there is a way to circumvent the use of a mercury
thermometer while achieving an attractive design. Wall-Mounted
Room Thermometer uses heat sensitive liquid crystal sheets to form
a becoming thermometer that makes the mercury variety obsolete.

CONSTRUCTION NOTES

Liquid crystal sheets are available in different heat sensitivity levels.
Although each liquid crystal sheet changes its color when subjected
to increasing or decreasing degrees of temperature, different sheets
show different colors when exposed to the same temperature conditions. For example, at 75 degrees Fahrenheit one sheet might
show red while another shows blue. Wall-Mounted Room Ther-

mometer is the result of exploiting this feature of the liquid crystal sheets. Creation of Wall-Mounted Room Thermometer requires several sheets of liquid crystal with various degrees of thermal sensitivity, as well as an insulative backing material.

The liquid crystal sheets are first cut to the desired size to be placed on the insulative backing and framed. Pieces of the liquid crystal sheet should be arranged in order of their temperature sensitivity so that a viewer can make an easy visual interpretation of the registered temperature.

Each unique temperature sensitive area of Wall-Mounted Room Thermometer should be labeled with its corresponding temperature value. A viewer of the thermometer must understand, however, that only one specific color seen under a particular value indicates the stated temperature. For example, if the color red is chosen as the indicating color and red is seen in the 75 degree F zone, then the room's temperature is 75 degrees F.

The insulative backing is an important element of Wall-Mounted Room Thermometer. A piece of Styrofoam or foam core board used as a backing for the thermometer will act as a buffer from false temperature readings. A wall's temperature may be significantly different from that of the room.

OPERATION

Because of its extreme sensitivity, placement of Wall-Mounted Room Thermometer should be carefully planned. Study the temperature of the wall on which you plan to hang Wall-Mounted Room Thermometer. Despite the insulative material placed between the crystal sheets and the wall, a wall that is inordinately cold or hot compared to the room itself will skew the readings of the thermometer.

51

Random Switch Generator

I N THE CONVENTIONAL HOUSEHOLD, YOU FLICK ON A SWITCH
and a specific action happens. For instance, turn on the switch
that is connected to the blender and the blender starts. This sequence of events is not so simple in the high-tech household. In
this case, turn on a switch and any of a number of different actions
can result. This unpredictable switching is the domain of Random
Switch Generator.

Basically, Random Switch Generator takes a given input—the
action of a switch, and provides a random output—the lighting of
one of several bulbs. Granted, this random result would be impractical in the average household situation, but there is application in
certain displays and games.

CONSTRUCTION NOTES

The 4017 Decade Counter/Divider chip (Radio Shack #276-2417)
fires LEDs at a pulse set by the 555 Timer IC (Radio Shack
#276-1723) (see Table 51-1 for a complete parts list). The pulse
rate of this 555 chip is adjustable via potentiometer R1 (see Fig.
51-1). This flexibility makes the Random Switch Generator adaptable to a number of different situations.

If Random Switch Generator fails to light the LEDs after it is
breadboarded, check the polarity of the LEDs. One lead of the LED

Table 51-1. Parts List for Random Switch Generator.

```
C1- .01mf Capacitor
IC1- 555
IC2- 4017
L1-L10- LEDs
R1- 1K Resistor
R2- 1M Resistor
R3- 1K Resistor
S1- Momentary SPST
```

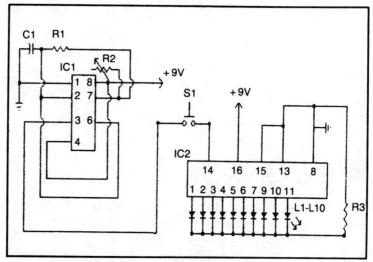

Fig. 51-1. Schematic diagram for Random Switch Generator.

represents the anode and the other is the cathode. In this project, all of the anodes should be connected to the pins (1-7 and 9-11) of the 4017, while the cathodes all connect to resistor R3.

OPERATION

A contact at switch S1 causes the 555 to pulse. When this switch is broken only one of the LEDs will remain lighted provided the power remains active in the circuit. If the sequential firing of the LEDs appears too slow, adjust R1 for a higher clock speed from the 555 Timer. When this adjustment is complete the Random Switch Generator will light a different LED for each switch pressing.

52

IR Switch

J UST WHEN YOU FINISH CLEANING YOUR HOUSE, DO YOU
sense a sudden anxiety concerning the whereabouts of your
children and the family pet? Do you worry about your kids getting
hurt in your home or about your home getting hurt by the kids?
Because people have so many important daily concerns, it is difficult for them to constantly monitor all rooms and all household activities. Assistance in this matter is readily accepted whenever it
is available.

Besides the obvious home dangers from which children should
be protected (such as unmonitored stairwells and cabinets full of
cleaning solution), a high-tech household occasionally has to be protected from the children which reside in it. Gingerly placed art objects are not immune from a child's or pet's rambunctious play.

While no parent can constantly monitor all household activities,
an electronic assistant can help perform this task. One electronic
monitoring device is capable of constantly keeping watch over
anything in its path. Because this monitoring device never sleeps,
it is able to watch for intruders as well as observe children and pets.
The electronic monitoring device that functions in all of these
capacities is IR (infrared) Switch.

An example of an easily acquired and easily employed IR
Switch is the Radio Shack Announcer With Invisible Infrared
Pulsed Beam (Radio Shack #49-201). This IR Switch consists of

a single transmitter/receiver unit and a reflective panel. The Radio Shack IR Switch works by emitting a beam of infrared light and receiving the signal as it is returned by the reflective panel. Whenever the beam is interrupted, an alarm is sounded from the IR unit.

An area can be monitored by placing the IR Switch unit so that the emitted beam of infrared light spans the area to be monitored. IR Switch is placed at one endpoint of the monitored area and the reflective panel is placed directly opposite the switch at the second endpoint.

By placing IR Switch so that the beam is at a low level, a child or pet breaking the beam will set off the alarm and immediately draw the attention of an adult. Low beam placement is ideal for monitoring child and pet safety situations (that means both the safety of the child and pet, as well as the safety of priceless objects they might come into contact with).

High beam placement is well suited for intruder detection. When high beam placement is used, only an intruding adult will break the IR beam and activate the switch. Children are too small to accidentally cause the alarm to sound.

53

Sound Switch

Y OU HAVE JUST SETTLED INTO YOUR FAVORITE CHAIR AND
the stereo system is belting out the latest high-tech musical
offering when you notice a distracting glare from a distant lamp.
You have two choices—get up and go turn it off or press a button
on the sound chirper which remotely turns off the lamp. While this
second choice is definitely the best, it can only be accomplished
through the use of a Sound Switch.

There are numerous sound activated switches (for example,
Radio Shack #61-2660) currently available on the market. All of
these consist of two separate elements: the hand-held chirper
transmitter or signaling device and the switch controlling receiver.
In operation, the chirper emits a sonic frequency with each
keypress. These sound vibrations are read by the receiver and set
off a trigger which controls an internal switch. This switch toggles
between an on and an off state. Therefore, with each chirp from
the transmitter, the receiver turns the switch on or off.

Prior to attempting sound control with Sound Switch it must
be connected to the household current. From there any appliance
can be plugged into the receptacle provided on the switch. In order
to ensure correct operation, the appliance's main power switch must
be turned on. To control the appliance, just press the chirper
transmitter button. Using Sound Switch does not eliminate the more
conventional on-off operation of the appliance, however. Because

of the chirper's high frequency nature, this silent control won't cut into your music enjoyment either (but, watch out for dogs). So turn off that annoying lamp, but do it quietly and effortlessly, with Sound Switch.

54

Temperature Switch

THE GREATEST THREAT TO HIGH-TECH ELECTRONIC EQUIP-
ment is heat. Excessive heat build-up caused by an unventilated case can permanently destroy delicate ICs and other heat sensitive components. Even with a liberal number of "flow-through" ventilation openings, 120 Vac (volts alternating current) powered equipment will overheat. In this situation, only forced air ventilation will provide the necessary cooling.

Using the forced air method of ventilation is both bulky and energy consumptive. The bulk comes from the electric fan that forces the air over the sweltering components. As the fan runs it uses electricity and wastes energy. A better alternative would be a "smart" electric fan (unfortunately, the problem of bulk will have to remain) which runs only when heat becomes excessive. Temperature Switch monitors the surrounding air and turns on an electric fan when a set temperature level is reached.

CONSTRUCTION NOTES

Temperature Switch is an extremely simple project. All that is necessary is a temperature control unit or thermostat that can run on line voltage and control a small electric fan (Radio Shack #273-241).

In order for Temperature Switch to function properly, there

are several important construction considerations that must be made prior to operation. First, decide upon the fan's relationship to the ventilation opening. Do you want the fan to exhaust the hot air or to pull in cool air? The orientation of the fan's blades will satisfy either of these requirements. In most cases, however, it is better to have the fan exhaust the overheated air.

A second important consideration is the placement of the thermostat. This location should be determined only after the fan's location and operation have both been established. The reason for this is that after the thermostat turns on the fan, the equipment's cooling progress will be monitored by the thermostat to ensure proper heat reduction. Therefore, position the thermostat at the edge of the fan's air flow.

One final construction point centers on the number and location of ventilation openings. This is not just a matter of taking a drill and poking holes all over the chassis. Instead, careful thought must be given to the flow of the air circulated by the fan. These precautions translate into adequate holes for the fan's air intake and a large number of openings near the top (hot air rises) of the fan's opposing case side.

OPERATION

A good thermostat sets a thermal activation level. This setting should be at least 10 degrees Fahrenheit below the equipment's critical temperature. Under operational conditions, when this temperature level is reached the thermostat will trigger the fan into life. In a typical configuration, the fan will then draw cool air from the front or bottom of the chassis and exhaust the heated air along the case's upper rear panel. This process will continue until the equipment's inside temperature drops between 10 and 15 degrees F.

This cyclic cooling process of Temperature Switch consumes less energy than its constantly running counterparts. While no promises can be made about substantial cost savings, there will be less unnecessary power drain during periods of limited operation. In other words, Temperature Switch is ideal for equipment that is temperature sensitive, but is used for only short periods of time.

55

Door-Open Alarm

W ITHIN EVERY HOME, THERE ARE AREAS THAT MUST BE monitored against unwanted entry. An area that deserves special safety consideration is a cabinet containing valuables. While a wall mounted safe box (hidden by a classic painting, of course) has a certain romantic appeal, it is not a likely fixture in most homes. A better solution is to protect your cabinet full of valuables with a Door Open Alarm.

Door-Open Alarm emits an audible tone when the cabinet door to which it is attached is opened. This audible tone is loud enough to alert you to the possible danger to your valuables.

CONSTRUCTION NOTES

Door-Open Alarm is based on the 555 Timer IC and a door-open detection switch. The ideal door-open detection switch is the normally-closed variety, because it prevents the switch contact from completing a circuit while a door is closed. A contact is made, instead, when the door is opened and the switch is released to its normal electrically closed position. The released switch then causes an 8 ohm speaker to emit its warning tone.

Door-Open Alarm is a simple circuit requiring only two resistors and two capacitors in addition to its 555 IC, its switch, and the speaker (see Table 55-1). If you find the tone generated by Door-

Table 55-1. Parts List for Door-Open Alarm.

```
C1- 4.7mf Electrolytic Capacitor
C2- .1mf Capacitor
IC1- 555
R1- 100K Potentiometer
R2- 1K Resistor
S1- Normally-open SPST
```

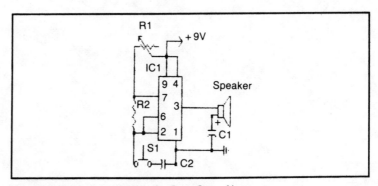

Fig. 55-1. Schematic diagram for Door-Open Alarm.

Open Alarm to be offensive, you can alter its pitch by changing the value of capacitor C1 (see Fig. 55-1).

OPERATION

Installation of Door-Open Alarm necessitates the placement of the project's normally-closed switch so that when your cabinet door is closed, the switch is depressed. When the safety protected cabinet door is opened, the switch is released and Door-Open Alarm is activated. The tone is only silenced when the cabinet door is once again closed.

56

Time-Delay Switch

I T'S NO FUN TO BUMP YOUR SHIN ON A BEDSIDE TABLE AS YOU stumble towards your bed in a darkened room. Inevitably, a room's main light switch is located five to ten feet away from your bed. This requires you to navigate the distance from the light switch to the bed each dark night.

A small light source, controlled by Time-Delay Switch, allows you to find your way to your bed before the light automatically turns off. For convenience, Time-Delay Switch and the light source are placed next to the standard wall mounted light switch. You are safely tucked under the covers without any injuries when the light is extinguished.

CONSTRUCTION NOTES

As this is a single IC circuit (see Fig. 56-1), the only chip required for Time-Delay Switch is the 555 Timer. Other components include a 6 volt relay to which the light source is connected, two diodes, two capacitors, and a potentiometer for controlling the timing length of Time-Delay Switch (see Table 56-1). A normally open push-button switch is used to trigger Time-Delay Switch. The relay coil is energized by IC 1 and the relay contacts close the circuit for the light source. The potentiometer regulates the length of time that the relay is active and, consequently, the duration of the light

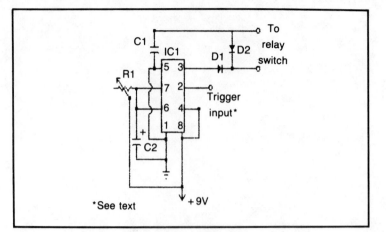

Fig. 56-1. Schematic diagram for Time-Delay Switch.

Table 56-1. Parts List for Time-Delay Switch.

```
C1- .01mf Capacitor
C2- 10mf Electrolytic Capacitor
D1- 1N914 Diode
D2- 1N914 Diode
IC1- 555
R1- 1M Potentiometer
```

source. You can experiment with different settings of this pot to arrive at an appropriate duration for the light source to remain lit.

OPERATION

Time-Delay Switch is well suited for wall mounting next to your normal light switch. Just press the push button of Time-Delay Switch when you turn out your room light. Depending on your setting of the potentiometer, you have up to ten seconds to find your way to your bed before Time-Delay Switch's light is turned off.

Although ten seconds sounds like a short amount of time, you'll discover that you have plenty of time to find your way to bed. Your shins will thank you for your considerate treatment as you cease bludgeoning the furniture with them. Most importantly, however, other family members will not hear your late night howls of pain, because Time-Delay Switch now lights your way to bed.

57

Radio Cube

W HETHER ITS PURPOSE IS FOR ENTERTAINMENT OR FOR information, a portable radio provides an invaluable service to household members. For example, the portable radio, matches, and candles are the devices immediately sought during power failures and weather emergencies. The only drawback to using a portable radio is its inability to comfortably fit into its high-tech surroundings. Let's face it—most portable radios are ugly. A radio cannot serve its intended functional purpose if its owner hides it away because of embarrassment.

As a solution to the problems of both beauty and convenience, Radio Cube takes a portable radio and transforms it into a beautiful and functional tool. In this new form, Radio Cube becomes an attractive and useful addition to a home's interior design scheme.

CONSTRUCTION NOTES

The parts required for constructing Radio Cube are the internal circuitry of a functional portable radio and materials for constructing its new enclosure. Radio Cube's enclosure dimensions are completely dependent on the size of the components (transported from the portable radio) that will be placed within the cube. Be sure that enough room is allowed for circuit board and speaker mounting.

Although you can use any convenient material for Radio Cube's

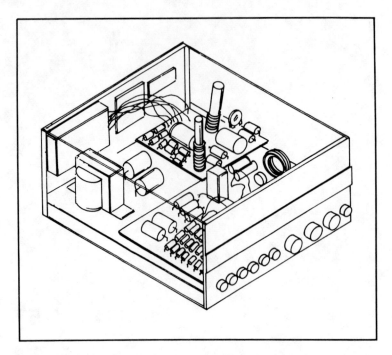

enclosure, clear Plexiglas makes a particularly attractive enclosure because the radio's internal structure is clearly exhibited. Mark and drill the component and board mounting holes, as well as a series of holes near the desired speaker location before joining the sides of the cube together. The holes near the speaker location provide sound output.

Mount Radio Cube's power, volume, and channel selection controls on the exterior of Radio Cube. External mounting of these controls eliminates the need to constantly reopen Radio Cube just to turn the "cube" on.

OPERATION

Radio Cube is operated in exactly the same manner as you would operate any other radio. The pleasant exception is that Radio Cube is custom designed for both your aesthetic and functional needs. Radio Cube is an attractive addition to its surroundings. Your original ugly duckling radio is now a Cube Radio swan.

58

Remote Weather

WHAT IS THE MOST FREQUENTLY DISCUSSED SUBJECT IN the United States? The answer will probably surprise you—it's the weather. Is it going to rain tomorrow, will it be sunny on Thursday, what was the temperature today? This kind of talk seeps into our conversations daily. Not only does the weather dominate our social interactions, its also influences our lives. All hyperbole aside, to be ignorant of the weather is more than a failing social grace.

The only problem with evaluating the weather from within the high-tech household is one of isolation. An enclosed, climate-controlled living area is not the best environment to determine the outside temperature. This project is one solution—Remote Weather.

Most of the conventional weather instruments can be purchased in either an analog or a digital version. The analog variety is typified by the standard mercury (or red alcohol) thermometer. A digital thermometer on the other hand is a thermoelectric couple that connects to a digital display for a numeric readout of the current temperature. An even greater asset of the digital thermometer is its ability to provide secondary information (high and low temperatures for the day, the current inside temperature, a temperature alarm). This secondary information faculty is far superior to any of the capabilities of the analog version.

Remote Weather effectively uses the primary and secondary

information abilities of digital weather instruments. A completed Remote Weather station is composed of the instruments that will supply the required outside environmental data. These instruments must be placed in a suitable location and then calibrated for the expected weather conditions.

CONSTRUCTION NOTES

Only two weather instruments will be necessary for the average Remote Weather station: a multi-function thermometer and precipitation indicator. Both of these devices will need to have their sensors installed in a suitable external location. In order to ensure accurate readings, this location must be away from any sheltering windbreaks or overhangs.

In the case of the thermometer, the probe can either be in direct sunlight or placed in the shade. The most beneficial readings will come from a thermometer probe that is located in a shady, wind-free area. Additionally, the probe must not rest too near a house opening such as a window. Drafts from cracks around the window's frame (yes, all window frames have some cracks) and radiated heat from the glass panes could cause inaccurate readings.

Similarly, the precipitation indicator needs to be away from any major buildings. Stray rain splatters, shielding overhangs, and windbreaks all contribute to false readings. This isolation distance does not need to be great—at least 2 feet from any form of obstruction at or near the same height.

OPERATION

By following the probe placement guidelines discussed above, reliable weather information is provided by the digital thermometer and precipitation indicator. Because these data are collected and displayed on interior control consoles, whenever weather information is required just push a button and read the LEDs. These digital readouts will eliminate all of the problems associated with dressing for the weather—if you ask Remote Weather first.

59

Remote Telephone
Ringer/Lighter

HOW CAN YOU TELL IF THE TELEPHONE IS RINGING? IF YOU are gifted with the sense of hearing, the sound of the telephone's bell serves as your indicator. If your hearing is impaired, however, the telephone is forever silent. While this scenario might seem exaggerated, hearing impairment can be artificially induced.

Slip on a pair of high fidelity headphones and you are totally isolated from the outside world. No other sound, not even the ringing of a telephone, penetrates the stereo system's aural environment. For the sake of this argument—*you* are hearing impaired.

What every hearing impaired person needs is an alternate method to signal an incoming telephone call; they need a Remote Telephone Ringer/Lighter. This project substitutes the flash of an LED for the ring of a telephone's bell.

CONSTRUCTION NOTES

There are a total of six components required for the construction of Remote Telephone Ringer/Lighter (see Table 59-1). The only IC is the TCM1512A Ring Detector/Driver (Radio Shack #276-1302). This chip draws its power from the telephone's ring voltage.

The positive and negative telephone terminals must be connected to pins 1 and 8 of the TCM1512A, respectively (see Fig.

Table 59-1. Parts List for Remote Telephone Ringer/Lighter.

```
C1-  1mf Capacitor
C2-  10mf Electrolytic Capacitor
IC1- TCM1512A
L1-  LED
R1-  2.2K Resistor
R2-  100K Resistor
```

59-1). Prior to reaching pin 1, the positive signal passes through capacitor C1 and resistor R1. These two components serve as blockers and current limiters before the telephone's voltage reaches the Ring Detector/Driver chip.

The entire benefit of Remote Telephone Ringer/Lighter is in its ability to silently indicate a telephone call. Therefore, the selection of a lamp should be given considerable thought. Ideally, a high-brightness, red incandescent lamp (e.g. Radio Shack #272-331) should be used. The chosen lamp should be mounted prominently on the top of Remote Telephone Ringer/Lighter's case.

OPERATION

Remote Telephone Ringer/Lighter can be either permanently or temporarily mounted on your telephone. The temporary method, using standard telephone jacks and plugs, is the best. In fact, by connecting a switch between the positive and negative telephone lines either a sound or a silent "ring" is possible.

Once construction is complete, full-scale operation can begin. Any incoming call will cause the lamp of Remote Telephone Ringer/Lighter to glow brightly during each ring. This lamp oscillation continues until the telephone receiver is picked up or the caller gives up. Never again will a hearing impairment let a call go unanswered. The only problem is that Remote Telephone Ringer/Lighter can't discriminate between a phone call from a friend and an annoying solicitation.

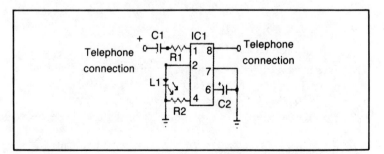

Fig. 59-1. Schematic diagram for Remote Telephone Ringer/Light.

Wireless Stereo Connections

A DD SEVERAL COMPONENTS TO THE AVERAGE STEREO SYS-
tem and you have a nightmare—a cable nightmare. Each
amplifier, cassette deck, tuner, or frequency equalizer contributes
three or more tentacles to this growing cable hydra. Additionally,
each speaker is attached to the main stereo unit through a wire um-
bilical. This increasing wire fantasia becomes even uglier when the
speakers are moved away from the stereo unit.

Other than adding to this cable propagation, speakers present
the stereo owner with yet another problem; the problem of awkward
speaker wire placement. Invariably, the ideal speaker location is
at a distance from the stereo unit. In this case, the word "distance"
translates into speaker wire and this wire runs across the floor to
be tripped over. There are wire placement alternatives, however.
Such an alternative might be running the wire across the ceiling.
Now the only problem is the sight of the wire dangling from the
ceiling. A better solution to this entire speaker wire problem is
speaker connections that don't use wires—Wireless Stereo Connections.

By using infrared transmitters and receivers to carry sound,
long speaker wires can be completely eliminated. Basically, this
is the theory behind Wireless Stereo Connections. While this is the
ultimate solution to a common problem, stereo owners with high-
fidelity demands might not find Wireless Stereo Connections ap-

propriate. This is a "medium fidelity" project that should be experimented with before it is made a permanent part of your stereo system.

CONSTRUCTION NOTES

There are two separate circuits that make up Wireless Stereo Connections for each speaker. One circuit is a transmitter and the other is a receiver. The transmitter is constructed around the 324 Quad Op Amp (operational amplifier) (Radio Shack #276-1711) IC. The receiver uses a TL084CN Quad Bi-FET Op Amp (Radio Shack #276-1714) chip. Figures 60-1 and 60-2 provide the pin assignments for these two ICs. A complete project parts list is given in Table 60-1.

In the transmitter (see Fig. 60-3), the sound is converted into an IR beam that is produced by the IR Emitter LED. This beam is detected in the receiver by an IR Detector phototransistor and sent into an amplifier. It is this power amplifier that actually drives the speaker. This amplifier is placed with and needs to match the power requirements of the speaker.

There are two vital links in the Wireless Stereo Connections system: the IR Emitter LED and the IR Detector phototransistor. Excessive amounts of direct sunlight will interfere with the operation of Wireless Stereo Connections. Both of the IR sensitive components, therefore, need to be protected and isolated from these stray light elements. Additionally, room lighting conditions can also

Pin#	Assignment
1	Output
2	-Input
3	+Input
4	V
5	+Input
6	-Input
7	Output
8	Output
9	-Input
10	+Input
11	GND
12	+Input
13	-Input
14	Output

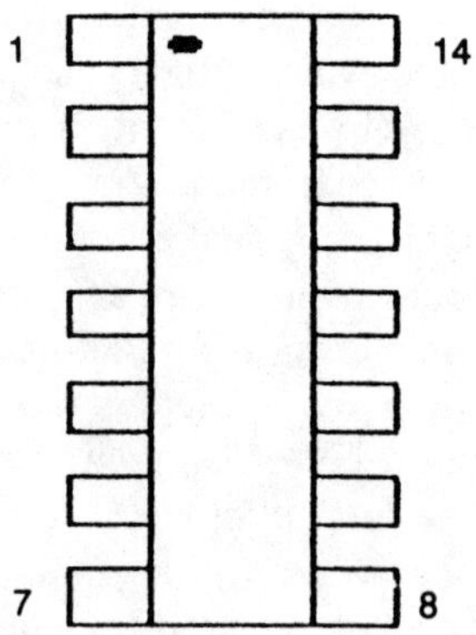

Fig. 60-1. Pin assignments for the 324.

168

```
Pin#          Assignment

 1    Output
 2    Inverting Output
 3    Non-Inverting Output
 4    V
 5    Non-Inverting Output
 6    Inverting Output
 7    Output
 8    Output
 9    Inverting Output
10    Non-Inverting Output
11    GND
12    Non-Inverting Output
13    Inverting Output
14    Output
```

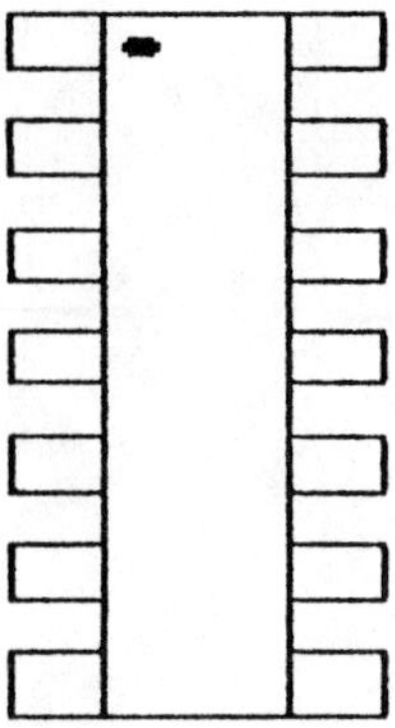

Fig. 60-2. Pin assignments for the TL084CN.

disrupt the effective transmission distance of Wireless Stereo Connections. In addition to isolating the IR components in order to reduce stray light elements, the use of lenses over the IR LED and the phototransistor will enhance communication by focusing the signal across the room.

Table 60-1. Parts List for Wireless Stereo Connections.

```
C1-  1mf Electrolytic Capacitor
C2-  10mf Electrolytic Capacitor
C3-  .1mf Capacitor
IC1- 324
IC2- TL084CN
L1-  Infrared LED Emitter
Q1-  MPS 2222A
Q2-  Phototransistor Detector
R1-  1K Resistor
R2-  1M Potentiometer
R3-  100K Resistor
R4-  100 Resistor
R5-  100 Resistor
R6-  220K Resistor
R7-  1K Resistor
R8-  220K Resistor
```

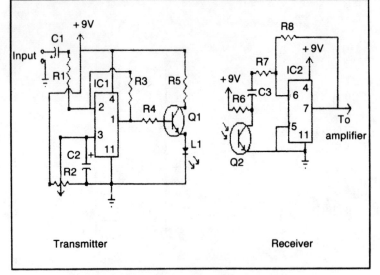

Fig. 60-3. Schematic diagram for Wireless Stereo Connections.

OPERATION

Both the transmitter and the receiver require 9 volt power supplies. Another independent power supply is necessary for the amplifier that drives the speaker. All three of these circuits (transmitter, receiver, and amplifier) will have to be active for music to be carried over Wireless Stereo Connections.

Connection of the transmitter to the stereo system is similar to attaching regular speaker wire. In other words, there is a positive (red) and a negative (black) terminal on the stereo. Just attach these two terminals to their respective points in Wireless Stereo Connections' transmitter circuit.

Under operational conditions, the sensitivity of Wireless Stereo Connections will depend on the room's lighting. The transmission and reception quality can be enhanced by shielding the IR LED and the phototransistor and by focusing the IR beam with lenses. If the quality of the reception is still poor after following these precautions, adjust the potentiometer until the best possible sound can be heard through the speaker. Remember Wireless Stereo Connections will not produce high-fidelity sound, but they will serve as a welcome reduction in your stereo cabling.

61

Intercom

E VERY HIGH-TECH HOUSEHOLD WITH MORE THAN ONE ROOM
suffers from a communication problem. This isn't a case of
not knowing who to talk to or of not having anything to say; it's
more a problem of trying to find someone.

An example of this problem is locating a family member in order
to announce that dinner is being served. Even a task as simple as
this is complicated when the location of the individual is unknown.
Then again, even if you knew the exact location of this person you
would still have to either yell your message or walk until you are
within earshot and deliver your notification. A superior method is
electronic communication via the Intercom.

Contrary to the open operation of IR Intercom (see Chapter
62), Intercom is a closed system. In other words, direct wiring connects the two communication stations. One added benefit of this
layout is a reduction in the overall parts count for constructing Intercom. Additionally, Intercom has provisions for two-way conversation between both stations.

CONSTRUCTION NOTES

Both the input and the output from both stations of Intercom are
driven by a 386 Low Voltage Audio Power Amplifier IC (Radio
Shack #276-1731). This versatile chip uses very little power and

Table 61-1. Parts List for Intercom.

```
C1-  .1mf Capacitor
C2-  47mf Electrolytic Capacitor
IC1- 386
M1-  Speaker/Microphone
M2-  Speaker/Microphone
R1-  1M Potentiometer
R2-  10 Resistor
S1-  SPDT Toggle
S2-  SPDT Toggle
T1-  18V Transformer
```

is ideal for battery operation.

A regular 8 ohm speaker is used as both the microphone and the speaker for each of the two stations (see Table 61-1). This dual usage is toggled by a two position switch. This switch is an SPDT (single pole, double throw) switch (toggle or push button) with one switch installed on each station (see Fig. 61-1). One position of each double throw switch will be labeled transmit (or talk) and the other will be receive (or listen). A special signaling procedure reminiscent of a pilot's "Over" will be needed to notify a listener that the conversation is awaiting their transmission.

Finally, if the output of Intercom is insufficient there is a modification that can be made to the 386. Pins 1 and 8 of this IC

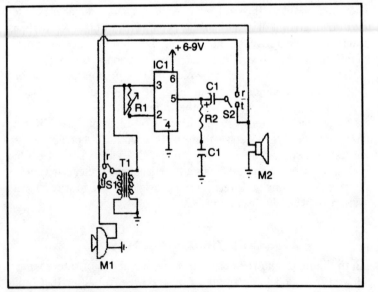

Fig. 61-1. Schematic diagram for Intercom.

control the gain of the chip. In its present configuration, Intercom is set for a gain of 20 dB (decibel). This level can be raised to 50 dB by placing a 10 microfarad capacitor between pins 1 and 8. A further increase to 200 dB is possible with the addition of both a 1.2K ohm resistor and a 10 microfarad capacitor between these same two pins. Both of these modifications should be tested on the breadboard before they are made a final part of Intercom.

OPERATION

Before attempting any adjustments of Intercom's circuitry, make sure that the two SPDT switches are properly connected and labeled. With the switches working correctly, place one station in the transmit mode and the other in the receive position. The potentiometer should now be adjusted until the volume is suitable for both stations.

Your last installation test concerns the length of the wire between the two stations. A long wire requires more power and a wire that is too long simply won't work with Intercom as shown. In order to use Intercom over great distances, additional power amplifiers are required. These amplifiers will be used to strengthen the signal to and from both stations. Experiment with various amplifier arrangements until your Intercom works perfectly.

62

IR Intercom

H OW MANY TIMES DO YOU FIND YOUR VOICE HOARSE FROM yelling to family members through hallways, down stairwells, or out the back door to your garage? When a guest arrives or a telephone call is received, the host or call recipient is rarely in your vicinity. You are forced to either conduct a house-wide search for the missing family member, or bellow out his or her name in hopes that he or she will respond. This scene creates an embarrassing moment for both the guest or caller and the door or phone answerer. Fortunately, an uncomfortable scene can be quietly eliminated with the use of IR Intercom.

IR Intercom consists of two parts—a voice transmitter and a voice receiver. A microphone in the transmitter accepts your spoken message so that it can be modified and carried via a beam of infrared light to the receiver. Within the receiver, the beam is translated back into a signal that can be easily amplified. Using the amplifier of your choice, the signal is then fed to a speaker.

CONSTRUCTION NOTES

IR Intercom is constructed in two separate units for placement in two different enclosures—the transmitter circuit and the receiver circuit (see Fig. 62-1). The link between the two circuits is the infrared light transferred between the IR Emitter/Detector Pair

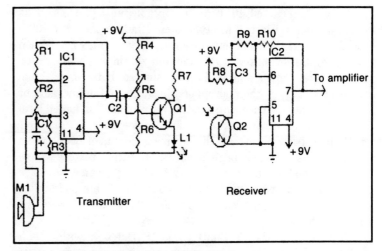

Fig. 62-1. Schematic diagram for IR Intercom.

(Radio Shack #276-142). The transmitting circuitry of IR Intercom uses the TL084CN Quad Bi-FET Operational Amplifier IC to modify a voice signal so that it can be sent to the receiver via the IR beam. A second TL084CN is used within the receiving circuitry to prepare the received IR signal for amplification. The remaining parts required for IR Intercom are listed in Table 62-1.

Table 62-1. Parts List for IR Intercom.

```
C1-  220mf Electrolytic Capacitor
C2-  .1mf Capacitor
C3-  .1mf Capacitor
IC1- TL084CN
IC2- TL084CN
L1-  Infrared LED Emitter
M1-  Speaker/Microphone
Q1-  MPS 2222A
Q2-  Phototransistor Detector
R1-  100K Resistor
R2-  1K Resistor
R3-  10K Resistor
R4-  1K Resistor
R5-  10K Resistor
R6-  1K Resistor
R7-  220 Resistor
R8-  220K Resistor
R9-  1K Resistor
R10- 220K Resistor
```

An omnidirectional, PC board mountable microphone such as the High Fidelity Electret Mike Element (Radio Shack #270-090) is used within the transmitter to pick up your voice message. When mounting the transmitter of IR Intercom within an enclosure, be sure to provide an opening in the enclosure so that a voice signal can be picked up by the microphone. A series of narrow slots or holes drilled into the enclosure over the microphone's mounted location will provide a perfect acoustical access area.

Both the transmitting and the receiving circuits of IR Intercom require 9 volts of power for their operation. Either battery or line voltage can be used to arrive at this 9 volt requirement for each circuit. If battery operation is chosen, a push-to-talk button installed within the transmitting assembly circuit will dramatically save the life of the battery.

Installation of the IR Emitter and IR Detector within their respective IR Intercom enclosures must be planned so that there is an unobstructed line of sight between the IR Emitter and the IR Detector when IR Intercom is in use. This means that the microphone must be placed within the transmitting assembly enclosure so that your head does not interrupt the IR beam as you speak into the microphone. Placing the microphone and the IR Emitter on opposite sides of the enclosure effectively eliminates the possibility of your head blocking the IR beam.

OPERATION

Proper IR Emitter to IR Detector signal exchange is the primary concern for installing the two units of IR Intercom. Be sure that the transmitting assembly is placed in direct line of sight of the receiving assembly of IR Intercom and that nothing obstructs the path of the IR beam. Fine tuning of the signal generated by the transmitter is controlled by the potentiometer within the transmitting assembly enclosure.

Enhancement of the IR beam transmissions over a long distance is accomplished by adding focusing lenses over both the IR Emitter and the IR Detector. Remember to maintain proper IR beam alignment when making these lens additions, however. Further signal improvement can be obtained by operating IR Intercom under darkened conditions. Installation of IR Intercom within a dimly lit hallway or stairwell prevents stray light from interfering with the IR beam signal. The worst enemy of IR Intercom, however, is direct sunlight. Sunlight will severely handicap the use of IR Intercom unless proper measures are taken. The IR Detector must be shielded from this intense light while still allowing it to receive signals from the IR Emitter.

Once IR Intercom is constructed and a suitable amplifying circuit and speaker have been connected to the receiver, inter-room communication can begin. If you would like to be able to get a response from the person you page on IR Intercom, you can add a second IR Intercom next to the first, but this time place the receiver of the second IR Intercom near the transmitter of the first IR Intercom. Arrange the second transmitter and receiver so that their signals are shielded from the first pair's IR beam signal. Now all you have to do is speak into the transmitter and listen for a reply on the receiver. Thanks to IR Intercom, you'll never again have to suffer from a hoarse voice.

63

Light Alarm

SECURITY IS A PRECIOUS COMMODITY. ALTHOUGH THOU-
sands of security systems exist, most of them are easily
thwarted. A little bit of cunning and effort is all that's required for
someone to pick a lock, avoid a light beam, or evade a motion detection switch. There is one security measure, however, that even the
most clever burglar or snoop cannot circumvent—Light Alarm.

Light Alarm is a small, light sensitive device that emits a tone
in the presence of light. If Light Alarm is placed within a desk
drawer containing sensitive material, the opening of the drawer
under normal room lighting conditions greets the drawer opener
with a noisy surprise.

CONSTRUCTION NOTES

A single IC, the 741C Op Amp, controls Light Alarm with the
assistance of a light detecting Cadmium Sulfide Photocell (Radio
Shack #276-116). The remaining parts for Light Alarm are two
capacitors, four resistors, one potentiometer, and an 8 ohm speaker
(see Table 63-1).

The power requirement for Light Alarm is +9 volts. Because
Light Alarm is well suited to portable use, a battery is the most
suitable power supply for this circuit. You can easily move the compact Light Alarm to protect various areas within your household.

**Table 63-1. Parts
List for Light Alarm.**

```
C1- 1mf Electrolytic Capacitor
C2- 4.7mf Electrolytic Capacitor
IC1- 741C
P1- CdS Photocell
R1- 1K Resistor
R2- 100K Resistor
R3- 470K Resistor
R4- 470 Resistor
R5- 50K Potentiometer
S1- Speaker
```

The volume of Light Alarm's emitted tone is controlled by the potentiometer (see Fig. 63-1). Adjustment of this pot selectively allows you to mildly embarrass a snoop rummaging through your personal belongings or to startle a burglar with an electronic scream.

The Light Alarm circuit must be placed within an enclosure so that the photocell is in plain view of any potential light source. External mounting of this photocell on the project's enclosure is, therefore, required.

OPERATION

Very little maintenance is required for Light Alarm once it is situated within the drawer it is protecting. Light Alarm must be placed so that room light immediately strikes the photocell when the drawer is opened. Just remember Light Alarm's presence when *you* open the protected drawer. You can save your eardrums a great deal of suffering by opening the drawer in darkness and covering the photocell before turning on the room light.

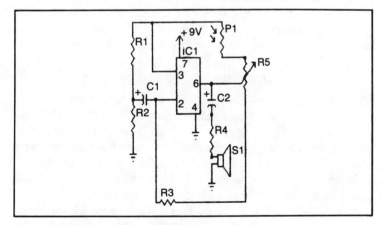

Fig. 63-1. Schematic diagram for Light Alarm.

64

LED Timer

E VERY KITCHEN COOKING RECIPE REQUIRES AN ACCURATE
timer. Without accurate timing a three-minute egg is usually
a runny mess. So, all that is really needed is a good timer. For the
high-tech household, however, there are additional requirements—a
functional timer must also have a suitable form.

The most commonly encountered kitchen timer consists of the
analog twist-dial variety. This timekeeper ticks down until the
preset time has expired and it "dings." The ding might be fine,
but what about the time? How can you tell when 1 minute has
passed if the timer is set for 3 minutes? LED Timer provides you
with a running digital display read-out for up to 9 minutes.

CONSTRUCTION NOTES

Three integrated circuit chips do the lion's share of the work in
LED Timer. The 555 Timer (Radio Shack #276-1723) supplies the
clock pulse, the 7490 Divide By 2 or 5, BCD Counter (Radio Shack
#276-1808) (see Fig. 64-1) translates the clock's pulse into a binary
output, and the 7447 BCD to Seven-Segment Decoder/Driver
decodes the binary output into a 7-segment numerical digit. All of
LED Timer's components are listed in Table 64-1.

Since LED Timer is designed for use anywhere accurate timing is required, only battery operation should be considered for

Pin#	Assignment
1	Input B
2	Reset Input
3	Reset Input
4	NC
5	V
6	Reset Input
7	Reset Input
8	Output
9	Output
10	GND
11	Output
12	Output
13	NC
14	Input A

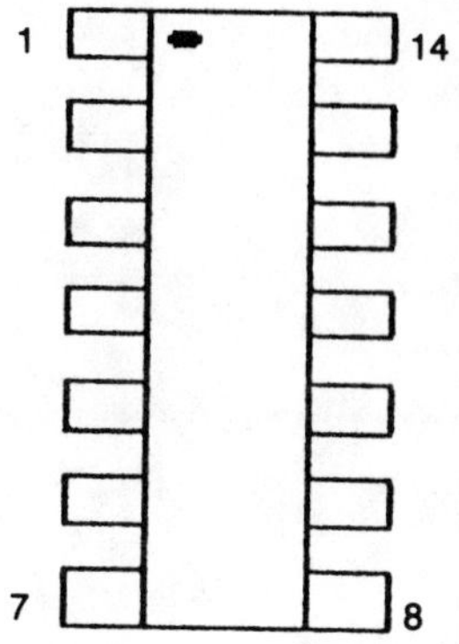

Fig. 64-1. Pin assignments for the 7490.

power. In order to conserve battery life, an optional power switch can be added to control the +5 volts (see Fig. 64-2). When S1 is turned on the timer starts its timing cycle. When S1 is turned off the timing cycle is stopped. The display will remain lighted until the optional power switch is turned off.

The ideal display for LED Timer is a single seven-segment LED display. A 7-segment display is only capable of generating the digits 0-9. Therefore, LED Timer can only display a maximum of 9 elapsed minutes. Another valuable feature of this display is that it can be driven directly from the 7447 with only 7 support resistors. The common anode type display (Radio Shack #276-053) with red LED segments also makes LED Timer highly visible in the kitchen environment.

Table 64-1. Parts List for LED Timer.

```
C1- 1mf Electrolytic Capacitor
D1- Common Anode 7-segment Display
IC1- 555
IC2- 7490
IC3- 7447
R1- 1M Potentiometer
R2- 1K Resistor
R3-R9- 330 Resistor
S1- SPST Toggle
```

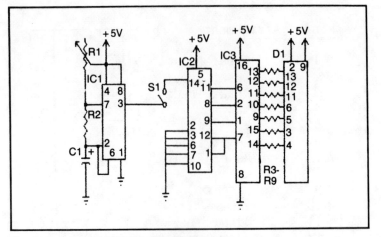

Fig. 64-2. Schematic diagram for LED Timer.

OPERATION

Calibration of LED Timer is required before final operation is possible. A highly accurate clock must be used to adjust the pulse of the 555. Turn the potentiometer until there is one count per minute on the 7-segment display. Several test runs should be made before LED Timer is placed on galley duty.

A typical timing chore for LED Timer begins with activation of the power switch (if the two switch method is used). When the event starts, flip the timing switch (S1). LED Timer now counts off each minute with an additive display (3 minutes of elapsed time displays as 3). On completion of the event, turn off S1 and the display stays lighted reminding you of the elapsed time. If you are finished cooking, the power switch is also turned off and LED Timer vanishes into its high-tech surroundings. Not bad for a redesign of the three-minute egg timer.

65

LEDminder

A NYONE WITH A BUSY DAILY SCHEDULE OFTEN REALIZES AT the end of a hectic day that they have forgotten to accomplish at least one task. Whether the unfinished job is trivial or monumental, eventually this malady of forgetfulness afflicts all of us. Fortunately, the peculiar habit of tying a string around one's finger to remember forgettable tasks has fallen into obscurity. A new electronic method now exists for remembering things to do. LEDminder is an electronic "finger string" that uses an LED display to remind its user of an unfinished task.

As a display on your desk or work area, LEDminder uses a 7-segment LED to show a pattern. Turn LEDminder on when you think of a task to be performed, and turn LEDminder off later, after the job has been completed.

CONSTRUCTION NOTES

Remarkably, LEDminder uses only a few components for its entire circuit (see Table 65-1). The only other ingredient that must be added to the LEDminder circuit is a 5 volt power supply.

The numeric LED for LEDminder is a simple Seven-Segment LED such as the Radio Shack common anode Seven-Segment LED (Radio Shack #276-053). Controlling the output of the Seven-Segment LED is a 7447 BCD To Seven-Segment Decoder/Driver.

Table 65-1. Parts List for LEDminder.

```
D1- Common Anode 7-segment Display
IC1- 7447
R1-R7- 330 Resistor
S1- 4-position DIP
```

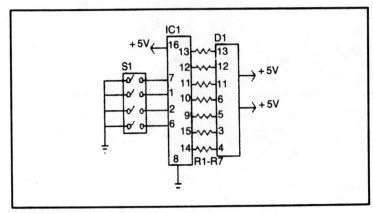

Fig. 65-1. Schematic diagram for LEDminder.

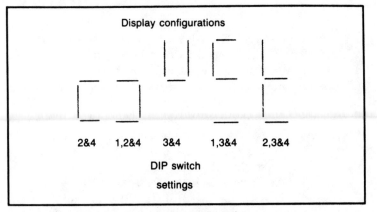

Fig. 65-2. Possible LEDminder display configurations.

The 7447 driver causes the pattern selected by S1 to be displayed on the segments of the LED. An optional power on/off switch connected between the power supply and pin 16 of the 7447 driver (see Fig. 65-1) will conserve the battery power supply's life.

Construction of LEDminder on a breadboard allows room for experimentation with the LED display output. By selectively channeling the output of pins 1, 2, 6, and 7 of the 7447 Decoder/Driver to ground, certain segments of the LED display are turned on. Breadboard jumper wires or a four position DIP switch (S1) placed

184

between ground and pins 1, 2, 6, and 7 of the 7447 IC allow selection of various LED segment combinations. Figure 65-2 illustrates several possible LED output displays and the settings required to achieve them.

OPERATION

Once installed within an appropriate enclosure, LEDminder is turned on to begin its reminding function. With the controlling DIP switch (S1), you can change the setting of the display at any time. A closed DIP switch position brings the signal of the associated 7447 pin to ground.

With LEDminder, you can now throw away your ball of string. You may find, however, that you need to construct a second LEDminder to remind you of the purpose of the first one.

66

Privacy Indicator

ONE OF THE MORE EXCITING ASPECTS OF PHOTOGRAPHY IS darkroom work. Taking an image from the initial idea to the final enlarged print is an art that demands long uninterrupted hours of work. Difficulty can sometimes arise, however, when you try to obtain those hours of darkness. Invariably, someone will enter the darkroom and turn darkness into light.

Many times this unwanted intrusion could be avoided with a suitable occupancy warning posted on the darkroom's door. An indicator that is equivalent to a hotel's "Do Not Disturb" sign would help protect a darkroom's light sensitive materials. Privacy Indicator is a high-tech warning flag that states the occupancy of a room. This does not limit Privacy Indicator to strictly darkroom work. Any situation that requires an occupancy warning is perfect for using Privacy Indicator.

CONSTRUCTION NOTES

The simplicity of Privacy Indicator's construction eliminates the need for ICs. The entire project consists of an 8-position DIP switch and a seven-segment LED display (see Table 66-1).

Privacy Indicator uses switch S1 as the display selector (see Fig. 66-1). Three parallel horizontal lines on the display (selected with S1) are used to signal occupancy. These segments correspond

Table 66-1. Parts List for Privacy Indicator.

```
D1- Common Anode 7-segment Display
S1- 8-position DIP
*Optional- SPST Toggle (S2)
```

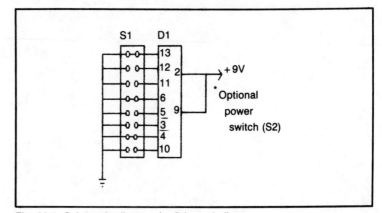

Fig. 66-1. Schematic diagram for Privacy Indicator.

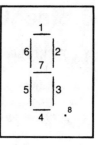

Fig. 66-2. DIP switch settings for Privacy Indicator.

to cathode a, cathode g, and cathode d of a 7-segment common anode display (Radio Shack #276-053). Figure 66-2 shows the S1 settings necessary for selecting the proper segments.

OPERATION

If S1 has been properly set, three parallel segments will light. This is the warning used to indicate room occupancy. Visual variations in the display are possible with different S1 settings. Experiment with other segment arrangements until the display is satisfactory.

Privacy Indicator should be attached to a conspicuous location outside of the sensitive area. Then turn on this high-tech "Do Not Disturb" sign whenever you enter the room and need uninterrupted working conditions. In the case of a darkroom equipped with Privacy Indicator, never again will anyone inadvertently walk in and destroy a day's work.

67

Biofeedback Box

W HETHER YOU ARE AN EXECUTIVE, A HOMEMAKER, A STU-
dent, or a member of any other stress-producing occupa-
tion, a difficult and unrecognized transition period exists between
your work periods and your relaxation periods. During the transition period occurring right after work or school, tension builds between husbands and wives, parents and children, or even
roommates. Finally, this tension erupts in arguments and a lack
of understanding between the parties involved. A unique side-effect
of stress related arguments is that, later, the arguers remain angry
or upset but forget the original causes of their quarrels.

The culprit in these unprovoked arguments is stress-related tension. The cure for such arguments is a recognition of one's own
stress and a good measure of concern for the other party. While
the concern and subsequent communication is purely human dependent, the stress relief can be electronically assisted. Biofeedback
Box helps you analyze your own stressful emotions before they
erupt negatively on a friend or family member.

CONSTRUCTION NOTES

Stress has several obvious side effects, one of which is an increased
volume of perspiration. Therefore, by measuring one's perspiration level, one can also monitor one's stress level. The amount of

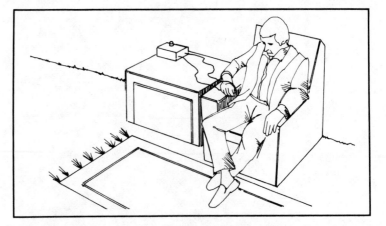

moisture present on your skin can influence the resistance of a small electrical charge across its surface. The measurement of this skin resistance is called the galvanic skin response or GSR. Biofeedback Box provides a method of detecting one's GSR level.

The construction of an ideal tool for GSR monitoring uses Radio Shack's CONTINUITY AND TONE GENERATING CHASSIS (Radio Shack #277-1014) as its basis. A beeping tone is emitted from the Continuity and Tone Generating Chassis as an electrical charge passes across the unit's leads. By soldering a metallic test lead to the end of each of the Chassis' leads, the two test leads can be easily held to monitor skin resistance.

OPERATION

Consciously control your temper after a hard day's work by using the relaxation techniques influenced by Biofeedback Box. Select a quiet room with a comfortable chair or couch and seat yourself in a relaxing position. Turn on Biofeedback Box and hold *both* of its two test leads between an index finger and thumb. Be sure that the two test leads do not touch each other.

Close your eyes and listen to the beeping tone produced by Biofeedback Box. A rapid tone describes a stressful feeling as indicated by your lower skin resistance. You must listen to the tone and consciously try to reduce the speed of the tone's beeping. As you control and reduce the speed of your breathing and concentrate on lowering your heart rate, your skin resistance should increase along with your relaxed state of mind.

When the beeping tone of Biofeedback Box is reduced to the slowest speed you can create, you know that you are finally relaxed. Don't be surprised if this process takes anywhere from ten minutes to one half hour. When you find yourself in a more gentle mood after relaxing your state of mind, be generous and let all members of your household use Biofeedback Box—the ultimate result will be complete family détente.

68

Plant Moisture Detector

DID YOU REMEMBER TO WATER YOUR DIEFFENBACHIA TO-
day? How about your Jade plant, does it need any water? The
watering of house plants is often drown or drought. While water
is beneficial to the life and growth of a plant, too much water can
swamp a plant, rot its root system, and kill it. Death by drowning
is not a suitable finale for your prized house plants. What you need
is an accurate watering indicator—in other words, a device that will
tell you when it is time to water your plants. Plant Moisture Detector satisfies this requirement.

Plant Moisture Detector works just like sticking your finger
into a plant's soil. The only difference is that the needle deflection
on Plant Moisture Detector's meter indicates the soil's moisture
level more accurately. In fact, after proper calibration, Plant Moisture Detector will not only save your plants from inadvertent drown-
ings, but it will also indicate plants that are slowly becoming
parched.

CONSTRUCTION NOTES

The bulk of the circuitry in Plant Moisture Detector is already constructed. A Continuity and Tone Generating Chassis (Radio Shack
#277-1014) is used to sense the water level data. The only other
parts necessary for completing Plant Moisture Detector are a dc

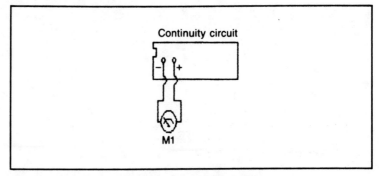

Fig. 68-1. Schematic diagram for Plant Moisture Detector.

(direct current) voltmeter and a test probe.

The dc voltmeter is attached at the speaker points illustrated in Fig. 68-1. Once this meter has been connected the speaker can be either removed or left intact. Leaving the speaker attached will provide Plant Moisture Detector with both an audio and visual indication of a plant's moisture level.

In order to make Plant Moisture Detector a functional project, a test probe must be soldered to the end of the Continuity and Tone Generating Chassis' twin lead cable. When planning the probe's design, make it long enough to reach into even the most awkwardly positioned potted plant's soil. One of the cable's leads is fixed in the probe's tip and the other lead attaches to the probe's shaft.

OPERATION

As with any indicating device, Plant Moisture Detector requires calibration prior to use. The best calibration procedure is to first test one of your plants with your current water sampling procedure (e.g. sticking your finger in the soil). Then test the same plant with Plant Moisture Detector before and after watering and record the meter's results. Follow this same procedure several times with all of your house plants.

By using your calibration results, either make a conversion chart (meter readings and their equivalent plant moisture levels) or a replacement scale for the meter showing moisture level instead of dc current. Plant Moisture Detector is now ready to take on the responsibility for your house plant's moisture levels. Only by turning green with envy will your neighbor's ivy look better.

69

Solar Powered Alarm

DO YOU WORRY THAT A LATE NIGHT POWER FAILURE WILL inadvertently make you late for work the next day? Are you tired of constantly changing the batteries of your alarm clock from fear that they will wear out and leave you snoozing through an important, early morning engagement? The sun is the world's oldest alarm clock and solar energy can be harnessed to power a high-tech alarm clock that never needs batteries.

Solar Powered Alarm uses silicon solar cells to capture solar energy as its power source. This power is used to sound an alarm tone generated by a mini dc buzzer. The alarm is silent during night-time darkness, but the bright morning sun makes Solar Powered Alarm sound a cheerful wake up call.

CONSTRUCTION NOTES

Construction of Solar Powered Alarm (see Fig. 69-1) is as simple as choosing a suitable silicon solar cell power supply and buzzer (see Table 69-1). The only consideration is that the power output of the silicon solar cell supply must be great enough to drive your chosen buzzer.

OPERATION

When Solar Powered Alarm is placed in a window with good mor-

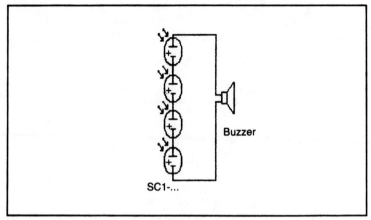

Fig. 69-1. Schematic diagram for Solar Powered Alarm.

**Table 69-1. Parts
List for Solar-Powered Alarm.**

SC1- Silicon Solar Cell(s)
DC Buzzer

ning sun exposure, you are assured of a daybreak wakeup call. Place Solar Powered Alarm away from the influence of street lights and other extraneous light sources before you retire for the evening. You will be awakened at dawn's's light by the buzzing of your Solar Powered Alarm. To turn the alarm off, simply place the alarm in a darkened area or cover it to eliminate sunlight from reaching the solar cells.

Extremely reluctant risers no longer have to worry about sleeping through the entire battery life of a battery powered alarm clock. Instead, the insistent drone of Solar Powered Alarm's buzzer is a call that cannot go unanswered. Now you only have to worry about cloudy days.

70

LED Night Light

WHEN YOU LEAVE YOUR HOUSE AT NIGHT, YOU HAVE TO perform several rituals. First, make sure that a light is left on to discourage any potential burglars. Next, the outdoor and/or garage lights are turned on and the door is finally locked as you leave. Upon your return, you discover a problem. The light that was left on to prevent burglary provides insufficient illumination to find your way safely through the house. What you need is an inexpensive and unobtrusive night light—LED Night Light.

LED Night Light is a small, portable red light that can be placed in any needed location. Its power is turned on as you leave at night to produce a bright red glow on your return. An added bonus of LED Night Light is the near invisibility of its red glow to outside observers of your house.

CONSTRUCTION NOTES

LED Night Light uses a special type of LED known as LED LIGHT BARS. LED Light Bars come in various sizes, colors, and shapes from numerous manufacturers. A small, high-efficiency, red, rectangular LED Light Bar is recommended for LED Night Light (see Table 70-1). Install a sufficient number of these LED Light Bars (see Fig. 70-1) to generate ample illumination (at least three).

**Table 70-1. Parts
List for LED Night Light.**

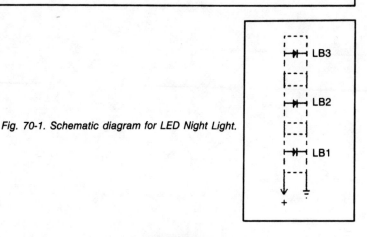

LB1-LB3- LED Light Bar

Fig. 70-1. Schematic diagram for LED Night Light.

OPERATION

Insert a battery and LED Night Light is ready to illuminate your next soiree departure. Just place your beacon wherever its shine will do the most good and turn it on. Later in the evening when you return, LED Night Light will guide you effortlessly about your house with its bright red glow.

71

LED Clock

DESPITE THE FACT THAT CLOCKS ARE PRODUCED IN A MIND boggling assortment of shapes, sizes, and styles, you can never find the one you most desire. You have a picture of the clock's intended location clearly fixed in your mind. You know the type of LED display that will look best for the clock, the type of enclosure the clock should have, and even the mounting method desired for your new timepiece. But, after picking through all of the merchandise in every store in your city, you come up empty-handed.

No one living in a high-tech household should have to put up with an inferior household fixture. After all, a clock is something that you will look at many times throughout a day. An undesirable clock enclosure will be both unappealing to read and an eyesore that detracts from the room's decor.

If, after all of your searching, you discover a clock whose only fault is its unattractive enclosure, a solution is available to you. A self-created enclosure, following your own design, can be constructed around this clock's internal structure. The result is LED Clock.

CONSTRUCTION NOTES

Begin by removing all of the purchased clock's case. After selecting the material to construct LED Clock's enclosure, lay out the purchased clock's components and design a suitable external appearance for LED Clock. Be sure to cut out all of the mounting areas for the display and any control knobs and dials before assembling the enclosure.

Depending on the intended mounting method for LED Clock, you may wish to position the LED display readout so that it is tilted for easy viewing. A clear plastic covering over LED Clock's display readout can even be used as part of the clock's final enclosure.

OPERATION

LED Clock is operated following the instructions of the clock's manufacturer. The only difference will possibly be in the location of controls and in the method of changing the battery. LED Clock can be displayed with a great feeling of satisfaction because you know that you have created the ideal clock for your room.

72

LED Message Board

I F SOMEONE RECEIVES A TELEPHONE CALL WHEN THEY ARE away from the house, how do you relay the message? Do you leave a note under a magnet attached to the refrigerator door? You can use this method elsewhere, but not in the high-tech household. In this interior design plan, paper and magnets are replaced with DIPs and LEDs.

Any message, whether written on paper or programmed into a computer, should be both eye-catching and informative. The information must accurately relay the message to the specified recipient. LED Message Board is designed to meet all of these requirements with a few special added features.

CONSTRUCTION NOTES

LED Message Board is a two-part project. The first part is easily acquired and ready-made—a small pocket computer. This can be any of a large variety of pocket computers made by such manufacturers as Radio Shack and Sharp Electronics. In fact, any calculator or computer that is battery powered, programmable in BASIC, and able to retain data in RAM (Random Access Memory) will meet this construction requirement.

The second part of LED Message Board consists of an alphanumeric display (Hewlett-Packard HDSP-6508), a power

Table 72-1. Parts List for LED Message Board.

```
D1- HDSP-6508 8-character, 16-segment Display
S1- 4-position DIP
*Optional- 8-position DIP (S1)
```

source, and a 4-position DIP switch (see Table 72-1). Any 8 character alphanumeric display will work in LED Message Board as long as its specifications are similar to HDSP-6508's listed in Fig. 72-1.

Follow the schematic diagram in Fig. 72-2 and LED Message Board is wired to produce an *asterisk*. There are 63 other possible characters that can be created on an HDSP-6508. Any one of these may be wired and substituted for the asterisk. Experiment with

Pin#	Assignment
1	Segment g1
2	Segment DP
3	Digit 1
4	Segment d2
5	Segment l
6	Digit 3
7	Segment e
8	Segment m
9	Segment k
10	Digit 4
11	Segment d1
12	Digit 6
13	Digit 8
14	Digit 7
15	Digit 5
16	Segment j
17	Segment CO
18	Segment g2
19	Segment a2
20	Segment i
21	Digit 2
22	Segment b
23	Segment a1
24	Segment c
25	Segment h
26	Segment f

Fig. 72-1. Pin assignments for the HDSP-6508.

199

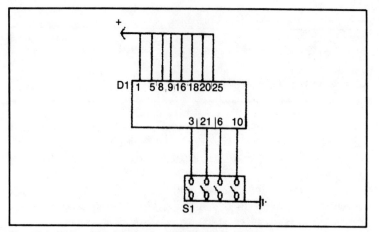

Fig. 72-2. Schematic diagram for LED Message Board.

the cathode pins until you find your desired character, then solder these connections instead of those diagrammed in the schematic. There is one creative limitation, however. Only a maximum of 10 segments per character can be lit at any one time.

OPERATION

The 4-position DIP is set to indicate two things: the presence of a message and the message's recipient. The bright red asterisk is a sure attention getter signaling every passerby of the presence of the message. This same red asterisk can also tell the passerby the message's recipient. Up to four different people (an 8-position DIP would create an 8 person LED Message Board) can receive messages through LED Message Board by assigning a specific character position to each person.

The pocket computer is used to hold the actual text of the message. This text is easily entered into the computer in the form of a short one line program. Your actual message is placed within the quotation marks of a PRINT statement. A format similar to the following should work for most pocket computers:

10 PRINT "TYPE THE MESSAGE HERE"

If your pocket computer has trouble with the syntax of this program, use any command that allows the printing of characters (i.e., a character string) on the computer's screen. Then whenever the message needs to be read just *run* this one line message program.

The operation of LED Message Board boils down to only a few simple actions: activate the LED alphanumeric display with the person's correct character (as selected via the DIP switch) and type in the one line pocket computer message program. Reading a message is just as simple: notice the presence of a message, find out who the message is for, and run the one line message program stored in the pocket computer. One final point worth considering is that by using LED Message Board, you will contribute to the reduction in paper usage thereby saving at least one tree from becoming a notepad.

73

Radio Control Circuit

E ASING THE BURDEN OF DAILY HUMAN ACTIVITIES IS ONE
major goal of modern technology. In many ways, modern
technology has already met this goal. An obvious illustration of
technology simplifying a human task is the ability of an electronic
device to remotely control an operation. Think of the satisfaction
you would feel, after a long workday, if you could relax and be able
to operate a few selected household appliances and even your
homemade robot from one central location. The ability to remotely
control electronic devices can be easily accomplished with a radio
transmitter and an accompanying radio receiver, known together
as Radio Control Circuit.

While a radio transmitter and receiver are physically separate
circuits that are used in separate locations, they can be considered
a single "circuit" because of the radio signal that is their common
bond. Each Radio Control Circuit has a number of channels which
the transmitter uses to broadcast control signals to the receiver unit.
Each channel is capable of carrying information for one specific
operation.

The job of the receiving circuit is to translate the signals it
receives so that the desired physical operations can finally be performed by servomotors. Servomotors are tiny electric motors that
are available in numerous configurations and can fulfill a wide
assortment of physical actions, such as precision movement, for-

Fig. 73-1. A complete Futaba 4L radio control outfit. In the back row, from left to right: 4 channel transmitter, 4M receiver, and battery pack. Additionally, there are three servomotors located in the front row.

ward drive, and reverse drive. Within your own Radio Control Circuit applications, you select servomotors that perform the actions required to control the desired activity. For example, activating switches that are rigged to control household operations or steer your homemade robot around on the floor are suitable applications that make optimal use of Radio Control Circuit.

CONSTRUCTION NOTES

Two simple methods are available to provide Radio Control Circuit for use with your desired activity: the modular method or the "ready to go" method. If you choose the modular method, you can purchase a Radio Control Electronic Kit containing a pair of radio control modules (Radio Shack #277-1012). The transmitter and receiver boards of this two channel system can be placed within your own project and coupled to the necessary accessories. These accessories are servomotors in the receiver and control switches in the transmitter. One final luxury for this method is a transmitter control panel. This control panel will contain the previously mentioned accessory switches that manipulate the transmission signal sent to the receiving circuit.

A "ready to go" method of preparing Radio Control Circuit is as simple as purchasing one of the many fine completed radio control outfits such as the *Futaba 4L*, 4 channel transmitter and a 4M receiver (see Fig. 73-1). The Futaba system is a completely self-contained transmitter unit which includes all the necessary switches and gimbals or joystick pots for the control of its four channels. The use of joysticks in the Futaba design permits continuous control over a precise range. As with the modular construction method, Futaba's receiving circuitry can be connected with servomotors for controlling your particular system.

OPERATION

Once your Radio Control Circuit is connected to the desired control system, all you need to do is select the appropriate switch or joystick positions to operate your circuit. In other words, for each joystick movement on the transmitter's control panel, a corresponding movement is made by a servomotor attached to the receiver. This "stick" movement is so precise in some of the "ready to go" units that it is proportional in its travel (i.e., a given joystick movement distance on the transmitter is equal to the same distance traveled on the receiver's servomotor). In fact, with proper handling, Radio Control Circuit will make a robot more than a slave—it will become a friend.

74

Light Pedestal

C ONVENTIONAL INCANDESCENT LAMPS, WHILE IDEAL FOR illumination, are usually restricted to conventional lighting fixtures. This physical limitation reduces the interior designer's selection when creating the more unconventional look of a high-tech household. The only remedy for a designer locked into this predicament is to make a new lighting fixture.

A lighting fixture can be either simple or complex, but no matter which direction is taken there are several design problems that need to be solved. Light Pedestal cuts through all of these problems and presents a solid solution that is ripe for experimentation. While there are hundreds of construction possibilities for Light Pedestal, the concept is both simple and sound—support a light source inside a covered, rectangular tank-shaped frame.

CONSTRUCTION NOTES

The following Light Pedestal construction information is presented only for illustration of one possible design. Feel free to create your own unique Light Pedestal using these notes as a guide.

Before attempting any construction, you should choose your materials very carefully. In every project that involves light, heat will be your worst enemy. This heat problem can be reduced by selecting low wattage lamps coupled to low voltage power sources.

Fig. 74-1. Light Pedestal prior to assembly and MonoKoting. The pictured parts from left to right, in the back row: MonoKote covering, heating iron. The two assembled "ends" and the four side pieces complete the foreground.

Notice that these precautions only reduce the heat buildup—they don't eliminate it. Therefore, ventilation holes are a necessity.

Virtually any material can be used for the frame of Light Pedestal. In this example, 1/2 inch square spruce sticks were cut to form a 12 inch by 4 inch by 4 inch wooden, rectangular tank-shaped frame (see Fig. 74-1). Before assembly, all of the spruce pieces were treated with a heat resistant primer. They were then glued and nailed into place.

A unique covering material was applied to this spruce frame. The material is called *MonoKote* (many other similar products exist under different names). MonoKote is a plastic film that is "glued" to a prepared surface by heat. This adhesion technique presents some interesting possibilities when used on Light Pedestal. Under typical operating conditions, MonoKote will become soft and movable when Light Pedestal is on, but it will tighten to a hard drum-like finish when the light is turned off and the heat is removed. Because of the danger involved in this transformation, MonoKote should be used with Light Pedestal only if lamp heat is reduced.

OPERATION

Immediately after Light Pedestal is turned on for the first time, monitor its heat buildup. If the heat begins to alter the shape of the frame and/or covering material, lower the wattage of the lamp, lower the power source's voltage, and add more ventilation holes.

If you continue to experience heat problems, an alternate light source is the only solution. One light source worth considering is the lamp from a flashlight. Several of these bulbs attached to the proper battery source will make Light Pedestal an ideal high-tech lighting fixture.

75

Rotating Display Case

V ERY FEW THREE-DIMENSIONAL OBJECTS ARE VIEWED FROM only one direction. In fact, the nature of a 3-D sculpture demands examination from various angles. This viewing technique, however, can present some problems in a home with limited space. How are your guests going to examine the back surface of your beautifully sculptured art objects? Only a host with nerves of steel would relish repeated handling of his objet d'art.

Rotating Display Case painlessly allows guests to view all sides of any displayed treasure. Additionally, this case protects a work of art from minor damage that is usually associated with open-air display. Rotating Display Case can be made in any size or shape that will safely hold your precious cargo.

CONSTRUCTION NOTES

In order for Rotating Display Case to practically display your high-tech art, all of its sides should be clear. Glass should be avoided at all costs for this panel and any other side of the rotating case. Plexiglas, on the other hand, makes the perfect construction material. Apply a quick-setting cyanoacrylate adhesive to the Plexiglas panels to finish the case portion of Rotating Display Case. Remember to leave a bottom panel free from the final case assembly process. This panel will be later attached with screws to allow easy

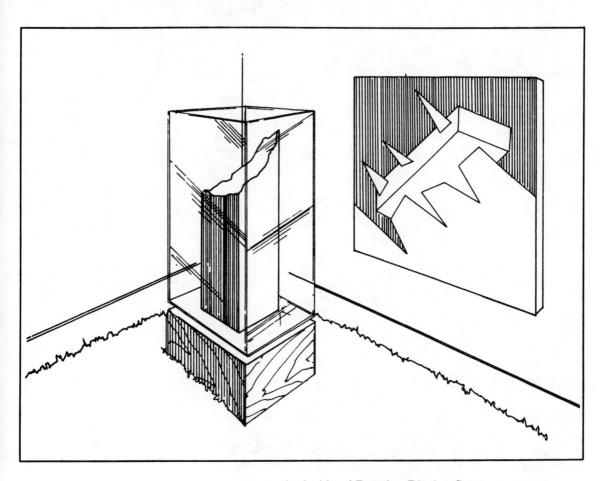

access to the inside of Rotating Display Case.

Constructing the rotation mechanism is just as easy as building the case. The final choice of a small electric motor for this purpose will depend on the weight of the Plexiglas case. Also, the motor should not directly drive the case. A set of reduction gears will be necessary to help the electric motor turn the display case at a reasonable revolution speed. Finally, an SPST switch is attached to this motor circuit to activate its rotation.

OPERATION

After the viewing material has been fixed to the base, attach Rotating Display Case's top to its motorized pedestal using the screws attached to the bottom panel. Your three-dimensional art is now ready for "all sides" display with just the flick of a switch.

76

Pressure Switch

BEING A CREATURE WITH BILATERAL SYMMETRY DOES HAVE its complications. While this orientation is fine for bimanual labor, any work that requires three inputs stymies the average human being. Sure our hands with their associated fingers can easily handle two manipulation requirements, but add one more and an impossible work barrier appears. Luckily, our symmetry also makes us bipedal and this dual-legged bonus enables us to manage additional work inputs.

Unfortunately, the human foot only makes a suitable input device in theory. Most people are unable to manipulate their feet with nearly the dexterity of their hands. Even soccer players have limited functional ability with their feet. Very few of these players are able to type a letter or cook a meal using solely their feet.

If the work assigned to a foot were modified to its abilities, then up to four chores could be accomplished by a working human. In fact, your average foot is made for "low-fidelity work," like "stomping." So, translate this stomping action into on and off functions and you have Pressure Switch.

CONSTRUCTION NOTES

Pressure Switch is basically a two wire sandwich. One wire with its insulation removed from a central contact area is attached to the top layer of a flexible material (e.g. latex rubber). The second wire with its insulation similarly removed is attached to a bottom layer of the same material. When this contraption is properly assembled, and the two wires make contact, an "on" switch action is performed. Conversely, when a foot is removed from Pressure Switch and the two layers separate, an "off" switch action occurs.

One modification of this project that will ensure consistent, reliable operation is the addition of a middle layer. This layer adds an insulative barrier between the two wires and prevents accidental switching. A hard plastic sheet less than 1/32 inch thick is used for this insulative layer. The two wires will make their contact through a hole cut in the center of this plastic sheet. This hole's size is determined by the size of the area needed to activate Pressure Switch. The area of activation now becomes the "hot" spot for operating the switch.

OPERATION

Both the top and bottom wire-carrying layers are pulled taut and their edges sealed before you operate Pressure Switch. This procedure adds resilience to the completed switch. After a few trial stomps, Pressure Switch is now ready to help your feet pull their own weight. Be prepared for a new problem, though. Running four separate operations with two hands and two feet will lead the average bimanual brain to a "quadlevel" mental overload.

77

Clear Wall Switch Covers

E XPOSED ELECTRICAL CIRCUITRY, AS MENTIONED IN THE IN-
troduction, is an extremely attractive design technique when
it is exhibited in the proper surroundings. Many common examples
of this design technique are found in large scale pieces of architecture such as office buildings and museums. But, you can achieve
equally exciting results with exposed electrical circuitry when working within the smaller scale dimensions of your own home.

The large scale of an office building or museum can support
a bold interior design technique. An exposed electrical fixture treatment within an entire building of this magnitude is quite appropriate. Within the smaller area of your household, however, such
a drastically implemented design scheme would overpower any
room and detract from its final appearance. Your best alternative
to this drastic measure is to use the "less is more" approach, by
only exposing your wall switches.

Within a household environment, design beauty must be
tempered with safety precautions. One way to implement exposed
electrical circuitry within your home, while retaining a wide safety
margin, is with Clear Wall Switch Covers. Clear, heavy gauge
plastic sheeting material, such as Plexiglas, is used to replace the
standard wall switch covers throughout your home, thus exposing
the electrical circuitry while physically separating it from accidental human contact.

212

CONSTRUCTION NOTES

Before you remove your present wall switch covers, be sure that the power to these switches has been turned off at your fuse box. This action is taken only as a protective measure against accidents; no alterations are made to any wall switch's circuitry during installation of Clear Wall Switch Covers.

A piece of clear plastic sheeting is cut to the desired size for each Clear Wall Switch Cover. Mounting holes and a cutout for the switch mechanism should be marked on the plastic sheeting. The original wall switch cover makes a perfect template for marking this pattern for each Clear Wall Switch Cover.

Remove the old wall switch cover and mount the new Clear Wall Switch Cover in its place. You are now ready to turn your power back on.

OPERATION

Your wall switches work in their usual manner, despite the addition of Clear Wall Switch Covers. The worthwhile benefits provided by Clear Wall Switch Covers are the beauty and protection they offer to your walls. The wider the plastic sheeting area chosen for Clear Wall Switch Covers, the less likely you are to find gummy fingerprints on the walls around your switches. Fingerprints are easily wiped off of your new Clear Wall Switch Covers, instead.

78

Ergonomic Seating

W HETHER YOUR WORK ENVIRONMENT IS IN YOUR OFFICE
or in your home, attention to bodily comfort will improve
your work output. Therefore, one of the most important actions
you can take toward improving your work output is to provide a
comfortable working position for your body.

Many people do not realize the incredibly large amount of time
they spend sitting at their desks. For some people, almost seven
hours out of an eight hour workday is spent in a single, seated position. Without the proper preventive measures, this type of
"marathon sitting" elicits such unpleasant side effects as backaches,
headaches, stomachaches, and leg cramps. Fortunately, preventive
measures are available in the form of ergonomic seating.

Ergonomics is, simply stated, the study of the physical relationship between humans and the products with which they interact.
A human being and the chair at which he (or she) sits, form a definite ergonomic relationship. After careful study of the requirements
of a human's body, a chair can be selected that is ergonomically
suited to his or her comfort needs.

TIPS FOR SELECTING ERGONOMIC SEATING

☐ Surprisingly, the human body has only one major requirement
relevant to ergonomic seating selection: a straight spine. When

214

your spine is kept straight, all posture-oriented ailments are re-solved. Backaches, headaches, and stomachaches are the results of slouching at your desk. Similarly leg cramps and lower backaches are caused by an improper relationship of your hips to your spine while seated. Therefore, select an ergonomic seating arrangement that is conducive to maintaining a straight spine.

☐ An ergonomic seating arrangement eliminates posture-oriented problems by providing two qualities: seat height adjustment and back incline adjustment. You should adjust your seat height so that your spine is kept straight and so that you neither need to slouch nor stretch to comfortably rest your arms on your desk at your normal working height. The degree of incline for the chair's back should be placed so that it gives support and assists in maintaining a straight spine.

☐ Further seating comfort is provided by a chair with casters. When used on a hard floor surface or a carpeted floor with a hard plastic floor pad, these wheels allow the sitter unrestricted movement. When the sitter is not hampered with an immovable chair, he or she is more likely to move his or her limbs more often. This freedom of movement releases muscle tension built up while you are restricted to a single position for an extended period of time.

☐ One final ergonomic seating trait that should be considered is a padded back and seat for the selected chair. Cushioned seating provides both comfort and an increased blood flow to a person's lower extremities.

FINAL RESULTS

If your requirements for ergonomic seating are followed, you will find yourself sitting at your job for longer periods of time. Your discomfort and physical stress will be eliminated and your produc-tivity will soar as you work in ergonomic comfort.

79

Clearing the Air

O NE SUBSTANCE THAT EVERY HOUSEHOLD HAS IN ABUN-
dance is dust. Fastidious homemakers thoroughly clean their
dwellings only to find that a fresh layer of dust builds up almost
immediately. This dusty build-up is not limited to visible surfaces
such as coffee tables and television screens. An endless supply of
dust covers every household fixture, as it inexplicably settles within
closed cabinets and inside the tiny crevices of intricately detailed
art objects. A homemaker's only recourse is to constantly repeat
his or her dusting activities.

Household dust is visually unattractive, but its worst
characteristics are its dangerous physical side effects. Dust and
microscopic particles such as those contained within smoke, are
a menace to both the human and the electronic occupants of a high-
tech household. Human reactions to these particles range from mild
sneezing to allergic reactions. A more costly casualty of dust and
smoke pollution is electronic equipment. Particles of dust and smoke
find their way between the contact points of switches and electrical
circuits causing poor connections and resultant poor circuit operation. The final result is an expensive television, computer, or
stereo system that malfunctions.

Computer disk drives also suffer a great affliction from dust
and smoke problems. Disk drive heads which read information from
the magnetic media of floppy disks are extremely sensitive to dust.

When these drive heads become coated with dust particles, the disks within the drives can become scratched and ruined so that their data are permanently lost. Fortunately, a few preventive measures can reduce the chance of this crisis ever occurring. Below are tips to help clear the air:

☐ The best way to eliminate dust and smoke related problems suffered by people and electronic equipment is to stop them before they start. Maintaining clean air filters in your home's heating and cooling systems removes the large dust particles from your home's atmosphere.

☐ Confinement is the key to the usefulness of smoke filtering ashtrays. Rather than allowing smoke to permeate a room's entire environment, the smoke filtering ashtray uses an air suction mechanism to draw local smoke-filled air through a purifying filter. This type of air clearing device is particularly useful to computer users that cannot (or will not) kick the smoking habit. Disk drives are safe from these users if a smoke filtering ashtray is nearby.

☐ Fine-filtered air purifiers can be considered an extension of your home's heating and cooling systems' air filters. The coarse fibers of your heating and cooling systems' air filters are able to screen out only large dust particles. The minute particles of dust and smoke that irritate your nose and your electronic equipment can be captured, however, within the fine textured filters of a fine-filtered air purifier. Ordinary room air is cycled through the fine-filtered air purifier to capture dust particles. In order to achieve the best results from a fine-filtered air purifier, its filters should be replaced often.

☐ One extremely unusual and effective dust removal method involves a direct attack on individual dust particles. The negative ion generator sends out negatively charged ions which become attached to dust particles in the air and the dust particles are thus given a negative charge. These negatively charged particles are easily collected on a positively charged surface. Well-made negative ion generators are equipped with their own positively charged surfaces to attract the dust and remove it from the environment.

80

Charge It

S TATIC ELECTRICITY CREATES SOME HAIR-RAISING EXPER-
iences that can, in turn, wreak havoc on a household and its
residents. Have you ever walked across a shag carpet to turn off
a light switch, only to be "zapped" by a mild spark as you touch
the switch? Have you and your spouse ever shared a kiss containing more than just a spark of love? Both of these occurrences are
the result of static electricity buildup. While these types of mild
shocks are harmless to people, electronic equipment can be ir-
reparably damaged by the shock of an innocent hand turning on
a power switch.

Any electronic equipment containing ICs must be protected
from the deleterious effects of static electric shock. Some of the
devices containing the ICs are microwave ovens, self-built electronic
projects, stereos, and computers. Protection of your equipment is
as simple as being careful about the clothing you wear or as complicated as purchasing anti-static mats on which to place delicate
electronic equipment. Following are tips for eliminating static electricity buildup:

☐ Your clothing has a great influence on static electricity buildup.
Wear a cotton sweatshirt rather than a sweater of synthetic
fibers, for example. As you sit at your computer keyboard, this
will reduce the possibility of discharging static electricity. The

same static electricity that causes your socks to cling to your sweaters when they are removed from a clothes dryer can zap your ICs when you touch your computer keyboard.

☐ Footwear can also minimize the chance for static electric damage to your electronic equipment. Rubber soled shoes insulate against static electricity better than do hard soled shoes.

☐ A drastic, but extremely effective, method for protecting your computer equipment from the damage of static electricity is to remove all carpeting from the computer environment. No carpet-generated static charge is built up when this bare floor method is employed.

☐ If you wish to keep the carpeting in your computer environment, you can find some degree of protection by placing an antistatic mat under the computer. This electrically grounded mat permits you to discharge yourself on the mat before turning on the computer and its associated equipment.

☐ A hard plastic floor mat placed in your work area underneath your desk and chair assists in eliminating the continuous static electricity buildup caused by rubbing your feet inadvertently across the carpeting underneath your desk.

☐ Static electricity thrives in dry environments. Controlling a room's humidity level consequently controls a room's static electricity level. By adding moisture to your household, you can reduce static electricity—especially during the wintertime dry season. A household or a room-based humidifying unit ensures a proper moisture level in the atmosphere at all times, therefore minimizing static electricity.

81

Fire Safety

AS THE AMOUNT OF ELECTRICAL EQUIPMENT PROLIFERATES within each household, homeowners must deal with the increased likelihood of electrical fires. The growing incidence of electrically related fires is not necessarily the fault of electrical equipment manufacturers or home project builders, but rather it is due to the improper use of the equipment. Additionally, greater emphasis needs to be given to the detection and elimination of fires once they start. Here are some tips for fire safety:

☐ The first steps in preventing household electrical fires are to follow correct installation and proper operation techniques for all electrically operated equipment. This applies to both manufactured and self-built electrical equipment.

☐ Household electrical outlets must never be obstructed by furniture or draperies in an attempt to hide their presence. Correct electrical power connection is truly a case in which form must follow function. Form may dictate the camouflaging of electrical outlets, but this can result in draperies or upholstery bursting into flames initiated by an electrical spark. Household electrical outlets must be unobstructed in order to be truly functional.

☐ Electrical cables must never be concealed underneath carpets. Although underlying cables make for a tidy looking room, they also make for a dangerous room. Repeated flexings of concealed cables as people walk across the carpet which cover them eventually causes the cables to fray and to expose bare wiring. Potentially, an electrical spark from this bare wiring will set the carpet on fire. There are many other attractive alternatives to cable placement than this dangerous method (see Chapter 83 for Cable Control).

☐ Once all of the precautionary measures are taken to prevent small household fires from occurring, a system to detect and eliminate minor fires must be employed. A combination of inexpensive wall or ceiling mounted smoke alarms (see Fig. 81-1) creates an early warning system for small fires as well as providing a means for their elimination.

☐ Fire alarms that use an ionization detection system are extremely sensitive to the minute products of combustion found in the initial phases of a starting fire. Unfortunately, a detection system as sensitive as the ionization type is often set off falsely by cigarette or cooking smoke, excessive dust, or even some aerosol sprays. Ionization type fire alarms should be placed away from heavy smokers or from kitchens to prevent constant false alarms. These ionization type alarms are ideally suited, however, for immediate fire detection protection near bedroom doors where room air conditions are usually unconducive to false alarms.

☐ Despite their slightly slower reaction time, photoelectric detecting fire alarms are usually less prone to false alarms. Photoelectric fire alarms actually "look" for the presence of smoke in a detection chamber within the unit. Because the photoelectric fire detection system lacks the extreme sensitivity of the ionization detection system, a photoelectric fire alarm adapts well to kitchen use and is less susceptible to false alarms caused by cigarette smoke.

☐ A well protected household requires the use of more than one fire alarm system. Your chosen system should ultimately have a combination of ionization and photoelectric type fire alarms for superior fire detection.

☐ One further consideration when purchasing your fire alarms is whether to choose battery or line powered alarms. Line powered alarms cause no worries about worn out batteries, but they are useless during power failures. Battery powered fire alarms, however, are independent from line power sources, but they are often left with discharged batteries if they are not checked regularly. Once again, a combination of methods provides the best results. Your house will benefit from a combination of battery and line powered fire alarm systems.

☐ Once you have selected and installed the appropriate fire alarm

Fig. 81-1. An installed ionization type fire alarm.

systems for your household, the remaining problem is to purchase suitable fire extinguishers. An all-purpose type of dry chemical fire extinguisher can be used on the types of fires that commonly occur in a household environment. Underwriters' Laboratories describes an all-purpose fire extinguisher as one that acts against fires in classes A, B, and C. This means that fires involving paper, wood, cloth, and some plastics (class A), or involving flammable liquids such as cooking oil, grease, or gasoline (class B), or involving electrical fires (class C) can all be fought with this all-purpose fire extinguisher type. Although fire extinguishers are available that only put out one or two of the listed classes of fires, an all-purpose fire extinguisher is the most reliable type for complete home use (see Fig. 81-2).

☐ In the event that your fire alarms alert you to the presence of a fire in your home, you must decide whether the fire is severe enough to make you vacate your house or minor enough for you to put it out with a household fire extinguisher. The answer to this question is based both on the size of the fire and on the type of fire extinguisher you have purchased for your home. You must always remember the limitations of your particular fire extinguisher: a single extinguisher has a chemical discharge time of only a few seconds. Furthermore, be sure that your extinguisher is of the correct class rating to extinguish the type of fire you are fighting.

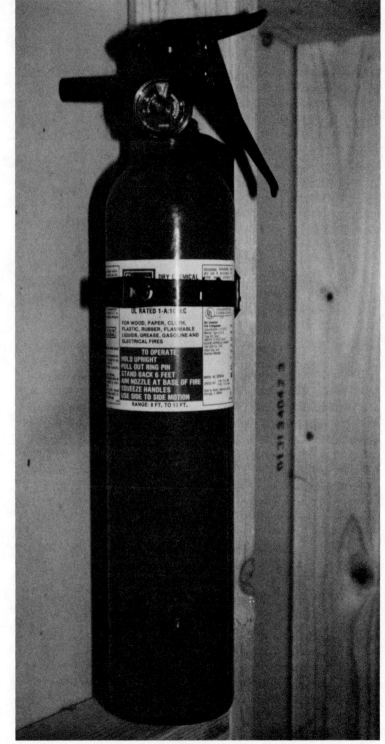

Fig. 81-2. An all-purpose, dry chemical fire extinguisher.

223

82

Power Allowances

W HETHER IT'S THE LAST FEW MINUTES OF THE FINAL NBA championship playoff game or the dramatic climax of the movie of the week, someone in the house turns on a hairdryer or a vacuum cleaner and scrambles the picture and sound on your television. You are the victim of power line noise.

You sit down at your computer to print out that fifty-page report you finished last night. You turn on your printer only to find that it is completely dead due to a blown fuse. You are the victim of an electrical power surge. Below are some tips for controlling power line problems:

☐ An electrical "power cleaner" must be used to solve the types of power line problems that are the culprits in the two scenarios discussed here. A simple line filtering device or surge protector placed between your household electrical outlet and any piece of sensitive electronic equipment will clean up stray signals or noise and smooth out power spikes and surges.

☐ The purpose of a line filtering device is to isolate a piece of equipment, such as a television set, from the interference of stray signals on your household power line. This interference is an electrical abnormality caused by a motorized unit plugged into the same electrical outlet or household ac circuit. A power filtering unit removes abnormal signals from power lines, leav-

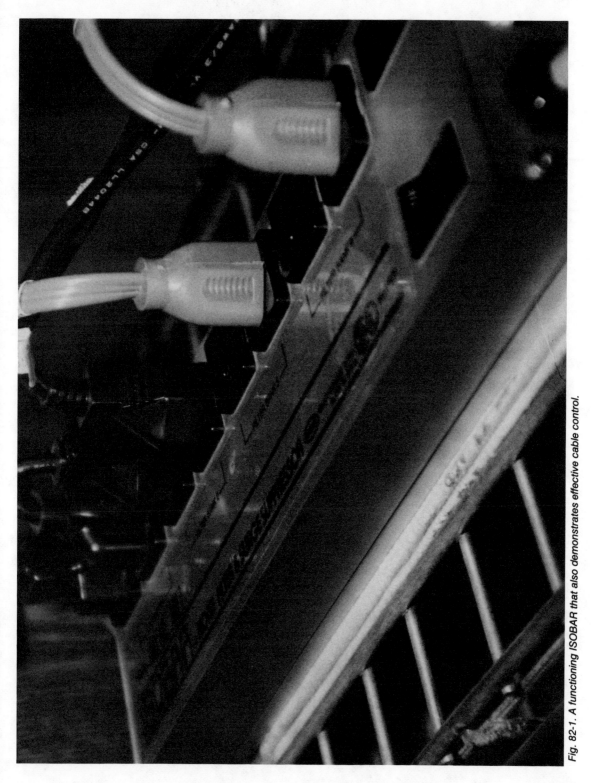

Fig. 82-1. A functioning ISOBAR that also demonstrates effective cable control.

ing only a "cleaned" energy source on which the television can run.

☐ A surge protector smooths out surges or spikes of electrical energy so that your electronic equipment receives a constant flow of good, clean electricity. The contact of a circuit breaker within the body of a surge protector is broken whenever an exceptionally large surge or spike of power is transmitted through your household power line. The surge protector consequently takes the brunt of the power spike or surge that would have potentially damaged equipment directly connected to the household power supply.

☐ One example of a combined line filter and surge protector is the ISOBAR NOISE FILTER AND SURGE SUPPRESSOR manufactured by GSC Electronics Corporation. This unit provides a filtered power supply from which surges and spikes are minimized. A rest switch reestablishes your power circuit after a power surge triggers the circuit breaker. Figure 82-1 shows an ISOBAR installed in a typical household power arrangement.

83

Cable Control

T HE LIFE-GIVING CONNECTION TO ALL AC OPERATED ELEC-
tronic equipment is the electrical power cable. Because each
piece of equipment requires its own power supply cable, a household
electrical outlet quickly becomes a rat's nest of cable ends. Excess
cable lengths are heaped into coiled piles, tucked underneath
carpets, or strewn across walking areas leaving an unsightly and
dangerous mess.

While such cable placement methods are often regarded to be
the only option, they should be avoided in order to maintain an attractive and safe household. Cables that lie across walking areas
make an excellent boobie trap for household intruders, but it's much
more likely that such cables will first trap and injure a household
member. Likewise, burying cables underneath carpets is also an
undesirable option because of the fire hazard they create (see
Chapter 81 for tips on household fire safety). Here are some tips
to help you with your cable control problems:

☐ Poor architectural planning of permanent electrical fixtures
often results in a room with a single outlet for ac voltage.
Thoughtful placement of electronic equipment partially over-
comes this problem, but all of a room's electronic equipment
cannot be placed within the immediate vicinity of a single electrical socket. A solution is found in carefully routing electrical

cables throughout a room while maintaining their concealed state.

☐ Cables can be removed from areas of heavy walking traffic by tacking them around the parimeter of a room with cable clips. Depending on the variety of clip selected, a cable is slipped through or snapped into a securing fixture of the cable clip (for example, Radio Shack #278-1640 or #278-1639 cable clips can be used). The clip is then affixed to a wall by means of either an adhesive backing on the clip or with an integral nail. By placing cable clips at the appropriate intervals, a cable can be routed around floors, up walls, or even around ceiling perimeters.

☐ When a number of cables are to be directed towards a power outlet, they can be grouped together with wire ties (such as the Radio Shack #278-1632 type) for easy and compact management. Wire-tie mounts (Radio Shack #278-441) can then be used to control the placement of the tied cable.

☐ In many situations, it is convenient to extend a power source to your equipment rather than bringing many equipment cables to a single power socket. A power extension cord with multiple outlets can be directed to any room location with the use of cable clips. Be sure, however, that you do not exceed the power draw of a wall outlet by connecting too many pieces of equipment to the single power extension cord.

☐ Multiple outlet electrical plugs that increase the number of sockets at an electrical outlet ease the burden of many small appliances competing for a single outlet. Multiple outlet units that add four or more additional sockets are plugged directly into your regular wall outlet. Alternatively, multiple outlet power strips that combine additional outlets with an extension cable are also available.

84

Computer Lighting

C ONCERNS ABOUT PRODUCTIVITY HAVE MADE CORPORA-
tions aware of proper lighting conditions for their employees
working with computers. An extended period of time spent star-
ing at a computer monitor screen induces severe eyestrain in computer users when proper ergonomic lighting conditions are not
provided. Corporations realize this fact and correct such lighting
problems to reap the rewards of increased employee productivity.
When computers are used within a household, however, this essential aspect of proper lighting is overlooked. Poor lighting is a real
headache for home computer users.

Fortunately, home computer users are able to create healthful
lighting conditions for extended computer use within their own computer environments. The answer lies in choosing the correct type
of light source and in the proper placement of the selected light
source.

The most flagrant lighting abuse for home computer users is
an inadequate amount of lighting. Quite often, home computer users
depend on a room's single ceiling light as their only light source.
A computer monitor screen can be viewed with relative ease under
a single ceiling light because the text on a screen provides its own
illumination. Printed material, such as a list of budget figures or
a computer program listing, is often viewed alternately with the
monitor, however. When this happens, the user's eyes must con-

Fig. 84-1. Tensioned springs keep a quality clamp-on desk lamp's arm in a stationary, user determined position.

stantly readjust between the two vastly different reading material and light sources. The result is eyestrain. This problem is alleviated with the use of local lighting.

Proper local lighting must be provided at the desk or table on which a computer is used. The user's work surface is then clearly illuminated and any shadows caused by the person's body blocking a ceiling light are eliminated. The most convenient type of desk or table top light source is the clamp-on desk lamp with a positionable arm (see Fig. 84-1). Unlike a stand-alone table lamp, a clamp-on desk lamp can be moved into a position that best suits an individual user in terms of his or her height and seating arrangement.

One type of desk lamp that should definitely be avoided within the computer environment is the type with a high-intensity light source. The contrast between a relatively dark monitor screen and a piece of paper brilliantly illuminated by a high-intensity lamp is so great that severe eyestrain is the unpleasant and painful result.

Ambient room lighting is equal in importance to desktop lighting as a concern for the computer user. Although the use of fluorescent lighting is almost universal in office settings, this is one area in which ergonomics has been disregarded by corporations. Fluorescent lighting creates a constant buzzing noise that is extremely annoying. Beyond the human comfort aspect of fluorescent lighting, electrical interference is also associated with the buzzing of these lights. Because of the sensitivity of computers, the use of fluorescent light in close proximity to them should be avoided. A soft white incandescent light source of about 60 watts provides excellent illumination for a computer environment while providing silent performance.

85

Printer Noise

A COMPUTER USER WHO IS ENTHRALLED WITH HIS OR HER latest program creation or word processor text is oblivious to the noise of a printer as the great work is converted into hard copy. Unfortunately, such enthusiastic computer users are often as oblivious to time as they are to noise. When a work is completed at two o'clock in the morning and all other family members are fast asleep, the sound of a clattering printer gives them an exceptionally rude awakening.

Whether it occurs during daylight hours or at night, computer printer noise is an irritant that does not belong within a high-tech household. It is quite simple, however, for the dedicated home computer user to rid the house of obnoxious printer noise without giving up their favorite pastime. Acoustic sound deadening devices are easily contructed so that printer noise is restricted to the area immediately surrounding the printer. Try some of these tips to subdue printer noise:

☐ A vibration absorbing pad placed underneath a printer prevents the desk or table on which the printer rests from becoming a resonating chamber that amplifies the printer's noise. The dimensions of a vibration absorbing pad should be large enough so that the area under the printer is completely covered and the printer's feet rest on the pad.

☐ Foam core board is an excellent material for forming a vibration absorbing pad. Consisting of plastic foam sandwiched between two pieces of heavy cardstock, foam core board can be purchased from most art supply stores. A board must be at least 3/8 of an inch thick to provide adequate sound deadening quality. It is possible to laminate two sheets of the foam core board together for increased effectiveness. Simply cut a piece of the board to fit the dimensions of your particular printer. Small rubber cushion feet with adhesive backings are then placed underneath your vibration absorbing pad. The use of these feet prevents the pad from "walking" off of the desk or table due to the vibration of the printer.

☐ Another useful method for muffling the noise of a printer is to provide a dead air space around the operating unit. This air space is provided with a printer enclosure. Plexiglas or a similar form of heavy gauge clear plastic sheeting is a good material for a printer enclosure because the printer's operation can be viewed through the clear material. However a clear enclosure will provide only moderate noise relief. An enclosure with sound deadening material fastened to its inside surfaces is the ideal way to control printer noise. The dimensions of your particular printer enclosure will depend on your printer, but optimal sound deadening is achieved by allowing several inches of air space between your printer and all sides of the printer enclosure. Two slots cut in the enclosure material permit computer tractor paper to enter and exit the printer. Ventilation may also be required.

☐ By combining both a vibration absorbing pad and a printer enclosure you can minimize the deafening noise generated by your printer.

86

Managing Everyday Paperwork

NO HOUSEHOLD IS FREE FROM THE CLUTTER OF EVERYDAY paperwork. Phone messages are stuck under magnets on refrigerator doors, notes are scribbled on loose scraps of paper, and appointment calendars and address books are made completely illegible with multiple erasures and rewritten entries. Inevitably, important messages are lost due to the inadequacies of this system of treating daily paperwork.

Consolidation of messages, information and address reference materials into a single, easily accessible information center is a difficult task, however. Although many family members dogmatically support their method of shuffling cluttered papers, there is one information organization system that most members of a household will greet with enthusiasm. Within the small enclosure of a portable notebook computer is found a single, attractive information storage center.

The compact size and battery operation of a portable notebook computer such as NEC's (Nippon Electric Company's) PC-8201A (Fig. 86-1) make this computer an ideal repository for household data. Software permanently stored within the PC-8201A's memory, as well as additional cassette tape based programs, allow household members to perform their note passing and message taking with electronic style. You can even throw away your calendar if you decide to use the NEC "Schedule Keeper" program supplied

Fig. 86-1. This NEC PC-8201A is ready for both quick note-taking and modem conducted telecommunications.

on a cassette tape with the PC-8201A.

For those people who cannot completely kick the paper habit, a printout can be made of any TEXT file notes within the PC-8201A's memory. The NEC PC-8201A's built-in text formatting facilities neatly arrange the text of a document file for printing.

PC-8201A TEXT files make perfect electronic note paper for holding telephone notes or personal messages. Each file should be named according to the person to whom the message is directed. Multiple messages for the same person can be defined by using a number after their TEXT file name (e.g. SARA1.DO and SARA2.DO). You must be careful, however, that you do not exceed the six character restriction for a TEXT file title length.

Designate a TEXT file with a name such as ADDRSS.DO to be used as an electronic address book and use a uniform format to enter each person's name, address, and telephone number. To access information from the file, simply enter the ADDRSS.DO file and use the "Find" command (F1). Be sure that the cursor is placed at the top of the entire file and then press F1. At the "STRING:" prompt, enter the desired person's name and you will be immediately transported to the location within the ADDRSS.DO file that the name occurs. A "Find" string containing only a portion of an entry word can also be used, with limited success, to locate a particular entry within the text.

Place your PC-8201A computer next to your telephone, as you would place a pad of scratch paper, for immediate access for note taking. This diminutive computer is not only useful in this location, it is also far more attractive than a pad of paper.

87

Computer-Aided
Floor Plan Design

DURING THE PLANNING STAGES OF A HOUSEHOLD'S INTERIOR design, many sketches are required for achieving the final appearance of each room. While freehand sketching of floor plans is a common and convenient method used by many individual home owners and by some interior design specialists, freehand drawings are inaccurate and difficult to reproduce. The difficulty of creating multiple drawings of a single room with each drawing possessing minor design alterations is a definite drawback of freehand sketching. These drawbacks do not mean that training in professional drafting skills is necessary for everyone planning interior design alterations, however.

Both individuals and professional designers can freely express their creativity when a computer software program is used to control the actual drawing functions. With the use of the AutoCAD 2 software package, by Autodesk, Incorporated, the computer's monitor screen becomes a sketch pad and hard copies of the sketch are then provided by a printing or plotting device. AutoCAD 2 is the only software required to recreate the skills of a draftsman for your own unique interior design applications (see Appendix B for a review of the AutoCAD 2 software package). Following are tips for designing a floor plan with AutoCAD 2:

☐ Install the 8087 numeric coprocessor IC within your IBM PC for enhanced operation of the AutoCAD 2 program. This chip will be automatically sensed by AutoCAD 2 and incorporated into its drafting functions.

☐ Select AutoCAD 2's GRID drawing aid to assist in accurate placement of room features. The use of the SNAP command automatically moves all drawn objects to their nearest grid point for a neat and accurate final design plan.

☐ As a scale reference aid, use AutoCAD 2's AXIS feature to label the graphics screen with a convenient scale value. Either English or metric units can be used.

☐ Use the LIST command as an automatic reference source to find the coordinates of any object drawn on the screen.

☐ For the design of individual rooms, create a basic room perimeter floor plan and save the file on a floppy disk. Variations on a single room's design can then be formed by filling in this basic floor plan layout and saving each altered plan under a different file name on the disk.

☐ Draw a floor plan for an entire level of your home and use AutoCAD 2's zoom feature to enlarge each room and fill in detailed illustration.

☐ Cross-hatching and other design overlays can be selected from a library of patterns and added to any AutoCAD 2 drawing. Additionally, user-designed patterns can be created and added to a library of their own. Therefore, virtually any texture or pattern can be incorporated into an AutoCAD 2 illustration without laborious hand entry.

88

Making Space Relative

R ESTRICTIONS GENERATED BY THE PHYSICAL DIMENSIONS of a dwelling are a common source of anguish to its residents. Unless major structural alterations are performed on a home, the physical dimensions of the rooms within the home are a permanent, unalterable consideration for design planning. Apartment and condominium dwellers are even more limited than are home owners in regards to structural redesign of their abodes—you can't just knock down a neighbor's wall to enlarge your master bedroom. Fortunately, such drastic measures as the addition or removal of walls, or the addition of entire rooms are unnecessary to create a comfortable and desirable living environment.

The space within a room is actually relative to the method and materials chosen to furnish it. Length, width, and height dimensions, however, are the ultimate yardsticks that limit the size of the furniture that can fill the room. Your room design can make a small room look relatively spacious or a large room look relatively cozy. The key to managing household space is in arranging household furnishings within each room for optimal space economy. Try some of these tips for making space relative:

☐ Furnish small rooms sparsely. A small room is made to seem larger by the use of minimal furnishings and by the reduction of clutter such as display items on shelves or table tops.

☐ Create areas of open floor space in small rooms. Furniture should be placed around the perimeter of the room so that an open walking area is available in the room's center.

☐ A light colored wall treatment within a small room produces a spacious feel for the room's occupants. The use of additional lighting helps to create a similar open feel inside rooms with a slightly darker wall coloring.

☐ The use of a reflective surface, especially over an entire wall area, adds a false feeling of depth to a small room. Reflective mylar sheeting placed over a framework is much simpler to install than a similar reflective wall surface created by glass paneling.

☐ Concealed placement of electronic projects reduces the clutter of small rooms, thereby making the room seem larger than it really is.

☐ Select track lighting for additional light in small rooms to eliminate the need for space-occupying floor or table lamps. Track lighting systems to take up space, but this space is on the ceiling where its loss is less obvious. See Chapter 91 for a detailed description of track lighting techniques.

☐ Particularly large rooms can serve the purpose of several smaller rooms by selectively grouping furniture. For example, when a dining room table is placed in one area of a large room, a living room can be created next to this area by using the furniture itself to give the impression of walls. The back of a couch, for example, would provide the primary wall-like structure separating the dining room area from the living room area.

☐ Large rooms can benefit from the enclosed feeling created by the use of medium to dark colored wall coverings.

89

Room Personality

UNLESS YOUR HOUSEHOLD POSSESSES POLTERGEISTS, THE only personality that it will reflect is your own. Every aspect of your household—the appearance of its furnishings the colors of its walls, its methods of lighting, and the sounds that it makes—influences visitors and residents alike. Pulling these elements together in an appealing fashion is the key to designing a personality for each room in your home. The final result should be pleasing both to visitors and to household members.

The initial impression that your household makes on a guest may be extremely important to you, but the guest's interaction with your household's personality is quite brief. The extensive amount of time spent by household members interacting with a household's personality is much more significant than a guest's brief time. All members of a household should be pleased with the home with which they interact on a daily basis. This fact demonstrates the need to carefully and personally shape the personality of each room in a house to reflect the feelings of its occupants. Most importantly, however, the shaping of a room's personality is a vital element of interior design that brings all elements of a room's fixtures together. Try some of these tips for shaping a room's personality:

☐ Maintain a theme throughout the design planning of a room. Demonstrate this theme with basic elements such as wall color, wall covering, lighting, furnishing, and electronic project installation.

☐ A sterile, high-tech personality can be achieved within a room by focusing on the electronic elements of the room. Stark, light colored wall treatment along with exposed electrical fixtures and prominent "form and function" project placement help to create this atmosphere.

☐ A contemporary room setting, suited to your own personal tastes, can easily incorporate high-tech electronic projects without taking on a sterile personality. Within this contemporary environment, electronic-oriented room sculptures (such as Weather Balloon Sculpture in Chapter 19) can be displayed without their high-tech nature becoming the focus of attention.

☐ Concealed placement of electronic projects allows high-tech devices to be incorporated inconspicuously into rooms lacking a high-tech room personality theme (e.g. colonial).

☐ Bright lighting should be used in utilitarian settings, such as within kitchens, or within areas where a stark room personality is desired.

☐ Soft room lighting should be used to create a soothing atmosphere. This type of soft lighting is especially beneficial when other light sources are used as a center of attraction (see Chapter 20 for Tube Lights and Chapter 19 for Weather Balloon Sculpture). A dimming switch for ceiling lights allows a wide range of mood-setting light levels.

☐ Projected colored lights alter a room's personality according to the color chosen for projection. See Chapter 90, Painting with Light for further information on mood setting with colored lights.

☐ Subtle control of room personality is accomplished by influencing the sounds the room's occupants experience. Electronic projects for the creation of wind sounds, surf sounds, and music box sounds are located in Chapters 6, 4, and 3, respectively.

90

Painting with Light

O NE OF THE MOST OVERLOOKED AREAS FOR CREATIVE LIGHT-
ing within a household setting is the use of colored lights.
Most home owners feel that only one type of light exists for their
home—white. There is an occasional use of a yellow outdoor bug
light, or a black light in the kids' room, but there is seldom any
serious utilization of colored light as a genuine room feature.

An entire room need not be bathed entirely in a single bright
color. Selective spotlights projected onto a wall's surface is a much
more suitable approach. The best vehicle for colored spotlighting
techniques is the track lighting system (see Chapter 91 for instruction on using a track lighting system). Each spotlight unit of the
track lighting system can be covered with a different color of gel
filter. As an alternative to the track lighting system, carefully placed
floor-based lamps can also achieve attractive colored light settings.
Here are some tips for painting with light:

☐ Use three light sources for projecting the colored light. Each
light source can then contain one of the three primary colors—
red, blue, and green.
☐ Project three primary colored light sources onto a wall, mixing
the spots of color. Secondary colors will be created where the
primary colors overlap.
☐ Use a white wall as a projection background to achieve the true

primary and secondary colors.

☐ Use a colored wall as a projection background for unusual color effects and interaction with the primary colors.

☐ Use multiple spotlights each projecting the same color for a more thematic and subdued colored light background.

☐ Display the wall, painted with the primary colored lights, under various general room lighting conditions. Full room lighting, no room lighting, or subdued room lighting each bring an unusual appearance to the colored lighting effect.

91

Track Lighting

C EILING LIGHTS PROVIDE ADEQUATE GENERAL ILLUMINA-
tion for the rooms that contain them. Likewise, table top and
floor type lamps are suitable for the illumination of specific,
predetermined areas of a room. These three types of lighting, however, are not always flexible enough to be easily repositioned within
a room's setting. Once you have established a lighting and furnishing arrangement for a room, any future alterations of the room's
design must be worked around the limitations of the available light
sources. Static lighting methods are not easily manipulated to suit
new room designs. Track lighting, on the other hand, is one light
source that is adaptable to almost any room situation.

The concept of track lighting is quite simple: a power "track"
is first mounted on a room's ceiling or wall, then a number of track-
compatible spotlights are guided onto the track. Both physical support and power to the spotlights are provided by the power track.
Once installed, the spotlights can be moved to any position along
the track while retaining their connection to a power source. Depending on the type of track lighting selected, the spotlights can
be controlled by individual power switches mounted on each
spotlight or by an overall power switch that controls the electricity
supplied to the track itself.

Track lighting spotlights can be individually positioned as a
utilitarian light source for certain household members without

disturbing others. For example, one household member can use a spotlight for reading without disturbing someone else who is watching television.

Track lighting spotlights can draw attention to certain areas of a room, for example, to illuminate a piece of sculpture or wall mounted artwork. Also, when a room's furnishings are rearranged, the track lighting spotlights can be slid into positions that best illuminate the new design setting.

The mood or personality of a room can be shaped by a specialized variation of track lighting. Multiple colored filters can be placed over track lighting spotlights for artistic illumination (see Chapter 31 and Chapter 90 for tips on this method of painting with light).

92

Bookshelf Lighting

AVID READERS OFTEN COMPLAIN OF INADEQUATE LIGHTING conditions. Fortunately, most of these readers are able to find a well lighted reading environment within their households, although a few devoted readers are forced to settle for dim, eyestraining conditions in which to pursue their passion. Finding a light by which to read a book is only a small portion of a reader's search, however. The reader must first peer through cramped, dimly lighted bookshelves to select the desired reading material. Providing adequate bookshelf lighting is a cure for this problem.

Use of an external light source to illuminate a bookshelf is usually unproductive. An external lamp fixture becomes a physical obstruction to someone examining a bookshelf and it also creates a shadow of that person which obscures the books' titles. Internal lighting is the most logical solution because the light is local and it is directed onto the books' titles. Try these tips for bookshelf lighting:

☐ Choose a cool light source, such as the fluorescent variety, to illuminate your bookshelf. Fluorescent lights that are especially designed for placement under cabinets can be purchased and used for bookshelf lighting.

☐ Select a bookshelf with a rimmed shelf edge to allow concealed placement of a light source. An under-cabinet fluorescent light readily adapts to placement directly behind such a rim.

☐ Allow plenty of space between the tops of the tallest books on your shelves and the light source. Ventilation and cooling are provided by this arrangement, as well as a light path for illuminating the books' titles.

☐ Make use of a power switch to the light source if one is available. Heat build-up is prevented by turning the bookshelf light off when it is not in use.

93

A View on Windows

ENERGY CONSCIOUS HOMEOWNERS HAVE TURNED TO HOUSEhold insulation techniques in order to benefit from the resulting money savings. As a household's heating and cooling systems are made to run more efficiently, there is a savings in both operation time and operation costs of these systems. The owner of even the most extensively insulated home will receive only a poor return on his or her insulation investment, however, if one key element of energy theft is overlooked—the window.

Window glass has two characteristics that can be either beneficial or detrimental to a household: window glass transmits light and it also conducts heat. Of course, light transmission is beneficial for both emotional and practical reasons. A room filled with sunlight is both bright and inviting. Additionally, a room that is illuminated by sunlight requires less artificial lighting.

The heat conductivity of a window must be considered for each time of the year. Fluctuations in outdoor temperature from one season to the next are enough to warrant the development of a window energy saving plan. Window panes that are not insulated during the winter season conduct a home's heat directly to the icy outdoor environment. Conversely, sun drenched windows turn into heat radiators in the summer, thereby reducing the effectiveness of a home's air conditioning system.

Fortunately, there are many attractive ways to create energy

Fig. 93-1. Heavy gauge plastic sheeting has turned this drafty window into an insulated, diffused light source.

saving window coverings. These window coverings range from insulative materials that block out light to others that provide a visually innocuous temperature barrier. In a few cases, these materials even add to a room's high-tech interior. Consider, for your home, these tips for energy saving window treatments:

☐ Venetian blinds provide a wide range of positions that can be used to regulate the amount of light that enters a room. Furthermore, fully closed venetian blinds also help create an insulative dead air space between a window and the rest of the room.

☐ Tinted adhesive film, of the type that is used within automobile windows, can be used to cover windows exposed to large amounts of undesired sunlight.

☐ Styrofoam board, cut to a window's exact dimensions, can be placed against the window frame as an insulator against heat or cold. Additionally, a moderate amount of light is transmitted by Styrofoam. The Styrofoam board can be held in place through the use of hook-and-loop fastener strips or velcro strips attached to both the frame and the Styrofoam board. Therefore, if desired, the Styrofoam board can easily be removed from or placed over the window.

☐ Similar to the Styrofoam board concept, an insulator of both light and heat can be formed from foam core board. A single piece of this board can be used or several sheets can be laminated together for greater insulative strength. The foam core board is cut to the dimensions of the window and held in place as described above.

☐ Heavy gauge plastic sheeting can be used to provide an insulated space between a window and a room. This method is also beneficial to illumination if textured plastic sheeting is used (see Fig. 93-1). Certain types of plastic sheeting possess texturing that will diffuse incoming light.

☐ An extremely attractive, as well as practical, insulative window covering is one made from a quilted fabric. This window covering should contain an insulative batting material that has been quilted between two nonporous fabric layers. It is the quilting, with its dead air spaces, that gives this design its insulation value. The addition of internal magnets to the window quilt's outside seams facilitates a tight fit around a metal flanked (either natural or artificially attached) window frame.

94

Room Acoustics

I SOLATION FROM EVERYDAY HOUSEHOLD NOISE IS A DIFFICULT
goal to attain, especially when the household sports high-tech
features. Noisy kitchen appliances, television sets, workroom power
tools, and computer printers are all irritants to someone seeking
relaxation from a hard day's work. People who make an office in
their home especially desire a silent work area, remote from other
household members and their associated noisy activities.

Thoughtful planning of room acoustics will make any room a
silent haven from household noise or will confine loud noises to a
single area within a household. By following a few basic rules of
acoustics (the study of controlling sound transmission and reception), sound deadening materials and methods can be used to shield
an area from noise.

Reflective surfaces such as hard walls, floors, and ceilings
transmit sound more easily than soft, padded surfaces. Cover as
many hard surfaces as possible within a room to provide the most
effective acoustic sound deadening. Cover floors with carpet and
heavy carpet pads to minimize sound vibration transmission.

Acoustic paneling is available in dimensions large enough to
reach from the floor to the ceiling of most rooms. This acoustic
paneling can be applied to all wall surfaces to provide the highest
degree of sound deadening. While acoustic paneling makes an attractive wall covering material by itself, this material can easily

Fig. 94-1. Acoustic panels reduce annoying sound reflections in this suspended ceiling.

253

be covered with fabric to more closely interact with a room's decor.

Do not forget to include the ceiling in your design plans for controlling room acoustics. Acoustic material in the form of ceiling paneling or tiles assists with absorbing sounds within a room (see Fig. 94-1).

Make use of natural sound deadening materials within rooms. For example, a large, heavily padded sofa can be placed along a living room wall to help reduce loud television or stereo noise transmitted to other areas of the household.

A room that has been set aside for the use of a computer and its associated printer equipment can be sound deadened with both carpeting and acoustic paneling to restrict the noise to the area within the room. An added benefit of this acoustic deadening treatment is the reduction of noise for the person using the computer equipment. Computer room noise can also be checked by the use of printer enclosures and vibration absorbing pads for computer printers (Chapter 85 presents instructions for designing your own versions of these printer noise reducers).

95

Speaker of the House

PEOPLE PLACE A GREAT DEMAND ON THEIR STEREO SYSTEMS. As manufacturers improve the quality of their turntables, tuners, amplifiers, tape decks, frequency equalizers, compact disk players, and speakers, they experience increased sales of these units. A combination of even the finest of these components, however, will create sound output of an inferior quality if the acoustic environment of the system's room is poor. Therefore, just as people demand enhanced fidelity from their stereo equipment, they must likewise provide an acoustic environment equal to the demands of their system's sound output.

Good quality sound from stereo speakers is as dependent on the placement of furnishings in the room containing the stereo system as it is on the speakers themselves. With careful placement of a room's furnishings and the addition of acoustic materials to control sound, the speakers of your house will recreate stereo sounds the way your stereo system was intended to play them. Try these tips for enhancement of speaker output:

☐ Elevate speakers above the floor level (at least 10 inches). Do not place speakers in corners, if possible.

☐ Place speakers on opposite sides of a room so that a balanced stereo sound is achieved. One specific area within the room will ultimately be the optimal spot for listening, although the sound quality will be satisfactory for listeners throughout the room.

- [ ] Acoustically "insulate" a room containing a stereo system from other household noises with acoustic paneling. This paneling also serves to improve the sound quality within the room and to keep the sound away from other household rooms. Further tips for controlling sound are located in Chapter 94, which is completely devoted to techniques for room acoustics.

- [ ] Be careful not to overly deaden a room's sound transmission with acoustic wall coverings. the volume of your stereo system will become muffled, requiring you to boost its volume in order to compensate for the acoustic deadening.

- [ ] Don't block the path of a speaker's sound output with furniture. A padded chair placed in front of a speaker will absorb or muffle a large portion of the speaker's high-frequency output.

- [ ] Placement of a stereo component system within the same room as its associated set of speakers is optional. Speakers can be remotely controlled by speaker wires connecting the speakers with a stereo component system located in another room (see Chapter 83 for Cable Control).

- [ ] Balance the furniture placed in a stereo system's room with the output of the speakers. The output of one speaker should not be muffled more than the other speaker by room furnishings.

- [ ] One specific area of a room should be designated for optimal listening conditions. From this location, your stereo system should be adjusted for balanced sound output and other tonal qualities. Your particular room arrangement will influence every aspect of sound output, so individual adjustment is required.

96

Room Traffic Control

DIRECTING THE FLOW OF BUSY HOUSEHOLD ACTIVITY IS equivalent to highway traffic control. The shortest distance between two points is a straight line and most family members stubbornly follow this rule within their home. The results of this behavior include shins that are knocked into protruding coffee tables, hips that are slammed into display cabinets filled with delicate antiques, and a jungle path that is worn into a particularly popular area of carpet. These activities are quick and convenient for family members, but they are extremely destructive to furnishings and body parts. The solution to these problems is found with the use of Room Traffic Control.

By selectively placing furniture within a room, the convenience of walking through the room is retained while the unpleasant consequences of poor Room Traffic Control are avoided. Room Traffic Control has one additional benefit, however. Selective traffic flow draws attention to the artistic elements of a room.

Room Traffic Control involves the movements of people within a specific room as well as the flow of activities from one room to another. The most important consideration for furniture placement is the comfort and convenience of the people occupying the room. For example, regardless of plans for room traffic flow, lighting fixtures should be placed near the sofas and chairs in which readers will sit and not placed as a sort of bizarre traffic diversion. Traffic between rooms must be considered only after the requirements regarding the internal activities of the room are met.

Use furniture placement to direct traffic flow around delicate items such as stereo systems, televisions, and cabinets filled with antiques. For example, people will take a wide path around a large piece of furniture such as a sofa. By placing the delicate item near the sofa, the walker's path will require them to also avoid this delicate item.

Place furniture in a manner that creates a sort of speed reducer for rambunctious children. Instead of providing a straight running path through a room, arrange the room's furniture so that the children must slow down to walk around the furniture.

Distribute areas of heavy traffic by creating several paths to achieve the same common activity. Heavy carpet wear is reduced by allowing several paths to lead to a light switch, for example.

Room traffic can also be specifically directed to allow only one path to lead to a given destination. This technique is used to direct the attention of someone walking through a room to view a particular item, such as a piece of artwork or sculpture.

97

Carpet Capers

EACH ROOM WITHIN A DWELLING HAS SPECIFIC REQUIRE-
ments dictating the material selected to cover its floor. For
reasons of aesthetics, carpet is the almost universally desired floor
covering material. Carpet has a variety of useful benefits besides
beauty, to include thermal and acoustic insulation, that make this
type of floor covering ideal for many room environments. Because
of the large variety of carpet types currently available, however,
carpet selection is a painstaking task. A carpet that is attractive
when it is purchased can easily become a matted mess after a short
period of time within an inappropriate room environment.

When planning the floor covering of the rooms within your
household, consideration must be given to the activities that take
place in each room. Furthermore, the nature of certain types of floor
coverings must also be weighed against these room activities. You
might ultimately discover that the best floor covering for a room
is no covering at all.

Rooms with a high incidence of food or water spillage accidents,
such as kitchens and bathrooms, should be covered with a low pile
carpet rather than with a shag carpet. Low pile carpets are cleaned
more easily and dried more quickly than are the shag variety. Op-
tionally, a hard vinyl sheet or tile floor surface, instead of carpet,
can be used to facilitate the clean up of accidents within these
rooms.

Carpeting within kitchens, bathrooms, or any other area of the household likely to attract dirt, should be protectively treated. Alternately, some types of carpets are factory protected by their manufacturers. All types of carpet provide noise insulation for a room. Heavily padded carpet creates greater sound deadening, however, than lighter weight carpet.

A room containing a computer is especially sensitive to the type of carpet used to cover its floor. The danger of static electricity build-up, a notable side effect of carpeting, is a hazard to computer equipment. One option that ensures safety of computer equipment from carpet-generated static electricity is to eliminate carpet completely from the computer room environment. If you choose to cover the floor of your computer room, however, be sure to select a low pile carpet and not the shag variety (see Chapter 80 for further suggestions for static elimination).

Carpet designed with built-in anti-static qualities is an excellent alternative to a bare computer room floor. This type of carpet reduces the static electricity generated by walking across its surface. Static electricity generated by a computer user's feet rubbing against the carpet beneath a computer desk or table is eliminated by placing a hard plastic mat over the carpet to cover the entire work area.

98

Ceiling Coverings

A LTHOUGH FEW PEOPLE LOOK ABOVE THEIR HEADS WHEN
they enter a room, the style and design of a ceiling enhances
or detracts from the impression that a room gives to its occupants.
The selected ceiling treatment influences the mood of a room and,
to some extent, an occupant's perception of ambient light. This relationship between mood and ambient light is exemplified by both
the bright ceiling treatment of work environments and the muted
colors and dim light source of a ceiling within an intimate room
setting.

A ceiling provides an artistic work area for subtly controlling
light perception, room personality, and even sound transmission
within a room. Although the ceiling is often the most overlooked
aspect of a room's interior design, it is one of the most influential
aspects of a room's total appearance. Here are some tips for planning ceiling coverings:

☐ Cover a ceiling with a light, almost reflective color to enhance
ambient room light. A light colored ceiling will act to reflect
local room light instead of absorbing it.
☐ Paint a ceiling in a softly colored hue to carry out the color
scheme of the rest of the room. Light reflected from this type
of ceiling surface will enhance the native colors of the walls and
furnishings within the room.

Fig. 98-1. An example of a suspended ceiling with fluorescent lighting.

☐ Suspended ceilings coupled with fluorescent lighting are most applicable within work-intensive areas of a household. Kitchens, workrooms, family rooms, and bathrooms are the greatest beneficiaries of this type of ceiling lighting (see Fig. 98-1).

☐ In addition to providing overall, intensive lighting throughout the room, suspended ceilings with fluorescent lighting also provide an acoustic deadening area. This sound insulation is especially useful for family rooms because the sounds of noisy activities are confined within this limited area.

☐ Acoustic paneling or tiles can be added to rooms with normal ceilings just as easily as they are used within rooms sporting suspended ceilings. Once again, a degree of sound insulation is provided by this porous, acoustic deadening material.

99

Bed Coverings

T HE LARGEST AND MOST IMPOSING PIECE OF FURNITURE occupying a bedroom is, naturally, a bed. Night stands, chests of drawers, and dressing tables are all utilitarian accouterments designed to supplement the bed. Because of the large expanse of a room that a bed occupies, the type of material used to cover the bed plays a major role in the room's interior design.

A bed is, therefore, an ideal vehicle for expressing a room's personality. Bed coverings range from the reserved and simple to the elaborate and ornate. The only rule to follow when covering the beds in your household is to maintain a harmony and interaction between the design of the bed covering and the rest of the room. These tips for selecting bed coverings can help achieve that harmony:

☐ Use a simple, single-colored bed covering within a room having extreme elaborate or thematic design patterns. A multicolored, patterned bed covering is sure to clash with a patterned wall covering or a heavily decorated room.

☐ A room possessing a moderately complex decor can support a slightly more elaborate bed covering. If a single-colored bed covering is selected for such a room, a textured pattern within the covering is visually appealing without detracting from the room's decor.

264

Fig. 99-1. This traditional quilt is the Log Cabin–Barn Raising pattern. Additionally, note that this quilt is made from lightly patterned fabrics which give a solid "feel" to the displayed results.

- Bed coverings are dependent both on the climate of the area in which you reside and on seasonal changes. In areas of warm climates (or during the summer months), a lightweight bed covering serves a decorative purpose and can be removed from the bed while you are sleeping. Conversely, energy saving plans can be incorporated into your bed covering selection. Thick quilts keep those people living in cold climate areas and trying to survive the winter months, warm throughout the night while allowing their thermostats to be set at lower temperatures.
- Regardless of your outdoor climate, a bed covering or quilt can be created precisely to your own design specifications. These custom-made bed coverings are in the form of heavy quilts for cold climate dwellers or in the form of pieced or appliqued quilt tops without the usual thick quilt batting for people in warm environments.
- Pieced or appliqued bed cover designs come either from modifications of traditional quilt patterns or from entirely self-created patterns.

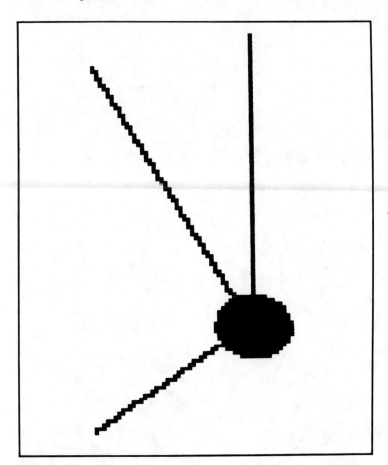

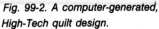

Fig. 99-2. A computer-generated, High-Tech quilt design.

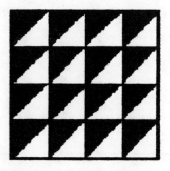

Fig. 99-3. PC Paintbrush was used to create this contemporary quilt pattern.

☐ Traditional pieced or appliqued patterns often have a geometrical design that aptly suits the decor of a high-tech bedroom (see Fig. 99-1). By escaping from the gingham and calico fabrics commonly associated with old-fashioned quilt work, modernistic bed coverings can be created from these standard designs. Solid colors should be selected from traditional cotton blend fabrics or from slightly more exotic silks and synthetic fabrics to achieve this high-tech look for your bed cover.

☐ Creation of your own high-tech bed cover design is one way to ensure that the final bed covering will exactly match the decor of your room. Within a high-tech setting, the best bed covering patterns incorporate sparse design layout, solid fabric colors, and abstract and geometric design themes (see Fig. 99-2).

☐ To aid in the planning of your self-created bed covering pattern, a computer program, such as FONTRIX, PC Paintbrush, or AutoCAD 2, is extremely helpful. Initially, an overall plan of the entire bed cover top can first be formed with one of these programs (see Fig. 99-3). Then the actual pattern pieces can be created with a program and dumped onto a computer printer to make final hard copy pattern pieces. A complete description of each of these programs is located in Appendix B.

100

Countertop Storage

H IGH-TECH INTERIOR DESIGN IS AS CONCERNED WITH THE
planning of concealed space as it is with the planning of visible space. An appropriate example of this statement is the space
utilized by a kitchen. A kitchen is really furnished in three distinct
manners. Refrigerators, stoves, microwave ovens, and kitchen
tables are the obvious outward kitchen furnishings. Concealed kitchen furnishings include the many small appliances, such as
blenders and food processors, that must be stored within a kitchen's
cabinets and drawers. The third area exists between these exposed
and concealed areas. This area, which alternately displays appliances for use and stores them when they are not in operation,
is the kitchen countertop.

Because the countertop is usually the only work area provided
within a kitchen, having full use of this area is essential. The
countertop is, however, often plagued by the overflow from bulg-
ing cabinets. A countertop cluttered with too many appliances is
both useless and dangerous. Fortunately, interior design planning
for your countertop will prevent this cluttered state from occurring and will give you a safe and spacious kitchen work area. Try
these tips for planning countertop storage:

☐ Avoid the tangle of several electrical appliances competing for
the same electrical outlet. Additional outlets can be provided

Fig. 100-1. A cutting board concealed under a High-Tech kitchen counter top.

with the use of a multiple outlet power strip. Depending on the type of unit you purchase, your multiple outlet power strip can be wall mounted for easy access and use.

☐ The clutter of excess appliance electrical cords is both inconvenient and potentially dangerous. If you are satisfied with the current placement of your countertop appliances, the electrical cords of these appliances can be shortened to the exact required length to reach to your power outlet socket. You can perform this operation yourself with the use of replacement wall plugs. Any hardware store offers two-pronged and three-pronged wall plugs that can be used for this purpose. Two pronged replacement plugs should never be used for appliances with three pronged, grounded electrical plugs.

☐ When you make new appliance purchases, select appliances that possess the ability to be mounted underneath cabinets. Countertop space is saved every time an appliance can be suspended, above the counter's surface. Wall mounted appliances are also effective countertop space savers.

☐ Heavy appliances that are permanently mounted within cabinets but that can be swung out and locked into place for use, save the strain of lifting heavy appliances onto a countertop for use.

☐ Additional countertop storage is created within a cramped kitchen by using a concealed cutting board. Requiring only a few inches of the area directly underneath your countertop for installation, the cutting board can be pulled out as a horizontal surface that becomes an extension of your normal countertop space (see Fig. 100-1).

101

The Model Child's Room

ADULTS AND CHILDREN HAVE ALWAYS HAD A FASCINATION with miniature representations of airplanes, ships, and cars. While model kits of these real-life objects provide hours of enjoyment while they are being built, the finished models require a large area for their display. Model airplanes are the biggest offenders which create inefficient use of space. A model airplane's wings and fuselage are relatively slender when examined independently, but when the model is considered as a whole unit, the completed airplane takes on monstrous proportions.

It is not necessary to forgo the entertaining and educational hobby of model building because of household space limitations, however. Instead, solutions are found in the use of extremely small scale models and thoughtfully designed enclosures for model display.

Select extremely small models of either 1/144 or 1/300 scale. Companies such as Crown and Hasegawa manufacture 1/144 scale kits while Nichimo produces 1/300 scale kits of excellent quality. The carefully executed detail of the plastic parts and the inclusion of scale decals within these companies' kits provide for an extremely realistic final appearance of each model. As an example of the minute size of these airplane models, a veritable squadron of 1/144 scale airplanes can be placed on top of the wing area of a 1/32 scale airplane (see Fig. 101-1).

Fig. 101-1. Four 1/144 scale aircraft rest comfortably on the wing of this 1/32 scale Revell Lockheed P-38J Lightning.

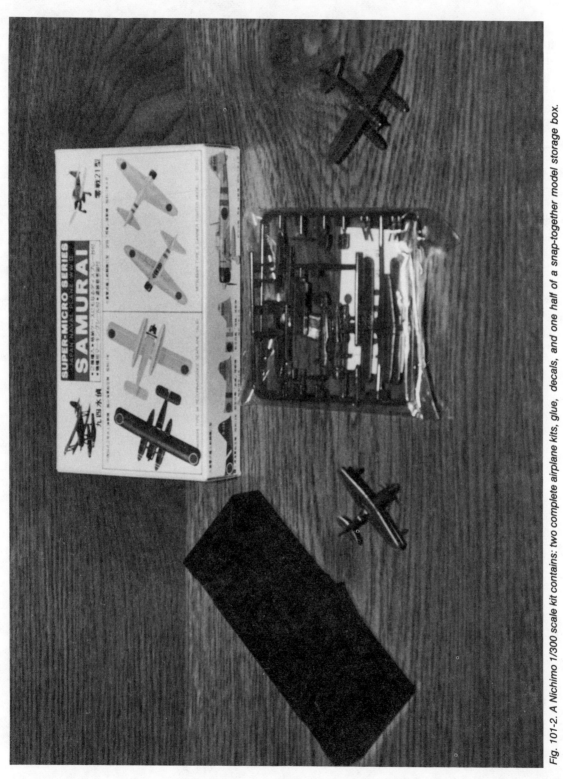

Fig. 101-2. A Nichimo 1/300 scale kit contains: two complete airplane kits, glue, decals, and one half of a snap-together model storage box.

Nichimo 1/300 scale airplane kits have the added benefit that each kit contains two airplane models plus one half of a snap-together model storage box. When you purchase two of these kits, you receive the complement to this storage box, giving you a complete container for holding the four assembled model aircraft (see Fig. 101-2).

Due to their minute detail and small nature, 1/144 and 1/300 scale model airplanes are difficult to paint in their traditional scale color schemes. This drawback can be transformed into an advantage by using these model aircraft as high-tech artistic design forms. Several airplanes can be painted a single color that complements the decor of a room in which the models will be displayed. No specialized detailed paint work or decal application is therefore required. Such models are an attractive addition to a living room, as well as to a child's room.

Because of the extremely delicate nature of assembled models, it is difficult to safely dust these small craft without the risk of damaging their fragile parts. The most logical alternative to the hazards of constant dusting is to provide a dust-free environment for your assembled models. This dust-free environment can also incorporate a display showcase design. A five sided enclosing cube (consisting of four sides and a top) made from clear, heavy gauge plastic sheeting provides a dust cover that can be set in place over your collected arrangement of models.

Appendices

Appendix A

Instructions and Tips

for Project Preparation

A CHOICE IS MADE AND A PROJECT IS SELECTED FOR ADDITION to a high-tech household. The unusual nature of this book's projects, however, requires you, as the builder, to take a new approach to the preparation and display of each project. Whether you are a steadfast electronic project enthusiast, a computer user, or an interior designer wiring his or her first circuit, conventional ideas must be disregarded. At least, these ideas must be tempered with a previsualized goal of the project's final place in the household environment. Three specific areas in which a new attitude is necessary are the way in which the circuit is built, the enclosure in which it is placed, and the way the final project is displayed.

Experienced project builders may be old hands at soldering and printed circuit board etching, but use of the modular IC breadboard socket is a method of project wiring available to all levels of project builders. Circuits are easily transferred from the printed page onto a breadboard by using easily cut jumper wires and no soldering. Project builders wishing more stability for their projects can quickly translate the breadboarded circuits onto a solderable printed circuit board. Radio Shack's MODULAR IC BREADBOARD SOCKETS (Radio Shack #276-174 and #276-175) and EXPERIMENTER'S PC BOARDS (Radio Shack #276-170) are well suited to these tasks and are used for the examples within this appendix.

In some ways, the familiar, boxy metal or plastic electronic project cabinet has become an outdated relic. However, where its form has lost its appeal, its functionality remains unquestionable. The use of purchased storage cabinets and suggestions for the creation of more aesthetically pleasing enclosures from easily acquired materials are addressed later in this appendix.

Finally, techniques for displaying the newly created high-tech projects are discussed. In fact, some projects are showcased as a form of sculptural artwork. Placement of these projects in relation to other such projects, and with regard to the room itself, is as important as the actual installation methods. Also, certain projects, especially those which are strictly sound-oriented, may be deemed appropriate for concealed placement.

JUMPING TO CONNECTIONS

A great equalizer in the electronics community is the modular breadboard socket. This tool may be unfamiliar to those who have never before constructed an electronic project. But, electronics enthusiasts have long employed these reusable boards to test circuits before committing their designs to hard-wired or etched printed circuits. The reason for this pretesting is quite logical: why solder expensive components to a board when a project's resultant function or design may prove to be undesirable?

The design of a modular breadboard is simple: a hard plastic board provides a gridwork of connection slots into which the leads of electronic components are inserted (see Fig. A-1). Electrical connection points are located underneath this grid. Without the use of soldering techniques, component leads are pinched in place by the underlying contacts. The connection slot spacing of "IC compatible" breadboards is designed so that integrated circuit chip pins fit neatly into the slots without being bent. Thus, an additional benefit of the modular breadboard is its ability to accept ICs plugged directly into the board without the use of an IC socket. If a builder decides to "scrap" a project, an IC is easily extracted and ready for use in another project.

Modular breadboard sockets are sold by a wide variety of manufacturers, but one particularly accessible type of breadboard is that sold by Radio Shack. This board comes in two sizes: the Modular IC Breadboard Socket (Radio Shack #276-174), roughly 2 inches by 6 inches, and the miniature Modular IC Breadboard Socket (Radio Shack #276-175) measuring 2 1/8 inches by 3 5/8 inches. These two breadboards are designed so that they can be joined together in many combinations to fit virtually any project size. The modular nature of these boards permits one to be linked with another by means of a tightly fitting "rim" on each edge of each board.

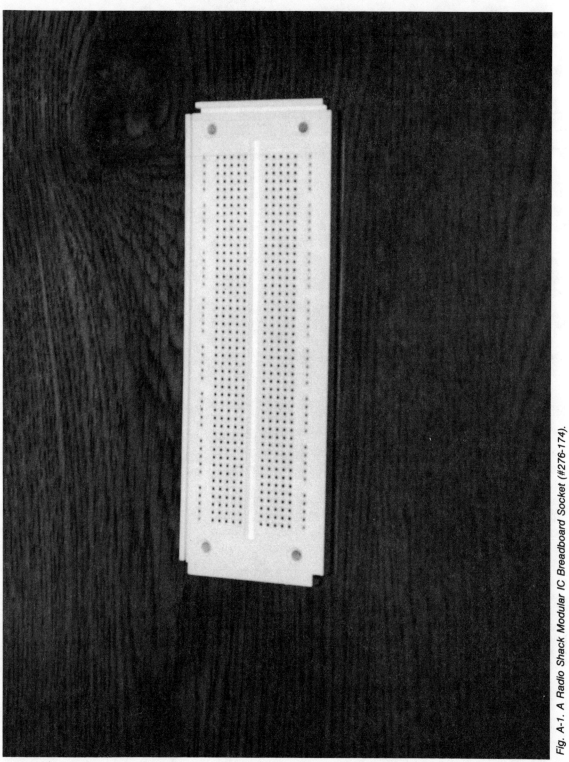

Fig. A-1. A Radio Shack Modular IC Breadboard Socket (#276-174).

When a project is constructed on a Modular IC Breadboard, the underlying pattern of connection points must be kept in mind. The two strips of connection points, labeled X and Y, located along the right and left sides of the Radio Shack boards each form a completely interconnected strip (see Fig. A-2). Each strip forms an integral "jumper" along which component connections are made. An ideal use for these strips is to designate one as a power line and the other as a grounding strip. Any circuit connection requiring power, for example, can be slipped into the most convenient slot on that line.

Other connection points on each breadboard are united with their neighbors in strips of five horizontal connection points. These sets of connection points are numbered down the length of the board. A separation down the center of the breadboard creates an inactive zone between a five connection strip on the right and a similar strip on the lefthand side. This inactive zone permits an IC to be placed onto the board across this gap without connecting opposing IC pins.

Component leads are connected on a breadboard by making use of adjacent connection points, that is, by placing appropriate component leads next to each other on the board (these leads can even be placed within the same slot). Alternatively, jumper wires are used for connecting from one component to another over the surface of the board. Small pieces of wire wrap wire, with their ends stripped (approximately 1/4 inch of the insulation is removed from each end), are perfectly suited for such jumper applications.

The use of Modular IC Breadboards for initial circuit preparation is ideal for the beginner to the electronic field, or even for the intermediate project builder. A circuit is tested, and if the final result is not suitable, modifications can be made or all of the components removed and the only loss is that of time. If, on the other hand, the builder decides that the project is worthy of a permanent place in their high-tech home, the breadboarded circuit can be transposed in its exact form onto a PC board using the same

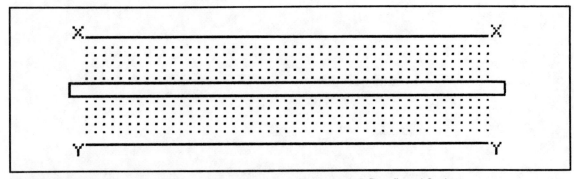

Fig. A-2. The two interconnected strips are labeled X and Y on the Modular IC Breadboard Socket.

component placement and identical jumper wire locations.

SELECTING A CIRCUIT BOARD

When purchasing a blank board to solder a circuit's components onto, three considerations are in order. First of all, a pre-drilled board is absolutely necessary; no one wants to drill dozens of holes to stick component leads into. Not just any pre-drilled board will do, however, because the chosen board must have "IC" spacing between its holes. This permits IC sockets, or even an IC, to be soldered directly onto the board. Secondly, the board should have solder ringed, or "pre-tinned" holes. This feature simplifies the soldering process by helping the solder stick to the board and making a secure connection with component leads. Finally, both sides of a PC board should be examined before purchase to ensure that the board does not have a specialized pattern of solder tracings that will make transferring a breadboarded circuit to this board difficult or even impossible.

Despite all of these warnings, PC board selection is really quite simple. Project builders using Radio Shack Modular IC Breadboards will find transposition of their circuits to a hardwired state easier than expected thanks to two other related Radio Shack products: the Experimenters' PC Board (Radio Shack #276-170) and the MODULAR BREADBOARD SCRATCHPADS (Radio Shack #276-185).

The Experimenter's PC Board is specifically designed to imitate the function and connection points of Radio Shack's Modular IC Breadboard. This means that specialized tracings *do* appear on one side of the Experimenter's PC Board. But these tracings are necessary to emulate the vertically and horizontally oriented connection points of the breadboard. Because of this direct emulation, a breadboarded circuit can be copied component for component, jumper wire for jumper wire, into the corresponding holes of the Experimenter's PC Board.

The copying process has one hitch, however; it is easy to lose one's place when moving components from the breadboard to the PC board. It's no fun to test a completed, soldered circuit only to find that a mistake has been made in the transposing process and that the circuit doesn't function properly. This does not mean, however, that two complete sets of components must be purchased (one to leave on the breadboard and another to solder onto the PC board, using the filled breadboard as a guide). Radio Shack's Modular Breadboard Scratchpads permit the circuit to be sketched as a guide for component and jumper placement. These note sheets illustrate the connection points of both the Modular Breadboard and the Experimenter's PC Board. Once the component layout is sketched on the scratchpad, components are removed from the Modular Breadboard and soldered to the Experimenter's PC Board using the scratchpad sketch as a reference source.

Because some circuits are not large enough to require an entire large Modular IC Breadboard, they are planned on the miniature Modular IC Breadboard. But only one size of Experimenter's PC Board exists, matching the size of the large breadboard. In order to save both space and money, however, one of these Experimenter's PC Boards can be cut into two pieces for the construction of two separate circuits. A small handsaw, such as the X-Acto RAZOR SAW BLADE (#234), is an ideal and easily acquired tool for this purpose. A careful cutting job and a light sanding of the board's rough edges creates two ready-to-use miniature PC boards.

EFFECTIVE SOLDERING TECHNIQUES

Before the first drop of solder is run onto a PC board, an overall concept must be planned for fitting the completed circuit into an enclosure. Small enclosures are usually preferred over larger cabinets simply because of their low profile and discreet appearance. Space is limited within the narrow confines of such a project enclosure, however. Once the appropriate components are in place, the project board starts to look like a miniature city skyline.

It is easy to think of a two dimensional circuit schematic diagram and to forget that the finished, hard-wired circuit will exist in three dimensions. Capacitors, resistors, and ICs give a considerable amount of depth to a finished project board. Fortunately, the effects of these tall components can be minimized.

It's perfectly acceptable (and even strongly recommended) to leave all component leads at their full length while they remain on a breadboard. These ungainly components, however, do not permit placement of a project into a sleek, decorative enclosure if they are soldered to a PC board in this manner. With only a few exceptions, all components must be soldered to a PC board as closely as possible. One exception is, of course, leaving adequate jumper wire lengths for external enclosure mounted components such as switches and LEDs.

Both component selection and mounting methods directly affect a project board's depth. For example, the selection of a horizontally oriented, miniature "PC mountable" potentiometer over a standard vertically oriented potentiometer may save up to 1/2 inch of a board's height. Likewise, flat, rectangular metal film capacitors offer a space savings whenever capacitors of their value are required (usually .01mF to 1.0mF) (see Fig. A-3).

If a disc or monolithic capacitor is used on a circuit board, the leads can be bent so that the capacitor lies nearly flat against the board (see Fig. A-4). The capacitor can be pre-fitted before solder-

Fig. A-3. A .47mf metal film capacitor and a 10K potentiometer neatly nestled in a surrounding field of "regular" capacitors.

283

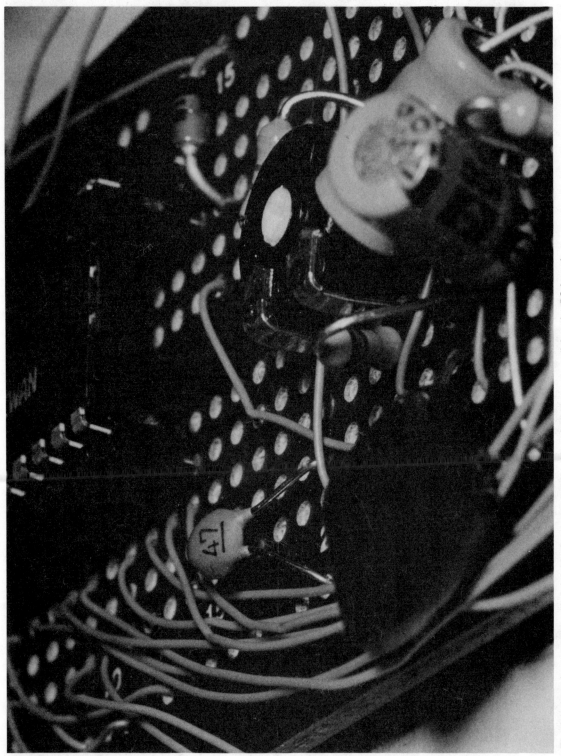

Fig. A-4. In order to conserve height, this disc capacitor has been folded over parallel to the PC board.

ing and the appropriate bends made with a pair of needle-nosed pliers. Be sure that the leads of any component are slipped through the PC board holes as far as possible before soldering them into place. Excess lead material can be clipped from the back side of the board *after* the solder connection has been made. A precautionary note is in order regarding overly zealous board compacting. Do not condense a board's components so tightly that undesired leads might touch; a short circuit is the almost inevitable and unwanted result. Also, some components will emit heat during operation. Therefore, some component spacing and enclosure ventilation may be necessary.

One way to minimize circuit board component crowding is by special mounting of resistors and diodes. A common method for mounting resistors or diodes is to lay them flat against the PC board. This method is impractical, and occasionally impossible, on an Experimenter's PC Board. A superior method is to stand the resistor or diode on end and fold one lead down until it is parallel with the other (see Fig. A-5). The component leads can then be placed in adjacent holes.

One low profile component that is a necessity for any PC board using ICs is the IC socket. An IC socket is soldered to a PC board to hold an IC. Therefore, the IC is free to be inserted into or extracted from a socket at any time. Acting as a safety measure, the IC socket prevents the damage that might be caused to a chip by a hot soldering iron if the IC is soldered directly to the PC board. Integrated circuit chips are quite delicate and excessive heat or static electricity will damage them. After the project board has been completely soldered, the ICs are finally added to the circuit.

PROJECT PACKAGING

The most easily acquired enclosure for a finished project is a metal or plastic project cabinet from a nearby electronic parts store. Unfortunately, if appearance is any indication, many of these enclosures belong in a 1950's science fiction movie. The outdated visual impact of these cabinets virtually disqualifies most of them for prominent display in a high-tech household. One pleasantly appealing exception to this type of enclosure is a set of sloped cabinets from Radio Shack (Radio Shack #270-282, #270-264, and #270-266). The modern, wedge-shaped design of these cabinets makes them attractive for household display. Another slightly less becoming, but even more functional, project enclosure that is also available from Radio Shack is the EXPERIMENTER BOX (Radio Shack #270-627). This rectangular enclosure's 6 1/4 by 3 3/4 by 2 inch dimensions ideally suit it for containing a project finished on an Experimenter's PC Board.

A local electronic parts store is one of the last places most peo-

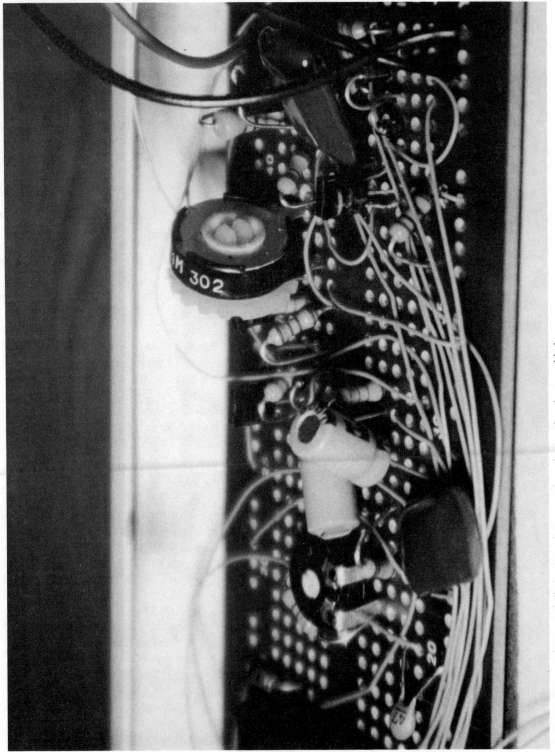

Fig. A-5. These resistors and diodes have been stood on their ends prior to soldering.

ple would look for objects to display in their home, whether it is high-tech oriented or not. This problem of finding an appealing project enclosure is easily overcome by the use of a little creative effort. A self-styled project enclosure is often the most appropriate type for a high-tech household. Materials for building custom-designed project enclosures come from such convenient sources as art stores and hobby stores (especially those that carry model airplane supplies).

Product developments in the radio controlled (R/C) airplane hobby industry have made new, inexpensive types of sheet plastics and associated adhesives available to the general public. This means that working with a sheet of PLEXIGLAS or other type of heavy gauge plastic sheeting is no longer as difficult as it once was. A powerful cyanoacrylate adhesive such as SATELLITE CITY'S HOT STUFF or SUPER "T" will bond two pieces of Plexiglas together immediately. These new construction elements come together to form unusual project enclosures.

A unique project enclosure can be constructed out of Plexiglas with little effort and stunning results. A rectangular enclosure with a hinged lid is described here. Because Plexiglas or a similar type of heavy gauge plastic sheeting is available in a variety of colors and with a choice of either clear, opaque, or translucent, at least one style should match the decor of anyone's high-tech household. After the dimensions of the enclosure have been calculated, the chosen Plexiglas sheet is cut with a hand tool or a power jig saw. Do not remove the protective paper covering from the Plexiglas while cutting it to prevent the sheet from splitting or becoming scratched. The edges of the cut plastic can be sanded slightly if necessary. Any mounting screw holes are drilled at this time, before construction of the enclosure begins.

Construct all permanent sides of the enclosure by placing adjoining sides together and laying a thin bead of the liquid adhesive Hot Stuff along the edge of the joint. Be sure that all panel edges are perfectly aligned before cementing them together because the glue sets immediately. If you require a greater setting time allowance, the Super "T" adhesive is a more appropriate choice. This glue permits approximately 10 seconds of positioning time before setting up solidly.

The enclosure's hinged lid is created with the final Plexiglas sheet and two model airplane type nylon hinges, such as the Carl Goldberg brand of KLETT PINNED HINGES. These hinges are glued both to the box's lid and to its adjoining side panel. Internal hinge mounting is recommended to enhance the enclosure's appearance. Once again, be sure that all parts are properly aligned before cementing anything into place. If an accident does occur and two pieces of plastic (or two fingers) need to be unglued, a debonder solution is available. As a precautionary measure, a bottle of this debonder should be purchased at the same time that you purchase your glue. The nearly finished enclosure only requires the circuit board to be set in place and any mounting hardware to be attached. The project is now ready for household installation.

If a more natural look is desired for the project enclosure, these same steps can be followed using spruce, birch, or plywood sheeting instead of the Plexiglas. Many hobby stores carry these types of wood in 1/4 inch thick sheets. Hot Stuff or Super "T" can also be used for bonding these wooden panels together if the surfaces to be bonded are smooth and sealed with any standard wood sealer.

Less angular enclosures are designed with the use of *stretch-forming* techniques. Stretch forming is a variation on the common method of vacuum forming a heated plastic sheet. To stretch form, a desired shape is created first as a solid three-dimensional form and later formed in ABS or moldable styrene plastic attained from a local hobby store. The three dimensional form is carved with balsa wood and mounted on a post to hold it. The final form is covered with a sealant, such as glue or model airplane dope. After the sealant is dry, the form is lightly sanded.

A template roughly following the outline of the form is cut from a thin spruce sheet. The plastic stretch form sheet is reinforced around its edges by tacking it to a spruce framework, (matching the dimensions of the template). The reinforced plastic sheet is then placed on a rack in an oven preheated at a low to moderate temperature (approximately 300 degrees Fahrenheit).

When the plastic within the framework begins to sag slightly, it is ready to be formed. Remove the framed plastic sheet from the oven and place it over the spruce template. Now press the balsa form against the soft plastic and through the template opening. Be sure to press the mold slightly past the template opening to completely create the desired shape and to leave adequate room for final trimming. Work quickly but accurately because the plastic cools quickly. It is soon ready to trim and an X-Acto knife with a number 11 blade is an ideal tool for the job. If gluing is desired to mount the stretch formed shape, a cyanoacrylate glue can be used.

HIGH-TECH PROJECT DISPLAY

Displaying your final high-tech project in its custom enclosure, first requires planning and a reevaluation of the project's form and function. If a project is purely functional, its display may not even be necessary. Concealed placement is a valuable option, but you must be sure that if the project is concealed, its function is still performed. It would be silly to place Solar Powered Alarm (see Chapter 69) where the morning sunlight would not activate it!

Projects can be displayed in a manner that either purposely attracts attention or that simply allows the project to perform a function without intentionally being the center of attention. Two examples of this latter method are Remote Weather (see Chapter 58) and Musical Message Pager (see Chapter 47). These projects become important to the inhabitants of the high-tech household only when specific information is sought or given: the current weather conditions or a guest's arrival, respectively. Placement of these projects should be planned accordingly.

The point of prominent project placement requires further elaboration. Wall mounted projects, such as Liquid Crystal Wall Hanging (see Chapter 42), command considerable attention in their own right, and their placement depends strictly on the decor of the room in which they hang. Sculpture oriented projects like the Tube Lights (see Chapter 20) and Weather Balloon Sculpture (see Chapter 19) are definitely attention-drawing room accouterments. It is the size and the decor of each room that dictate both the positioning of each project and the number of projects that comfortably and handsomely furnish one room.

As a rule of thumb, evaluate the form and the function of each high-tech project prior to construction. The project's final appearance should be directed by its previsualized purpose and not by its physical dimensions. With this "yardstick" in mind, you will have no trouble designing your own high-tech household.

Appendix B

Computer-Aided
Interior Design Planning
with Apple and IBM Computers

W HETHER YOU ARE AN INDIVIDUAL HOME OWNER MAKING
household alterations or a corporate designer executing a
major interior renovation, a plan is required before any of the
physical work can begin. This plan can be in the rough form of a
sketch made on a napkin or in the elegant aspects of a professionally
drafted "blueprint." No matter what its format, however, a plan
basically presents a physical, two-dimensional (or, sometimes, three-
dimensional) illustration of an idea.

As an example, imagine this plan-less scenario, "I want a partial wall going from here to here, two bookcases built-in, and a bigger doorway." Without the aid of a plan it is impossible to measure
"from here to here" or properly identify the wall for the "built-in"
bookcases. Likewise, is a "bigger doorway" taller, wider, or both?
Granted, the ambiguity of this verbal plan can be clarified through
the use of accompanying hand gestures, but precision will still be
sacrificed. More importantly, what if you finish the plan-less design
and there has been an undesirable alteration? It's tough to go back
to the "drawing board" when the house has had major reconstruc-
tive surgery. A plan provides unlimited experimentation with design
possibilities.

With the need for a plan now firmly established, the next step
is creating one. There are hundreds of papers, pens, pencils, and
templates that will provide the would-be plan designer with ample

means for expression. With an appropriate selection of these materials, the plan-drawing session can begin. First, the measurements for the area are taken. Next, a plan scale is determined, and finally, the layout is composed. This entire process can be either simple or complex, rough or accurate. The choice is left to the discretion of the designer (or the requirements of the assignment). Regardless of the choice, major advantages of a written plan are its forgiveness of mistakes and receptiveness to experimentation. Remarkably enough, in order to appreciate these virtues, you will only need to invest in another sheet of paper and not rebuild a demolished room.

After several mistakes, redesigns, and redrawings, a problem in the plan-drawing concept will be noticed—wasted paper. Along with this paper consumption is the expenditure of time to prepare each new layout from scratch. Perhaps time is an endless commodity for the average dilettante, but to the professional draftsman time is money and wasted time is lost revenue. A solution to this problem can be found in the field of microcomputers. This high-tech equipment is a quick and powerful plan producer that will save paper, hours, and dollars.

Computer-aided design (CAD) links the attributes of the microcomputer—rapid calculations, extensive storage, and flexibility—with the requirement for accurate and precise plan drawing. No professional architect, interior designer, or draftsman should dismiss CAD as "gimmickry" and "unprofessional looking." A negative opinion of microcomputer-based design usually stems from a negative introduction to CAD caused by a poor programming implementation. Basically, the power of CAD lies in individual *hardware* (computer's and associated equipment) and *software* (computer programs) products. Unfortunately, the problem with CAD lies in selecting these best hardware and software products from the vast ocean of poor ones. In fact, without the proper hardware and software, CAD is as useless as the vague language used in the "verbal plan" scenario mentioned earlier. When armed with the best hardware and software however, professionals and amateurs alike can benefit greatly by adopting CAD the next time they contemplate "pen and ink" drawing (and redrawing).

Before CAD can be fully embraced, one final barrier must be hurdled—identifying the "best" hardware and software CAD products. At first, this proposition sounds like any other subjective exercise, but with CAD there is an important difference. In computer-aided design, the final output or drawing is the goal. In other words, a poor or inadequate final illustration translates into a poor or worthless piece of CAD hardware and/or software. By using this single criterion, CAD hardware and software were objectively evaluated. Six top products, three hardware and three software, emerge. The three CAD hardware products are: ENTER COMPUTER'S SWEET-P MODEL 100 PERSONAL PLOTTER, C.ITOH ELECTRONICS' 8510SCP COLOR DOT MATRIX PRINTER, and APPLE COMPUTER'S MACINTOSH. DATA TRANSFORMS' FONTRIX, INTERNATIONAL MICROCOMPUTER SOFTWARE, INCORPORATED'S (IMSI) PC PAINTBRUSH, and AUTODESK'S AUTOCAD 2 are the three outstanding software products.

In the six sections that follow, each of these products is reviewed in terms of its special CAD features. The intention of these review sections is to introduce the interior designer to the power of CAD and not to provide application instructions. That kind of information is most easily provided in the individual product's documentation. Excellent documentation and easy operation are two prominent features common to all six of these standout CAD candidates. Anyone with a modest knowledge of the microcomputer industry knows that good documentation is indeed a rarity and excellent documentation together with easy operation are usually an unfulfilled dream. This dream becomes a reality, however, in each of the following six CAD products.

SWEET-P MODEL 100 PERSONAL PLOTTER

Before Enter Computer entered the plotter scene, all of the commercially available pen drawing devices or plotters were large, complicated, and expensive. The Sweet-P Model 100 plotter, manufactured by Enter Computer, broke this mold and started a new trend which championed compact dimensions, a simple, English-like command language, and an unbelievably low price tag. Table B-1 cites some of the Sweet-P Model 100's remarkable specifications.

An initial examination of the Sweet-P's physical dimensions mistakenly identifies this plotter as a "lightweight;" that is, light in construction equals "light" in performance. In operation, Sweet-P is able to duplicate the performance of some plotters costing twice its price and still has features like its standard Centronics parallel interface, a feature that is absent from some of the more expensive models. In fact, this interface feature allows the Sweet-P to be connected to other computers, such as an Apple *II*e or an IBM PC, with only a cable modification. Figure B-1 shows the Sweet-P in use.

Sweet-P is able to plot points, draw lines, and print text on any 8 1/2 inch wide paper or transparency media up to 10 feet in length. This versatility would be worthless if the Sweet-P were difficult to command. In fact, all of this plotter's features are controlled through 19 simple, two letter commands. This command brevity makes programming the Sweet-P a snap (see Chapter 30 for a programming example).

Table B-1. Specifications for the Sweet-P Model 100 Personal Plotter.

```
Resolution: .004"
Pen Speed: 1.40-6.00 inches per second
Maximum  Paper Dimensions:  8.5 inches wide by  120
inches long
Maximum Actual Plotting Dimensions: 7.4 inches wide
by 120 inches long
Interface: Parallel Centronics
Plotter Control Commands: 19 commands
Physical Dimensions: Length 14 inches
                     Width 8.5 inches
                     Height 3 inches
                     Weight 7.2 pounds
Comments:  Can plot on either paper or transparency
media.
```

Commercial software offers an alternative to homemade programming for control of the Sweet-P. Packages like AutoCAD 2 (see the review later in this appendix) incorporate the Sweet-P as one of the possible compatible output devices. Basically, the installation procedure for a Sweet-P Model 100 plotter when using AutoCAD 2 only requires the plotter's selection from an options menu. Then, the Sweet-P is connected to the IBM PC and its pen is placed in the "upper right" position. The Sweet-P will now reproduce any plan or drawing that you create with AutoCAD 2.

Based solely on the final plotted product, the Sweet-P is a competent performer. Using only its black pen, the Sweet-P Model 100 is able to generate work that approximates finely detailed "pen and ink" drafting. Additionally, pausing the Sweet-P's operation to interchange pens allows full 4-color reproductions. Therefore, through some manual pen swaps, the Sweet-P is able to keep up with its more expensive competitors in the race for high quality color image generation. When its other features, ease of use, and low cost are taken into account this plotter stands alone. If these factors are important, then consider the Sweet-P Model 100 Personal Plotter as your CAD plotter.

C.ITOH MODEL 8510SCP COLOR DOT MATRIX PRINTER

The dot matrix printer is one of the most readily available peripherals in the microcomputer market. The dot matrix printer is also the most frequently purchased peripheral. An incorrect assumption based on the number of printer models available would be that there is a large number of diverse dot matrix printer features.

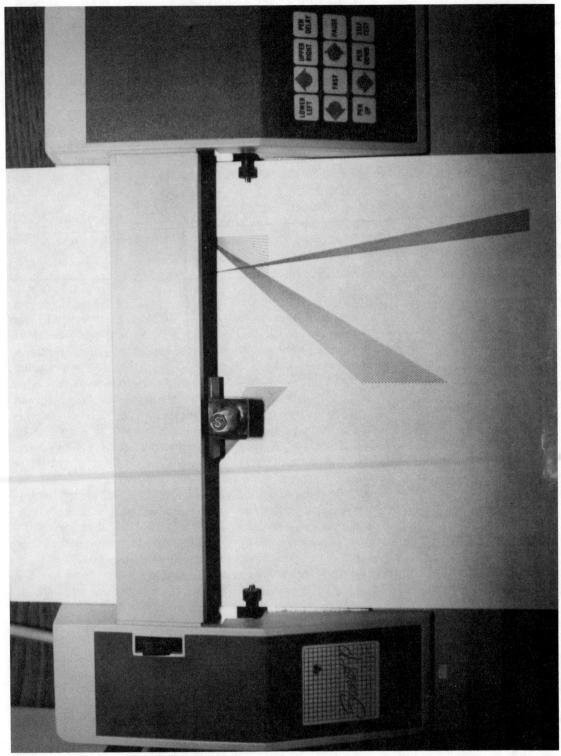

Fig. B-1. A Sweet-P plotter working with an IBM PCjr. This PCjr is using a Tecmar jrCaptain accessory board as the parallel interface.

C.Itoh Electronics manufactures a dot matrix printer that sports features unheard of in low cost printers—the Model 8510SCP Color Dot Matrix Serial Impact Printer. A high print speed, downloadable character facility, and full color printing ability are three of the outstanding CAD features combined into this single printer. All of the specifications for the 8510SCP are listed in Table B-2. If you wish additional information about dot matrix printers, please consult our book titled, *EPSON, EPSON, Read All About It!* (Addison-Wesley Publishing Company, 1985).

The 8510SCP's control code command language is both complex and, once mastered, quite powerful. The 72 commands provide extensive control over the printer's numerous features. This language includes codes for setting the graphics mode, activating a tab setting, and printing in a selected color (see Chapter 29 for a program demonstrating these features).

This revolutionary printer does have its drawbacks, however. One of the most exciting features of this printer is its special three color ribbon that can generate 8 different colors (see Fig. B-2). Unfortunately, most of the commercially available software packages do not support the 8510SCP's color printing facility.

Even though software like FONTRIX and PC Paintbrush (both are reviewed later) fail to utilize the full color palette of the

Table B-2. Specifications for the C.Itoh 8510SCP Dot Matrix Printer.

```
Text Resolutions: 9 by 7 dot matrix
Text Print Speed: 120 characters per second
Text Character Pitch: 6 variations
Text Weight: normal, draft, and emphasized
Text Character Sets: 3 different
Custom Character Resolution: 8 by 8 dot matrix
Graphics  Resolution:  4 modes;  640-1280 dots  per
inch
Paper Dimensions:  4.25-10 inches wide by unlimited
long
Interface:    Parallel   Centronics;   RS-232C   Serial
Option
Printer Control Commands: 72 commands
Ribbon: 3-color ribbon; yellow, red, and blue
Physical Dimensions: Length 17 inches
                     Width 11.5 inches
                     Height 5.25 inches
                     Weight 19.8 pounds
Comments: Can print with either tractor or friction
paper feed.
```

Fig. B-2. Only three colored bands are necessary for printing the C. Itoh's 8 color spectrum.

8510SCP, they do provide complete support of standard black and white printing. As the 8510SCP becomes more readily available so, too, will the presence of color printing software.

Based strictly on its other specifications, the 8510SCP is a superior performance CAD dot matrix printer. In fact, having a powerful capability like 8-color printing lying dormant inside the 8510SCP both enhances this printer's flexibility and increases its functional longevity.

MACINTOSH COMPUTER

Historically, CAD on the average microcomputer required the application of sophisticated software. In general, this point dictated the strategy of making sure that your intended system is able to run the necessary CAD software. This single option limitation presented an unreasonable restraint on choosing a suitable microcomputer. Times change, however, and so has the number of CAD computer options. Apple Computer is the provider of some relief in this selection process with a remarkable, self-contained CAD system—the Macintosh computer.

The Macintosh's flippant name belies its powerful computing potential (see Table B-3). Aside from its specifications, the Macintosh doesn't even look like a conventional microcomputer. Couple this point with Macintosh's unusual system architecture, its simple user interface, and its superior CAD abilities and it becomes

Table B-3. Specifications for the Apple Macintosh Computer.

```
Random   Access   Memory (RAM):    128K bytes   or   512K
bytes
Read Only Memory (ROM): 64K bytes
Display:   built-in 9 inch,   512  by  342 pixel
resolution
Disk Drive:   built-in 3.5 inch,   400K bytes storage
capacity
Microprocessor: 32-bit Motorola MC68000
Interface  Ports:   keyboard,  mouse,  second  disk
drive, RS-232C, RS-422, sound
Standard Software: MacPaint, MacWrite
Main Unit's Physical Dimensions: Length 9.7 inches
                                 Width 10.9 inches
                                 Height 13.5 inches
                                 Weight 9 pounds
Comments:  An optional Apple Imagewriter Printer is
necessary for a complete CAD outfit.
```

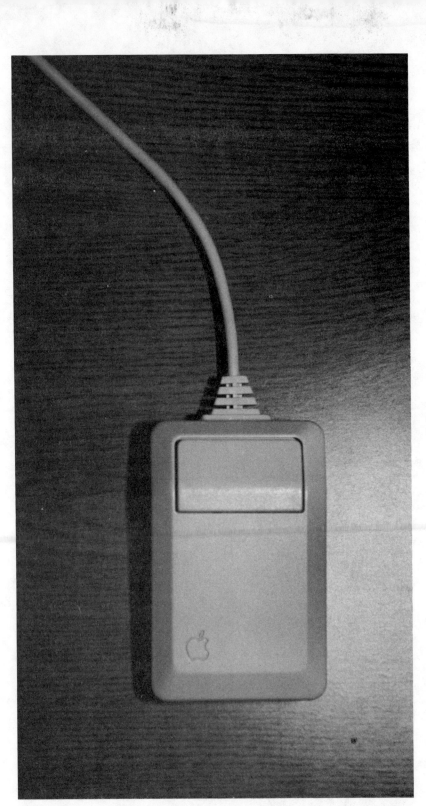

Fig. B-3. The Apple one-button mouse is a vital link in Macintosh's user interface.

obvious that the Macintosh is an intentionally unconventional microcomputer.

One of the more unusual of these unconventional features is the user interface. In a typical microcomputer system, the user interface is the hardware and/or software that facilitates the interaction of human being with computer. Under Macintosh's control, this interaction is both natural and painstakingly "non-computerese."

In order to reduce computer jargon to a minimum, every command is accessed through a network of elaborate "pull-down" menus. These menus guide the Macintosh user through program execution via the hardware portion of the user interface. Most computers use a keyboard similar to a typewriter's as their hardware user interface, but the Macintosh uses a one-button mouse (see Fig. B-3) for linking the human to the computer. Except for alphanumeric input, the rolling and clicking mouse handles all other computer operations. Therefore, working with a Macintosh becomes nothing more than a point and click process.

The two excellent software packages, MacPaint and MacWrite, that are standard with every Macintosh are easily adapted to CAD applications. MacPaint is basically a graphics development tool. Lines, textures, and circles are all in MacPaint's extensive drafting arsenal. With just the mouse, highly detailed drawings can be composed on the screen display. Finally, an optional Apple Imagewriter Printer is required for transferring the CRT compositions to paper.

Although limited text manipulation is possible with MacPaint, preparation of written documents is best accomplished with Mac-Write. Contrary to most word processors that are character oriented, MacWrite is a word processor that is based on a graphics environment. This presents the Macintosh writer with an overwhelming array of text fonts, point size, and weights. Just like the computer it was programmed for, a MacWrite document is impossible to mistake.

FONTRIX

The printed output of a MacWrite file has been the envy of many Apple IIe and IBM PC computer owners. These computer users admire the typeset quality of MacWrite's text, but they mistakenly felt that satisfaction could only come from a "Mactrade-in." Data Transforms took pity on these individuals and marketed a solution. They called their solution FONTRIX.

FONTRIX is a graphics based word processor that is able to create custom fonts. While the incorporation of a font editor into a word processor is not that revolutionary, the FONTRIX font editor is not restricted to alphanumeric characters. Any image up to a maximum 48 pixels by 48 pixels can be "edited" and assigned to a keyboard character. This new font is then saved on a floppy disk for later recall.

Like all of the products reviewed in this appendix, FONTRIX is both well documented and easy to operate. There are two versions of FONTRIX available: one for Apple II + /IIe computers and another for IBM PC computers with a minimum of 256K bytes of usable RAM (Random Access Memory). The notation of "usable RAM" is of special importance to IBM PCjr owners who wish to use FONTRIX on their computers. An IBM PCjr that contains 256K bytes of RAM does not have all of these bytes free for program usage. The relocated video RAM soaks up a major hunk of the memory. At least 320K bytes of RAM are necessary for an IBM PCjr to run FONTRIX.

Finally, if you should ever have any trouble with FONTRIX (which is difficult to imagine), be assured Data Transforms is a human company. Their staff will gladly address any topic or situation that you might find troublesome. Additionally, what better tribute could be paid to FONTRIX (for its power and ease of use) than to state that all of the schematic diagrams in this book were created under this program's expert guidance.

PC PAINTBRUSH

At first glance, PC Paintbrush looks just like MacPaint. They both have the familiar pull-down menus, the extensive side-bar toolbox, and the almost endless pattern and texture selections. Three differences, however, make International Microcomputer Software, Incorporated's (IMSI) PC Paintbrush a more attractive package: this program will run on any IBM PC computer (including PCjr), 20 different printers/plotters (unfortunately the Sweet-P is excluded) will work with this program, and, probably most importantly, PC Paintbrush is in color.

A special subprogram, FRIEZE, contained within PC Paintbrush can capture images generated by other software. Later, this image can be manipulated with PC Paintbrush's extensive toolbox. This ability can turn rather pedestrian Lotus 1-2-3 business graphs into professional printouts with very little effort.

Of the three major differences cited between PC Paintbrush and MacPaint, the presence of color is bound to raise at least a few eyebrows. An even bigger bonus, however, is PC Paintbrush's ability to print its colorful screens in a matching set of colors on the appropriate color printer or plotter. At present the list of supported color printers/plotters is limited to 11 candidates. This figure is constantly changing and IMSI's liberal update policy will keep any PC Paintbrush owner abreast with future developments.

AUTOCAD 2

Simply stated, AutoCAD 2, manufactured by Autodesk, Incorporated, is the state of the art computer-aided-design program. In fact, AutoCAD 2 is such a dynamic program that any critical design work that is to be performed on a microcomputer is best executed with AutoCAD 2.

A properly outfitted AutoCAD 2 system would include an IBM PC with at least 384K bytes of RAM, but preferably 512K bytes, a precision plotter (the Sweet-P Model 100 is supported), and a suitable drawing device (e.g. a mouse or a digitizing tablet). Remarkably, the AutoCAD 2 system's final price tag is actually determined by the user's needs and the purchase of the required support hardware.

An important point to remember, however, is that the selected support hardware also determines the quality and resolution of the final output. Therefore, AutoCAD 2 itself is only as good as the rest of the system. This is a superior approach when compared to other CAD software which is limited regardless of its support hardware.

AutoCAD 2's high performance is not obscured by either poor operation or poor documentation. Easy to follow menu paths provide an elaborate structure for the user to follow and modify. As one's proficiency level increases, with AutoCAD 2 custom menu system, items can be used for replacing lengthy command sequences. Additionally, a HELP command will instantly provide information on any operational parameter while AutoCAD 2 is running.

During a drafting session, AutoCAD 2 utilizes a drawing device for the input of graphic data. The data is placed on the screen either in precise measurements (GRID facility) or in a freehand mode (SKETCH). Chapter 87 gives a brief accounting of a typical AutoCAD 2 drafting session.

Although over one dozen CAD software products are now available in the microcomputer marketplace, AutoCAD 2 still remains unique. AutoCAD 2's deviation from the other CAD packages is due to its outstanding performance at a reasonable price. This combination is not provided by other manufacturers. As with the other five products reviewed in this appendix, AutoCAD 2 is an excellent CAD product.

Appendix C

Supply Source Guide

REFERENCES TO A VARIETY OF UNUSUAL MATERIALS FOR constructing high-tech projects have been made throughout this book. Because many of these materials are difficult to find in local electronics and hobby stores, this appendix provides a list of mail order houses through which these items can be purchased. Additionally, the names and addresses of specific product manufacturers are included.

Apple Computer, Incorporated
20525 Mariani Avenue
Cupertino, California 95014
Macintosh computer

Autodesk, Incorporated
2658 Bridgeway
Sausalito, California 94965
AutoCAD 2 software

C.Itoh Electronics, Incorporated
5301 Beethoven Street
Los Angeles, California 90066
8510SCP Color Dot Matrix Printer

DAK Industries Incorporated
8200 Remmet Avenue
Canoga Park, California 91304
AirEase negative ion generator
speaker systems

Data Transforms
616 Washington Street
Denver, Colorado 80203
FONTRIX software

Enter Computer, Incorporated
6867 Nancy Ridge Drive
San Diego, California 92121
Sweet-P Model 100 Plotter

Hewlett-Packard
P.O. Box 10301
Palo Alto, California 94303-0890
Fiber optic cable
HDSP-6508 alphanumeric display
LED light bars

Harry B. Higley & Sons, Incorporated
P.O. Box 532
Glenwood, Illinois 60425
Mabuchi electric motors

International Microcomputer Software, Incorporated
(IMSI)
1299 Fourth Street
San Rafael, California 94901
PC Paintbrush software

Jade Computer Products
4901 West Rosencrans Avenue
Hawthorne, California 90250
ISOBAR Noise Filter and Surge Suppressor

Light Impressions Corporation
439 Monroe Avenue
P.O. Box 940
Rochester, New York 14603
Fome-Cor brand, foam core board
Gallery Clips
Nielson aluminum frames
UF-3 Plexiglas

NEC Home Electronics, Incorporated
Personal Computer Division
1401 Estes Avenue
Elk Grove Village, Illinois 60007
NEC PC-8201A computer

Sig Manufacturing Company, Incorporated
401 South Front Street
Montezuma, Iowa 50171
Aeroplastic ABS plastic sheeting
Clear Plastic Sheets for stretch forming
Carl Goldberg brand, Klett Pinned Hinges
Foam Core Board
X-Acto Razor Saw Blades (#234)

Tower Hobbies
P.O. Box 778
Champaign, Illinois 61820
Futaba Radio Control transmitters, receivers, and
servomotors
Top Flite brand, MonoKote
Satellite City brand, Hot Stuff and Super "T"
cyanoacrylate adhesives

Bibliography

Brown, E., 1980, *Interior Views*, Thames and Hudson, London, England

Fisher, K., 1972, *Living for Today*, The Viking Press, New York, New York

Friedman, A., J. F. Pile, F. Wilson, 1982, *Interior Design an Introduction to Architectural Interiors,* Elsevier Science Publishing Co., New York, New York

Gilliatt, M., 1977, *Decorating, a Realistic Guide,* Pantheon Books, New York, New York

Heinz, T., 1982, *Frank Lloyd Wright*, St. Martin's Press, Inc., New York, New York

Hicks, D and N. Jenkins, 1979, *David Hicks Living with Design*, Weidenfeld and Nicolson Ltd., London, England

Kaufman, E., ed., 1955, *An American Architecture Frank Lloyd Wright,* Horizon Press, New York, New York

Kron, J. and S. Slesin, 1978, *High-Tech, the Industrial Style and Source Book for the Home,* Clarkson N. Potter, Inc., New York, New York

Pepis, B., 1965, *Interior Decoration A to Z,* Doubleday and Co., Inc., Garden City, New York

Rowntree, D., 1964, *Interior Design*, Penguin Books, Baltimore Maryland

Sullivan, L., 1947, *Kindergarten Chats and Other Writings,* (Isabella
  Athey, ed.), Wittenborn, Schultz, Inc., New York, New York
Sullivan, L., 1924, *The Autobiography of an Idea,* American Institute
  of Architects, Inc., New York, New York
Wright, F. L., 1939, *An Organic Architecture: The Architecture of
  Democracy,* London, England

Index

Index

Other Bestsellers From TAB

☐ **66 FAMILY HANDYMAN® WOOD PROJECTS**

Here are 66 practical, imaginative, and decorative projects . . . literally something for every home and every woodworking skill level from novice to advanced cabinet-maker: room dividers, a free-standing corner bench, china/book cabinet, coffee table, desk and storage units, a built-in sewing center, even your own Shaker furniture reproductions! 210 pp., 306 illus. 7″ × 10″.
Paper $14.95   **Hard $21.95**
Book No. 2623

☐ **HOW TO TROUBLESHOOT AND REPAIR ANY SMALL GAS ENGINE—Dempsey**

Here's a time-, money-, and aggravation-saving sourcebook that covers the full range of two- and four-cycle gas engines from just about *every* major American manufacturer—from Briggs & Stratton, to West Bend, and others! With the expert advice and step-by-step instructions provided by master mechanic Dempsey, you'll be amazed at how easily you can solve almost any engine problem. 272 pp., 228 illus.
Paper $10.95   **Hard $18.95**
Book No. 1967

☐ **DO-IT-YOURSELF DESIGNER WINDOWS**

If the cost of custom-made draperies puts you in a state of shock . . . if you've had trouble finding window coverings of any kind for cathedral or other problem windows . . . or if you're unsure of what type of window decor would look right in your home . . . here's all the advice and information you've been searching for. It's a complete, hands-on guide to selecting, measuring, making, and installing just about any type of window treatment imaginable. You'll even get an expert's insight into selection and installation of decorative storm windows and thermal windows, stained glass windows, woven or wooden blinds, and workable treatments for problem areas. 272 pp., 414 illus. 7″ × 10″.
Paper $14.95   **Hard $21.95**
Book No. 1922

☐ **MOPED MAINTENANCE AND REPAIR**

Guaranteed to save you time, money, and inconvenience, it is packed with practical troubleshooting and repair information, preventative maintenance tips, safety advice, even important facts on state moped regulations and operating guidelines. Generously illustrated, it provides solutions to these routine problems that plague every moped rider—flat tires, fouled spark plugs, broken or worn cables and chains, and more. 256 pp., 229 illus.
Paper $14.95   **Book No. 1847**

☐ **UPHOLSTERY TECHNIQUES ILLUSTRATED—Gheen**

Here's an easy-to-follow, step-by-step guide to modern upholstery techniques that covers everything from stripping off old covers and padding to restoring and installing new foundations, stuffing, cushions, and covers. All the most up-to-date pro techniques are included along with lots of time- and money-saving "tricks-of-the-trade" not usually shared by professional upholsterers. 352 pp., 549 illus. 7″ × 10″.
Paper $16.95   **Hard $27.95**
Book No. 2602

☐ **THE COMPUTER FURNITURE PLAN AND PROJECT BOOK—Wiley**

Now, with the help of this first-of-its-kind handbook, even a novice can build good looking, functional, and low-cost computer furniture that's custom-designed for your own special needs—tables, stands, desks, modular or built-in units, even a posture supporting kneeling chair! Computer hobbyist and craftsman Jack Wiley provides all the step-by-step guidance, detailed project plans, show-how illustrations, and practical customizing advice . . . even basic information on tools, materials, and construction techniques. 288 pp., 385 illus. 7″ × 10″.
Paper $15.95   **Hard $23.95**
Book No. 1949

☐ **MICRO MANSION: USING YOUR COMPUTER TO HAVE A SAFER, MORE CONVENIENT HOME—Bonynge**

Here's where you'll find everything you need to know to get the benefits of a computer home control system in the most economical, trouble-free way whether you only want to install a simple light, or you want a computer home control system that has it all—complete control of heating and cooling and improved security—this book is for you! 192 pp., 115 illus. 7″ × 10″.
Hard $18.95   **Book No. 1906**

☐ **BUILD YOUR OWN FITNESS CENTER**

This sourcebook gives you expert guidance on everything from planning your facility to constructing it, step-by-step. It shows you how to choose and install all the needed equipment, and in many cases gives you direction for building your own equipment and accessories for a fraction of the commercial cost! Plus, there's practical advice on the proper use of your equipment once it's installed. 224 pp., 301 illus. 7″ × 10″.
Paper $12.95   **Hard $18.95**
Book No. 1828

Other Bestsellers From TAB